Trail *of the* Great Bear

By Bruce Weide

The Offical Guidebook of the
Trail of the Great Bear Society

FALCON
PRESS®

ACKNOWLEDGMENTS

Numerous people assisted with the writing of this book and in the appropriate places, they receive their deserved recognition. (Thanks Beth Russell and Barney Reeves.) Of the people who made my journey up the Trail of the Great Bear more pleasant, one stands out in particular, Mary Porter. And to my friend (and editor) Mac Bates, your perverse sense of humor made my work more fun. I'll never forget the sage advise you passed on to me in a dream, "The way I was raised, when you get up in the morning, ya gotta go out and kick the chickens." I now live by that creed.

This publication is based on the Trail of the Great Bear concept. Text is based on material generated in the Trail of the Great Bear Study.

The sixteen-page color insert concept and text—Beth Russell
Assistance with maps, Canadian content, and editorial overview—Brian Reeves
A cooperative project of the Trail of the Great Bear and Falcon Press.
Trail of The Great Bear—P.O.B. 142-Waterton Lakes National Park, Canada TOK2MO.

Falcon Press is continually expanding its list of recreational guidebooks using the same general format as this book. All books include detailed descriptions, accurate maps, and all information necessary for enjoyable trips. You can order extra copies of this book and get information and prices by writing Falcon Press, P.O. Box 1718, Helena, MT 59624. Also, please ask for a free copy of our current catalog listing all Falcon Press books.

Library of Congress Catalog Card Number: 92-53086
ISBN: 1-56044-129-1

Manufactured in the United States of America.

Falcon Press Publishing Co., Inc.
P.O. Box 1718, Helena, MT 59624

FALCON
PRESS·

All text, maps, and photos by the author except as noted.
Cover Photo: Darrin Schreder, Mount Clementine in
          Glacier National Park
Back Cover: Mike Logan, Grizzly Bear
          Bruce Weide, Kananaskis Village

CONTENTS

FOREWORD by Beth Russell

It's a short stroll from my home to the top of the Prince of Wales Ridge in Waterton Lakes National Park. The view is supreme. To the northeast the Canadian Rockies abruptly give way to the grasslands of the Great Plains. Looking south, upper Waterton Lake is surrounded by the highest mountains in the region. Halfway along its length, the international border between the United States and Canada crosses unnoticed. Beyond is the rugged terrain of Glacier National Park. This is Waterton-Glacier International Peace Park. It was from this vantage that in 1985 I designed the Trail of the Great Bear concept.

That year I was fortunate to be part of Waterton's celebration of the centennial of the Canadian National Parks system. Canada was an early subscriber to the national park concept which was initiated with the designation of the world's first—Yellowstone. Today, that dream is shared around the world.

How incredible it seems that over 100 years ago, when the west was still considered to be a vast wilderness, individuals like John Muir had the foresight to dream and then bring to fruition the national parks program. During our 1985 celebrations, it became obvious that few people were aware of the origins of the parks, the significance of such a designation, or the issues facing parks today.

It seemed the time had come to restate the national park philosophy, to refocus attention on their goals and objectives, and to reignite a passion for our parks.

The Trail of the Great Bear concept is designed as a vehicle to further communicate such designations and to act as a tool for interpretation, environmental education, and sustainable development. I envisioned a scenic corridor that linked, via existing highways, the world's first national park, Yellowstone, to and through Waterton-Glacier, the world's first international peace park, to Banff, Canada's first national park.

The Spirit Bear, the great grizzly, is the Trail's symbol. How appropriate it is that the southernmost range of the Great Bear coincides with those lands preserved and managed in the world's first national park. Although most travelers will never see the awesome animal, the spirit of the bear prevails in the wildlands along the corridor and speaks of its precarious, yet still pristine state.

This spirit is yours to share along the Trail of the Great Bear. Each year, millions of people travel from around the world to visit our great parks. The Trail of the Great Bear will enhance those experiences by providing travelers with quality information about designated natural areas and the abundant opportunities for exploring the communities adjacent to them.

Great Bear information will encourage travel to areas outside national park boundaries. Itineraries will combine national parks with historic towns, native communities, state/provincial and national parks, forests and wildlands, as well as local recreation, art, and entertainment. The Trail of the Great Bear encourages travel to these larger regions, thus creating a deeper understanding of the broader ecosystems. It also contributes to the local economies by distributing the benefits of tourism throughout the area. The Trail of the Great

Bear encourages spring, fall, and winter visits which offer the most dramatic watchable wildlife displays and other unique seasonal features.

The Trail of the Great Bear strives to be a tourism model, embracing the comments of philosopher Lou D'Amore, who states, "Tourism transcends political boundaries and brings people of the world closer together through the understanding of different cultures, environments, and heritage. It is potentially one of the most important vehicles for promoting understanding, trust, and goodwill amongst the people of the world."

Interpretation is the key to accomplishing this tourism ideal. When I consider the events in my life that have empowered me with the ability to embrace the natural world and its many cultures, the bridge to understanding was interpretation.

From the joys of watching wildlife on a birding walk with Jim Butler, to the ability to see the past as presented by archaeologist Brian Reeves, interpretation allows us to look, to see, and to know.

From the magic of the natural world as expertly portrayed in Montana's Deparment of Fish, Wildlife and Park's film, "The Last Parable," to the holistic lessons of a universal sacred medicine as a circle revealed by native teachers, interpretation is unquestionably an essential element in our ability to consider Earth as a living whole, to embrace "Gaia." As the Trail of the Great Bear evolves, additional meaningful interpretive and educational experiences will become available for the Great Bear traveler, encouraging travelers to return time and time again.

Since its 1985 inception, the Trail of the Great Bear has been the recipient of significant support. The province of Alberta, the state of Montana, the American Recreation Coalition, Pannell-Kerr-Forster, regional tourism organizations, special interests groups, and many devoted individuals have contributed time and vision to the concept. Deep gratitude is acknowledged for Trail of the Great Bear founding supporters including: Mae Weber, Margaret Handford, Anne Dahl, Charlie Russell, Al Cluck, John Wilson, Peter Walsh, Brain Baker, Gerry and Leslie Muza, Chuck Jonkel, Bernie Campbell, Sandra Guedes, David McNeil, Brian Reeves, Shari Pullar, Marie Calder, Greg Bryan, John Dormaar, and the Trail of the Great Bear Study Committee and team.

A special thanks to Bill Schneider and Falcon Press, and Bruce Weide who, in sharing the vision of the Trail of the Great Bear, initiated this first Great Bear publication.

MAP LEGEND

MAP LEGEND:

Trail of the Great Bear Route	▬▬	Secondary, State or Provincial Hwy	[000]
Other Road	══	National Park	▬▬
Unpaved Road	= = =	River/Creeks	～
Interstate	(00)	Lakes	●
U.S. Highway	(00)	Peak	▲
Trans-Canada Hwy	◆1	Town/City	o
State and Provincial Hwy	(000) / ⬡	Place of Interest	▫
		Mountain Pass	) (

STATE/COUNTRY
– – – – – – – – – – – –
BOUNDARY

The maps in this guide are intended for general reference. Please consult state and provincial highway maps for detailed information.

The Greater Yellowstone Ecosystem, with its geothermal wonders, anchors the southern end of the Trail of the Great Bear.

INTRODUCTION

From Fire To Ice: The Trail of the Great Bear, describes sixteen contiguous routes that traverse some of the most incredible country on earth. Where else can you step out of a mall in your new Air-Jordans and, in less than an hour, watch a grizzly bear rake a huckleberry bush with her six-inch claws? How many places on this planet can you fly fish on a "blue-ribbon" stream ten minutes after a live presentation of Shakespeare? The journey begins in Greater Yellowstone, a realm of volcanic origins, and concludes on the Icefield Parkway to Jasper, Alberta. That's a lot of territory; it includes two nations, 2,520 mi/4,065 km of road, six national parks, a half-dozen provincial and state parks, six Indian reservations, eight national forests, ten wilderness areas, a dozen good-sized towns, and one major city.

One of the goals of this travel-guide and of the entire Trail of the Great Bear concept is to inspire you to slow down. Many people rocket from Glacier to Yellowstone National Park stopping only to refuel or empty their bladder. I've heard people boast of "doing the Icefield Parkway in a day." This is sad. If your vacation time is limited (and whose isn't), limit the amount of territory you want to cover. There's an old saying, "The runner sees no more than he who sits by a stream." Sure, you could jog along the trail overlooking Maligne Canyon in the morning and roar down to Banff in time to watch the sunset behind Vermilion Lakes. You could treat the natural wonders along the Trail of the Great Bear like a list of attractions to be checked off. But that can lead to the kind of mentality that thinks (if you can call it thinking) that in seeing one redwood, you've seen them all. "It takes time to live," a friend of mine once said. "But no one wants to take the time." The Trail of the Great Bear asks you to take time and invest yourself; this is an amazing chunk of the earth.

People's expectations of vacation are changing; they seek more than a rocket-trip from one national park to another; they want to return home with something more than plastic tomahawks and window decals. People are beginning to realize that while snapshots may capture the moment, memories are more than a moment frozen on paper. If you want to return home with something that adds more to your life than additional pages in a photo album, you must invest yourself in the journey. You have to explore. You have to discover.

Though I devote lots of words to beautiful sights and incredible scenes, I also mention some of the things we've lost or are about to lose. Grizzly bear, wolves, and bison no longer roam across the plains as they did within the memory of our grandparents. The awesome power of the Great Falls on the Missouri River has been tamed to produce electric energy. Our wilderness areas, while beautiful and inspiring, are basically museum pieces comprised primarily of rock and ice, and wildlife habitat continues to shrink like an ice cube in the Sahara. I mention such things, not to be an eco-soothsayer of doom and gloom, but with the hope that in realizing what we've lost, you'll appreciate more fully, and perhaps even feel compelled to protect, that which remains.

Take time, slow down, toss the watch in the glove compartment. Lay in a meadow and watch clouds change shape. Examine bear scat and learn what they're eating. Stop along a roadside and wander among the sagebrush, crush

Macdonald Lake is just one of the many spectacular mountain lakes found along the Trail of the Great Bear.

some leaves and inhale their pungent odor. Look for wolf tracks. Watch the social behavior of ravens. Take a nap beside a stream.

The Trail of the Great Bear is more than just a route to travel during vacation, it's a journey that combines movement, relaxation, learning, fun, observation, involvement, and understanding. Don't even think of completing the Trail of the Great Bear in one shot unless you've got a couple months (and even that's not enough time). Break the Trail of the Great Bear into segments, allow yourself five vacations (or more) to complete the journey; you won't regret it.

As for the descriptions that follow, each route is divided into eleven categories that are fairly self-explanatory. However, the following information may help.

How To Use This Guide

Title and Mileage; in most cases, the title provides the beginning and end point of each route followed by the distance it covers. For routes within the United States, the distance is expressed first in miles and then in kilometers; the reverse is true of the Canadian Routes. Where a noteworthy sidetrip or optional course of travel exists on a route, it is sub-divided.

For example, Route 5 begins in Missoula and ends in West Glacier; but along the way, Route 5A offers a sidetrip to the National Bison Range and Route 5B provides an east-shore alternative means of traveling around Flathead Lake.

General description furnishes a thumbnail sketch of what to expect from a route in terms of vegetation, natural features, and major attractions.

Unique features includes wilderness areas, national parks, museums, striking geologic formations, and other extraordinary, unusual, or distinctive features.

Wildlife viewing opportunities are places where the chances of seeing wildlife are exceptionally good. Bear in mind that, in general, the opportunity to observe wildlife along the Trail of the Great Bear is superior to almost any place in the world. However, even in the Northern Rockies, some locations stand out over others.

Activities is a list of outdoor pursuits that you could engage in on a particular route.

Events includes county fairs, Indian powwows, and events that either apply to Trail of the Great Bear themes or seemed particularly interesting.

Travel season notes whether or not a route is seasonal. While the Trail of the Great Bear can be traveled year-round, portions of some routes are closed in the winter. In such cases, there's always an alternate route. However, just because a route is designated for year-round travel doesn't mean that a winter snowstorm can't close it down temporarily. Listen to weather reports, use common sense, and pack equipment appropriate to the season of travel. The open and closing dates of a road are approximate and dependent upon the whims of the weather.

Services denotes towns where there is at least a restaurant, gas station, hotel or motel, and are listed as possessing basic service.

Road conditions and route description is a nuts-and-bolts explanation of how to follow a route, the specific highway numbers, and where and which way to turn. The listing also provides an idea of what condition the road is in.

Description provides a detailed account of the route that includes geologic information, historic facts and stories, where to observe wildlife, natural history, and whatever else seemed particularly interesting. This section also gives a brief account of events, historic sites, and museums in addition to the seasons and hours opened, and where to write or call for more information. In some cases, a hike, fishing spot, cross-country ski or float trip is suggested; but this book is not a definitive source for such information—it can't be. If the book included all that information, you'd need a trailer to pack it along. Because other guidebooks specialize in documenting places to fish, hike, climb, and float, it seemed pointless to reinvent the wheel.

For more information is used to recommend other books or information

The history of native cultures is documented along the Trail of the Great Bear at museums like Buffalo Bill Center in Cody, Wyoming. Photo courtesy of the Buffalo Bill Museum.

sources that will add to your enjoyment of a route; this category is used sporadically. For instance, *A River Runs Through It*, by Norman Maclean is an exceptional novella that utilizes the Blackfoot River as a setting; so, it's listed in Route 4. However, Hank Fischer's book, *A Floater's Guide To Montana*, is not listed. Why? Because Hank's book is pertinent to Routes 1 through 10. For books like Hank's, there's a special section in the appendix of this book.

Please, think of this book as a work in progress. While a lot of information is packed between the covers, undoubtedly there will be subjects and sights that you think should've been included. In some cases, I simply didn't have the time to learn or include them. In other cases, I purposely omitted information. After all, what fun is travel without exploration and what fulfillment comes from exploration that lacks discovery? And I'm sure that there are some mistakes in the book. Plans for the future include an update in 2 years that will include on-going Trail of the Great Bear developments. Any comments or corrections should be directed to the Trail of the Great Bear, 142 Waterton Lakes National Park, Alberta, Canada TOK 2MJ or Falcon Press.

"But I now leave my. . . .System standing thus unfinished. . . God keep me from ever completing anything. This whole book is but a draught—nay, but the draught of a draught. Oh, Time, Strength, Cash, and Patience!" Herman Melville, *Moby Dick*.

Eco-Buzz Words, Vegetation Zones, Geology and Bears

We hear the word *ecosystem* a lot these days; but what does this buzz word really mean? By general consensus an ecosystem refers to a zone where life is self-regulating—an area where species can maintain genetic diversity without migration in or out. Well, that sounds like a nice, tidy definition; but how big is an ecosystem? Now things start getting hazy because an ecosystem can be large or small. For instance, there are stretches along the Madison River where a distinct, profuse, and narrow band of trees, bushes, and grasses support a wide array of animals; this is called a riparian ecosystem. Step out of that ecosystem and you know it instantly because the profusion of plant life gives way to sagebrush and bunchgrass. The Greater Yellowstone Ecosystem, on the other hand, is an example of a large ecosystem.

While a number of plant and animal species can maintain a healthy existence within the bounds of both ecosystems, neither is entirely self-regulating or independent from its surroundings. White-tailed deer take from and contribute to a riparian ecosystem while inside of it, but then they leave and head out across an arid (steppe) ecosystem composed of sagebrush and bunchgrass. The Greater Yellowstone Ecosystem, if left to function on its own, would maintain genetically diverse populations of elk and grizzly bear. But what about trumpeter swans? They need a larger ecosystem, one that encompasses their entire migratory route.

Maybe we should simplify matters and just say that North America is an ecosystem. Won't work. What about migratory birds that fly to Central and South America? This brings us to one inescapable conclusion: The earth is an ecosystem, all other boundaries are contrived. Like John Muir said, "when we try to pick something by itself, we find it hitched to everything else in the universe."

Hopefully, one of the realizations that comes from traveling the Trail of the Great Bear is that boundaries are merely imaginary lines drawn by people for political convenience. While the federal governments of Canada and the United States require humans to stop at the international border, birds fly over it without batting an eye and grizzlies cross and never notice the difference.

Now that I've pummeled the word ecosystem, I have to admit that boundaries, contrived as they are, do help me understand and appreciate the life systems that surround me. The thing to remember is that boundaries, whether they mark the perimeter of an eco-zone or delineate a category, are a convenience not the rule. Here is some basic information full of generalities, boundaries, and categories that will help you better understand and appreciate the Trail of the Great Bear.

Greater Yellowstone Ecosystem

"Certainly it [Yellowstone National Park] is the largest relatively intact ecosystem remaining in the lower forty-eight states, but it is tiny when compared to the rest of the nation. You can drive through the area in almost any direction in a few hours. It is the largest, but it is not large." Franz Camenzind, wildlife biologist and filmmaker.

When Congress created the world's first national park, its primary concern was protecting the geothermal features and Yellowstone Lake. In his book, *Greater Yellowstone*, Rick Reese wrote, "Geology more than biology was the main criterion for the establishment of the park boundary. The concepts of watershed, wildlife migration routes, biological communities, and intact ecosystems were not known at that time."

Yellowstone's boundaries are merely politically determined lines drawn on paper; they pay absolutely no attention to the real life needs of wildlife. Back in 1882, after a visit to the park, General Sheridan (of Civil War fame) recommended a vast increase in the size of Yellowstone in order to make the area more suitable to the movement of wildlife. We can hardly blame Congress for not acting on his suggestion; a century ago, the land surrounding the park was wild. Today, though, logging, oil and gas development, mining, ranching, road building, dams, housing, recreation, and geothermal development surround and impact the park and many of the animals we see there.

The Greater Yellowstone Ecosystem is a region that extends beyond (and includes) the park. It encompasses habitat critical to the survival of wildlife within the park. Yellowstone National Park is a nice place for animals to live in the summer, but come winter, animals such as elk, deer, antelope, bighorn sheep, and bison move to lower elevations. Remember, the park is basically a volcanic plateau, most of which stands well over a mile/2 km high—not a cozy place to live in the winter. The seasonal migration of elk herds to outside the park is a good example of the arbitrary nature of the park's boundaries. The National Elk Refuge near Jackson, Wyoming, is proof of the need for winter habitat.

The grizzly provides another graphic example of how inadequate the park is for the overall survival of wildlife. Even by the most conservative estimates, more than forty percent of the habitat necessary to Yellowstone bears exists outside the park. In 1982, the former superintendent of Yellowstone Park, John Townsley, said, "It is blatantly clear that the grizzly bear cannot survive if Yellowstone National Park is its only refuge. It also needs portions of the five adjacent forests."

In one of those adjacent forests, the Targhee National Forest, more than seventy industrial and utility companies have applied for leases to drill into the Island Park Geothermal Area. Old Faithful is only 13 mi/21 km away from Island Park; will it be affected? Geothermal developers also see the Corwin Springs Known Geothermal Resource Area as a source of energy; Mammoth Hot Springs is only 4 mi/6 km to the south. The book *Greater Yellowstone* lists some of the consequences of drilling in other thermal areas, "In New Zealand, the Geyser Thermal Valley, which ranked fifth among the major geyser areas on earth, died shortly after the Wairakei plant was installed nearby. The Beowawe Geysers of Nevada were second only to Yellowstone on the North American continent prior to geothermal exploration from 1945 to 1958. During that period wells were drilled, and by 1961 all springs and geysers had ceased flowing."

Maybe it helps to think of the Greater Yellowstone concept in terms that hit a little closer to home. Think of the park as your heart and Greater Yellowstone as the rest of your body; both depend on each other, neither exists without the other. Due to its popularity, it seems that the boundaries of Yellowstone National Park will remain intact and the land within protected. The future of the surrounding area requires conscientious planning and consideration. This is why—as illustrated by elk, grizzly, and geothermal features—consideration of the Greater Yellowstone is so important. If a region is able to support a healthy population of grizzly bear, then you have a truly healthy ecosystem.

6

The Trail of the Great Bear encompasses the southernmost habitat of the grizzly in North America. Milo Burcham photo.

As Aldo Leopold wrote in 1948 in *A Sand County Almanac,* "The National Parks do not suffice as a means of perpetuating the larger carnivores; witness the precarious status of the grizzly bear; and the fact that the park system is already wolfless. The most feasible way to enlarge the area available for wilderness fauna is for the wilder parts of the National Forests, which usually surround the Parks, to function as parks in respect of threatened species. That they have not so functioned is tragically illustrated in the case of the grizzly bear." Leopold wrote those words in 1948! Nearly half a century has passed, and we are now beginning to treat the ecosystem concept as an idea that's worthy of implementation. Thinking in terms of ecosystems, of protecting a region like the Greater Yellowstone, is an idea worth immediate action.

The Mountains: How'd They Get Here And Why Are They So Pretty or Geomorphology 101

You need know only three things to understand mountains along the Trail of the Great Bear: deposition, uplift, and erosion. Long, long ago, in an ocean far, far away, sediment drifted down onto the sea floor. For 1.5 billion years, the sediment piled up (as much as 12 mi/20 km thick). Beginning 120 million years ago, this large section of ocean floor spent seventy-five million years engaged in a slow-motion collision with North America. Picture two pieces of (somewhat dry) pie dough being pushed together. They wouldn't meld, they'd bend, buckle, lift, snap, and stack. The same thing occurred with the earth's crust and the Rockies were born. The Rockies along the lower half of the Trail of the Great Bear experienced an additional boost by means of molten rock from within the earth that swelled towards the surface. Such a reservoir of liquid rock lifted the Yellowstone Plateau before finding its way to the surface and triggering a volcanic explosion of apocalyptic proportions. From Butte to Helena, however, the molten rock rose like bread dough and then, with only a few volcanic flare-ups, but no major fanfare, it cooled into granite.

As soon as the Rockies started to rise above sea level, erosion commenced. That's one consequence of living on a planet with enough gravity to keep us from floating away; what goes up, must come down—including mountains. While erosion sculpted the Rockies, the real artistry in landscaping occurred during the Wisconsin Glaciation some 12,000 years ago. Before that, the Rockies appeared round. During the ice age, glaciers enveloped entire mountain ranges. The ice chiseled away the roly-poly landscape and when the glaciers melted, they unveiled the rugged mountains we see today. A few hardy plants sprouted on the ice-scoured land and their roots worked through the rocks. With the help of weathering, soil formed. More plants and different plants grew. Then came the animals.

Wildlife

All animals, humans included, move through life with three basic needs: food, water, and shelter. The area in which a species can fulfill these needs is known as *habitat*. So, when someone says, "This is good bear habitat," you could translate that to mean, "Here's a few hundred square miles of forest, meadows, and streams, valley-bottoms that support a healthy number of deer and elk. There's less than .5 mi/1 km of roads per 1 sq mi/2.5 sq km of land."

Some animals are pretty picky about their habitat. The pika is a furry little creature that lives above tree line, among rocks and within easy reach of some vegetation. Humans, on the other hand, inhabit the earth from the equatorial tropics to the far frozen reaches near the poles.

The area an individual animal or common group of animals requires to live is known as *home range*. Your home range extends beyond your house; it includes the place where you work, buy groceries, shop for clothes, and go to church or school. A grizzly bear moves through a home range that can extend from a mountain top, where it licks up lady bugs, to valley bottoms thick with berries; their home range averages 80 sq mi/200 sq km, but can vary from ten to 380 sq mi/25 to 1,000 sq km. It just depends. And that's what makes natural history so fascinating; nothing is fixed or set in stone. A species may generally display certain behavior, but when it comes to individuals, it just depends.

Plants

Plants are a little more predictable. Nevertheless the boundaries between plant communities are fuzzy. For the purposes of this book, we'll stick to four basic vegetational zones (also called eco-regions and eco-zones):

1. Prairie/Plains consist of flat or gently rolling land vegetated with grasses, sagebrush, some cactus, and, along drainages, the streamside vegetation that makes up the all important riparian habitat such as cottonwood trees, alder, and willow. Prairie/plains eco-regions are generally found east of the Continental Divide.

The Frank Slide is a dramatic example of nature's power.

2. Montane vegetation is found from valley bottoms to the lower elevations of mountains. It includes forest, meadow, riparian, and wetland. Lodgepole pine, Douglas-fir, ponderosa pine, and aspen trees typify montane forests. The montane contains more species of plants and animals than any other zone along the Trail of the Great Bear. It constitutes a minor portion of the total area. For example, only five percent of Banff National Park's total land mass is montane and that area accommodates both man and wildlife. Careful consideration of the montane is required to accommodate both wildlife habitat and the needs of the human population.

3. Subalpine vegetation extends from the montane to tree line; this is the most extensive eco-region on the Trail of the Great Bear. The lower subalpine consists of lodgepole pine, limber pine, and Engelmann spruce which give way, in the upper subalpine, to western larch and subalpine fir. Krummholz, the miniature forests of stunted and wind-bent conifers, mark the extreme limits of the upper subalpine and the beginning of the alpine zone.

4. The sparse vegetation that exists in the alpine zone is characterized by small and hardy plant life that includes a variety of wildflowers, mosses, grasses, lichens, and heather. These plants—such as those easily viewed on the Beartooth Plateau (Route 1A), Logan Pass (Route 10A), Highwood Pass (Route 14), Bow Summit, and Sunwapta Pass (Route 15)—display amazing adaptations that allow them to survive in this harsh environment; some plants grow clustered together and close to the ground in order to take advantage of what little warmth exists, others possess waxy leaves that inhibit dehydration, and still others grow a vegetative fur that insulates leaves from the cold.

Living in Bear Country

"...In the evening the men in two of the rear canoes discovered a large brown bear lying in the open...and went out to attack him...four fired at nearly the same time and put each his bullet through him, two of the balls passed through the bulk of both lobes of his lungs, in an instant this monster ran at them with open mouth, the two who had reserved their fire discharged their pieces at him as he came towards them, both of them struck him, one only slightly and the other fortunately broke his shoulder, this however only retarded his motion...the men took flight...and the bear pursued. Each [man] discharged his piece at him as they had an opportunity they struck him several times again but the guns served only to direct the bear to them. He pursued two of them separately so close that they were obliged to throw...themselves into the river altho' the bank was nearly twenty feet perpendicular; so enraged was this animal that he plunged into the river only a few feet behind the second man...when the one who still remained on the shore shot him through the head and finally killed him; they then took him on shore and butch[er]ed him when they found eight balls had passed through him in different directions." (Captain Meriwether Lewis, May 14, 1805.)

Our modern society is slowly overcoming its fixation with taming everything wild. While we've dominated grizzlies as a species, the Great Bear as an individual remains indomitable. For this reason, if you're going to travel among bears, it's wise to learn how to live in the company of bears.

First, learn to distinguish the differences between a black bear and a grizzly. In terms of size and weight, there's a good deal of overlap; but, in general, grizzlies are larger than black bears. So, size isn't definitive and neither is color. In fact, to confuse matters even more, the taxonomist who set about classifying bears, decided to use color in the naming process. Black bears also come in dark brown, cinnamon, and blond. The grizzly, which is actually a species of brown bear, also ranges in color from blond to almost black. However, some of the hair on grizzlies is white, blond or silver-tipped creating a halo appearance. The face of a grizzly is flatter and the nose sharper than a black bear, which sports a Roman-nosed profile. Grizzly claws are longer than black bear claws, which are difficult to see. The shoulder hump on grizzlies is a distinguishing feature. However, there are some grizzlies in which the muscles that form the hump aren't well developed and there are some big, muscular black bears. Generalized classification of a group is generally effective; it falls apart, however, when you consider the wide range of diversity displayed by individuals in a group. Think of trying to come up with a system to easily identify humans when physical types range from Arnold Schwarzenegger to Michael Jackson to Woody Allen.

Understanding why a grizzly might act aggressively helps reduce the chances of a confrontation. Native People bestowed the title "Great Bear" on it and for good reason. Grizzlies ruled their world; no animal, human or otherwise, contested their crown. **The notion of backing down isn't common to grizzlies.** So, if you happen upon a carcass with a grizzly feeding on it (or a carcass all by its lonesome), just leave.

A male bear will kill cubs. Because grizzlies evolved on the plains, where there's no place to hide, mom presented the only line of defense when a mean male appeared. Female grizzlies become infuriated if they perceive a threat to their young. Should you spot a female with cubs, turn around, choose another destination, call the trip off (the lake will still be there tomorrow), or if you feel absolutely compelled to continue— detour around the bears and give them a wide berth (a 50-mile/80 km detour wouldn't be excessive). Here are some more preventative measures to follow while in bear country.

Be alert and watch for bear signs. Part of what makes travel through bear country so unique and special is that you're part of the food chain and must therefore conduct life in a very observant manner. With heightened awareness, your senses are elevated and everything stands out sharp, clear, and in bold detail. Keep looking ahead for trees to climb, should the need arise. Keep your camp area clean, especially your tent and sleeping bag. Hang your food at least 12 ft/4 m off the ground and don't store anything that might interest a bear (toothpaste, candy, perfume, deodorant, soap) near your sleeping area. Cook at least 100 ft/33 m from your sleeping area.

If you come upon a bear, remain calm; don't run, this could illicit a chase response. Speak in a nonthreatening and monotone voice as you slowly back away. Make yourself appear small, crouch and back away. Observe the bear; if he stands, this means the bear is curious, not aggressive. Should the bear huff or clomp teeth or rake a tree trunk with her claws, consider this a warning and back off. A bear standing sideways with his head down next to his front paws is displaying non-aggressive intentions. While bears seldom growl (like in the movies), a growl means go away. Don't stare at bears, this makes them feel threatened; think about how you feel when a stranger stares at you. If a bear puts her head down with ears laid back, think fast because this bear is about to charge.

Don't surprise bears; that's something that can cause them to charge. A survival mechanism, programmed deep inside the brain of most animals (and that includes humans), causes an instantaneous computation that elicits a *flight or fight* response. The calculation is based on distance. If there's enough space

Black bear.

between the bear and the surprise (that from the bear's point of view is a potential threat) then it can move away or choose other options. But if there's not enough space, then the bear eliminates the threat. So, what do you do if faced with the ultimate bear encounter?

Before going into that, let's put some perspective on bear attacks. Some people ruin their vacation by laying awake at night worrying about bears. Some people are scared of hiking in the woods because of bears. Some people even think the Rockies should be cleansed of bears thereby making the woods a safe place to frolic. But, the woods are safe, compared to other lifestyles.

In terms of threats to your safety, you're far safer among bears than you are among people or out on the road. The chance of being struck and killed by lightning (the odds 1:1,900,000) is more likely than being attacked by a bear. The odds of winning the California Lottery (1 in 13,000,000) are greater than being killed by a bear. The barking mutt in the camper parked in the Old Faithful parking lot poses more danger to you than a mountain lion. If ever faced with the decision of confronting Bambi or the Big Bad Wolf, choose the wolf; deer gore (sometimes fatally) at least a half-dozen people a year. So far there are no documented attacks on humans by a healthy, wild wolf in North America.

If fear of bears keeps you out of the forest, if fear of wolves prevents you from skiing a backwoods road beneath the full moon, if you never set foot in the ocean for fear of sharks— then you are letting your fears hold you back from wonderful, natural experiences. That's your problem. Don't make it the problem of bears, mountain lions, and wolves. Monsters dwell in our imagination, not the woods.

Now we return to our previously scheduled bear attack. You're facing a bear with a bad attitude; it charges. Most charges are bluffs. But when you're the one being charged by a bear, statistics aren't comforting. Can you reach a tree in time? If so, drop your pack and climb like crazy. While grizzlies can climb trees, for the most part, they won't climb very high if at all. Generally, bears equate tree climbing with submissive behavior which would leave them feeling unthreatened. This is also an opportune means of distinguishing a black bear from a grizzly. If it climbs the tree after you, it's a black bear; if it pushes the tree over then it's a grizzly.

Let's say the bear keeps coming; you're that one in a million person, the low number in a statistic. Spray bear repellent in the bear's face. If that doesn't work, or you forgot the bear spray, maybe it's time to play dead, but do this only as a last resort. Curl up in the fetal position with knees drawn up to protect the stomach and hands protecting the back of your head. One last word of advice, listen to your instincts. In such circumstances your instincts probably over-ride any kind of so-called rational thought process. A grizzly attacked a friend of mine. He tried to climb a tree but she pulled him down and started working him over. Instead of playing dead, he punched her in the face repeatedly while swearing at her. He still doesn't know if it was the blows to the face or the foul language that caused her to leave. He does know however that something from within overwhelmed him and he wasn't about to lay there playing dead. On the other hand, I've heard cases where the person's instincts said to play dead. What it all comes down to is, if the bear bites, you're on your own. *NOTE: The TGB does not encourage or promote direction interaction between the visitor and the bear.*

If you want to learn more about bears, read Steve Henero's *"Bear Attacks,"* and take one of the many outdoor educational courses offered through the Yellowstone Institute (on bears), 307-344-7381, Pine Butte Swamp (The Nature Conservancy), 406-466-5526, Glacier Institute, 406-888-5215, or Waterton Park Natural History Association, 403-859-2624.

Ring of Fire

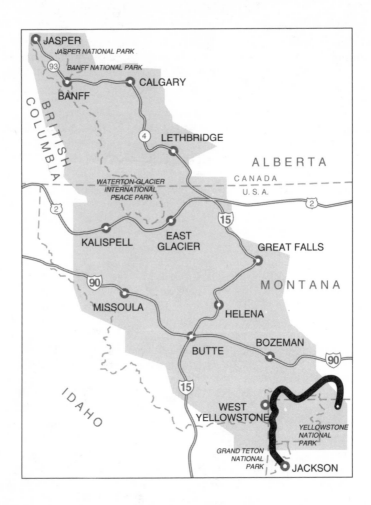

"Nothing can be done well at a speed of forty miles a day. . . The multitude of mixed, novel impressions rapidly piled on one another make only a dreamy, bewildering, swirling blur, most of which is unrememberable. Climb the mountains and get their good tidings. Nature's peace will flow into you as sunshine flows into the trees. The winds will blow their own freshness into you, and the storms their energy, while cares drop off like autumn leaves."

John Muir, 1898.

ROUTE 1—ACCESS TO THE TRAIL

JACKSON to WEST YELLOWSTONE   124 miles/200 kilometers

General description: Whether you start from Jackson or Cody, Wyoming, the beginning of the Trail of the Great Bear commences with a grand slam. Access Route 1A takes in Grand Teton and Yellowstone national parks. Access Route 1B follows the Beartooth Scenic Highway and passes through Yellowstone National Park.

From Jackson, Wyoming, Access Route 1A passes through Grand Teton National Park, along the shore of Jackson Lake, and up the John D. Rockefeller, Jr. Memorial Parkway into Yellowstone, the world's first national park. From the park's south entrance, the road gradually ascends through forests of lodgepole pine to the southwest shore of Yellowstone Lake, up to Craig Pass and over the Continental Divide and down to the Old Faithful area. Beyond Old Faithful, the route follows the Firehole River past world-famous geothermal features. From Madison Junction, where the Firehole River enters the Madison River, Access Route 1A passes through forests burned in the 1988 fires and on to the town of West Yellowstone, Montana.

Another place to start the Trail of the Great Bear is in Cody, Wyoming, home of the Buffalo Bill Historical Center. From Cody, Access Route 1B extends to Red Lodge, Montana, through an arid landscape east of the Yellowstone Plateau that is reminiscent of the West as portrayed in pulp fiction. Beyond the resort and ranching town of Red Lodge, the road ascends, via the incredibly engineered Beartooth Scenic Highway, up to the alpine world of the Beartooth Plateau. From the 10,947 ft/3,338 m Beartooth Pass, the highest driveable point on the Trail of the Great Bear, the route descends to the Northeast Entrance of Yellowstone National Park, and then continues through the Lamar Valley, past Tower Junction, and on to Mammoth Hot Springs, site of the Park Headquarters.

Access Route 1C provides a link between Mammoth Hot Springs and West Yellowstone and access to moose habitat, Roaring Mountain, and Norris Geyser Basin.

Unique features: The Teton Mountains, Old Faithful Geyser Area, Madison River, Norris Geyser Basin, Obsidian Cliff, Roaring Mountain, Mammoth Hot Springs, Lamar Valley, Beartooth Scenic Highway, Chief Joseph Scenic Highway, Buffalo Bill Historical Center.

Wildlife viewing opportunities: Oxbow Bend and Willow Flat turnouts in Teton National Park; Lewis Canyon, Willow Park, Lamar Valley, Mammoth Hot Springs Area, Upper Geyser Basin.

Activities: Backpacking, fishing, mountaineering, snowmobiling, cross-country skiing, downhill skiing, river floating, mountain biking, golf.

Events: Elk Antler Auction, Old West Days, Grand Teton Music Festival, Indian Art Show, Teton County Fair, Jackson Hole Fall Arts Festival, Arts for the Parks, Cowboy Songs and Range Ballads, Plains Indian Powwow, Cody Stampede, Red Lodge Mountain Man Rendezvous, Home of the Champions Rodeo and Red Lodge Parade, Festival of Nations.

Travel season: Jackson to the south entrance of Yellowstone National Park is open year-round. From Yellowstone's South Entrance to the West Entrance is closed from about November 1 to April 30.

Services: All services available in Jackson, Cody, Red Lodge, and West Yellowstone; limited services found in Cooke City, Silver Gate, Old Faithful, Mammoth Hot Springs, and Grant Village. Airports located in Jackson, Cody, and West Yellowstone.

Road conditions and access route description: Route 1A—From Jackson, drive north towards Grand Teton National Park on the well maintained, two-lane Highway 191. At Moose Junction, 8 mi/13 km beyond Jackson, either continue on Highway 191 or turn left (west) and follow the Teton Park Road for 20 mi/32 km on a paved two-lane road to Jackson Lake Junction. At the junction, turn left and stay with Highway 191 through the John D. Rockefeller, Jr. Memorial Parkway and into Yellowstone National Park where the road narrows and is no longer labeled as Highway 191. This National Park Service road crosses the Continental Divide three times and drops down from Craig Pass (8,262 ft/2,518 m) to Old Faithful and continues to Madison Junction. At Madison Junction, a left turn (west) leads to the end of Route 1A at West Yellowstone; a right turn leads to Mammoth Hot Springs via Route 1C. The road from the South Entrance of Yellowstone National Park to West Yellowstone is fairly well maintained though narrow at times and closed from about November 1 to April 30. Be prepared for slow traffic and vehicles that suddenly stop to view wildlife; the speed limit is 45 mi-/72 km-per-hour.

The route: The Trail of the Great Bear begins in Greater Yellowstone, a region formed by the earth's internal fire with the finishing touches sculpted by ice. Jackson Hole, the basin beneath the Teton Mountains, occupies the southern end of Greater Yellowstone. Humans first visited this beautiful, though inhospitable, basin more than 10,000 years ago. When viewed from Jackson's town square, it's hard to believe that, until recently, Jackson Hole existed as a no-man's land. One of today's big attractions, winter snow, limited the visits of Ute, Flathead, Shoshone, Nez Perce, Crow, Gros Ventre, and Blackfoot to spring and summer. The first European to venture through the Tetons and Yellowstone was John Colter and he traveled alone, on foot, and during the dead of winter.

After serving Lewis and Clark as a hunter for nearly three years, on the return trip and only a month away from St. Louis, Colter turned around and headed back into the wilderness (at least that's how whites labeled it; Native People called it home).

Following an unprofitable season of trapping, Colter started back towards *civilization* again. One his way down the Missouri River, Colter met the notorious St. Louis merchant and trader, Manuel Lisa. Lisa needed someone to tell the Crows, Cheyennes, and Shoshones about his new trading post (today, we'd call such a person an advertising agent). In November 1807, alone and on foot, Colter entered *terra incognita* equipped with only a thirty-pound pack, a rifle, and ammunition.

The following spring, he returned after walking hundreds of miles/kms, a journey that led him into present-day Jackson Hole and up through Yellowstone. Having escaped death at the hands of Blackfeet warriors three separate times (see Section 3), Colter finally left the Rockies for good. He returned to civilization, married, settled on a farm in Missouri, and within three years, died of jaundice at the age of thirty-eight. Bands of trappers constituted the next wave of Jackson Hole transients. A few decades after

The Tetons rise majestically from Jackson Hole.

the fur business went belly-up, rustlers, outlaws, and ranchers inhabited Jackson Hole. In 1897, the townsite of Jackson was laid out.

Jackson today

Today, Jackson is a progressive mountain town with an economy strongly based on tourism and outdoor recreation. Jackson Hole Airport serves the town of Jackson. Three ski resorts, Snow King (800-522-KING), Grand Targhee (800-443-8146), and Jackson Hole (800-443-6931), provide downhill skiers a chance to carve turns through Rocky Mountain powder. Jackson Hole is also an excellent area for cross-country skiing and snowmobiling. For specific information write to the Jackson Hole Visitors Council, P.O. Box 982, Department 8, Jackson Hole, Wyoming, 83001 or call 1-800-782-0011, extension 8. The Jackson Hole Visitors Council is extremely helpful.

On the Memorial Day weekend, Jackson kicks-off the summer tourist season, with Old West Days. Activities at this celebration include parades, street dances, beard-growing contests, Native dances, cowboy poetry, an amateur western swing dance contest, and an authentic Mountain Man

Rendezvous (307-733-3316). The Grand Teton Music Festival, held from July 10 through August 24 (8:00 and 8:30 p.m.), features 150 musicians from renowned orchestras throughout the world who perform classical and modern works at the Walk Festival Hall in Teton Village (307-733-1128).

On the last weekend of July, in Teton Village, national award-winning Native artists present their works and demonstrate artistic skills at the Indian Art Show (307-733-4913). The Teton County Fair and a special rodeo is held on the third weekend of August (307-733-3087). For a month, from mid-September to mid-October, the Jackson Hole Fall Arts Festival features Arts for the Parks (an exhibition of the top 100 paintings selected from an artistic competition dedicated to portraying United States National Parks, Monuments, and Historic Sites), in addition to dance, theatre, working demonstrations, workshops, quilting exhibits, and special events and exhibits (307-733-3316). The Jackson Hole Arts Center Hotline, 307-733-5465, provides current information on arts activities and events.

From June to September, the Snake River Institute offers seminars and workshops in the arts and humanities (307-733-2214). The Teton Science School operates year-round and conducts natural history classes for all age groups (307-733-4765, Box 68P, Kelly, Wyoming, 83011).

Jackson Hole is home to the National Elk Refuge, a winter sanctuary to Yellowstone's southern herd of 4,000 elk. Due to the loss of winter habitat in Jackson Hole, the Elk Refuge provides an artificial haven where elk are fed hay and pellets. From 10 a.m. to 4 p.m., December through March, sleigh rides depart from the visitor center (307-733-8084) every half-hour. The forty-

Fly fisherman on the Firehole River.

five-minute ride allows visitors a close-up view of elk. Come spring, the local Boy Scouts gather more than three tons of elk antlers that are sold at The Elk Antler Auction, held in mid-May from 7 a.m. to 1 p.m.

Grand Teton National Park

Upon leaving Jackson, a turnout on the edge of Highway 191/89/26, at the north end of town, overlooks an Elk Refuge slough where trumpeter swans and other water fowl make a temporary home. As you near the northern end of East Gros Ventre Butte (on the immediate left), prepare yourself to be blasted by a V.A.S. (visually amazing sight). The road ascends to the top of a floodplain and suddenly the Tetons appear, rising out of the earth like a surreal vision dreamed up by an Iowa corn farmer who longed for an escape from the flatlands. The Shoshoni called them the "hoary-headed fathers." Around 1820, French-Canadian trappers named the distinctive mountain landmarks, "Les Trois Tetons," The Three Breasts. One look at the Tetons proves the extent of a trapper's imagination and his obvious yearning for female companionship.

The Grand Teton towers 13,770 ft/4,197 m above sea level and over a mile above the valley floor. At the foot of the mountains, a fault stretches north-south. The Tetons mark the eastern edge of a block of the earth's crust that tilted upwards as the fault block next to it tilted down and formed Jackson Hole. Wind, rain, and ice chiseled sedimentary rock away and exposed a resistant core of basement rock that is nearly as old as the earth itself.

During the last ice age, glaciers carved the jagged alpine features in the range. A mere nine million years old, the Tetons are the youngest mountains in the Rockies and still growing.

In 1929, Grand Teton National Park only included the mountain range. Congress tacked on the Jackson Hole portion in 1950 and the park now protects 485 sq mi/1,242 sq km. Turn at Moose Junction to visit the Moose Visitor Center and watch an excellent computer simulation that depicts the formation of the Tetons. The visitor center also issues backpacking (no fee) and boating permits ($5 for non-motorized craft and $10 for motorized).

Entrance fees charged for Grand Teton and Yellowstone are $10 for a seven-day pass to both parks. At $25, the Golden Eagle Pass can prove a good investment as it admits the permit holder and accompanying passengers to all United States parks for a calendar year. The Golden Age Passport, for people over sixty-two, and the Golden Access Passport, for the handicapped, are free and entitle the holder and accompanying passengers to enter all parks and also a fifty percent reduction in campground fees.

The steep solid rock that forms the Teton Range attracts climbers from around the world. The park requires climbers to sign out prior to and sign in immediately following a climb; this can be accomplished, from early June to mid-September, at the Jenny Lake Ranger Station. The Exum Mountain Guides operate a climbing school and guide ascents in the Tetons (Box 56, Moose, Wyoming, 83012; 307-733-2297).

Farther up Highway 191/26/89, the Snake River Overlook provides a classic view of the Tetons; this is where Ansel Adams shot his famous black-and-white photograph of the mountains. Just beyond Moran Junction, the Oxbow Bend Turnout is a good place to observe bald eagles, great blue herons, moose, beaver, osprey, and otter (especially in the early morning). A little ways farther, at the Willow Flats Turnout, the wet meadows and willow thickets make good wildlife habitat; watch for moose feeding in this area. The Colter Bay Visitor

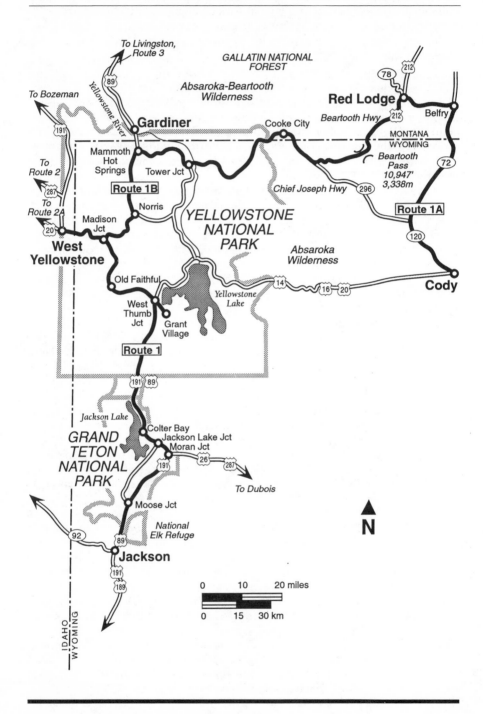

Center issues permits and displays exhibits of Native American artifacts and art.

You can see a lot by driving but you'll notice more on a walk. The *Teewinot*, Teton Park's information newspaper, lists some self-guided interpretive trails and rangers can recommend a trail suitable to your level of fitness and time available. Because most of the National Park campgrounds, in peak season, fill up by late morning, it's best to find a campsite prior to departing on a day hike. Of the five campgrounds, Gros Ventre, at the southern end of the park, is the slowest to fill.

The Volcanic Time Bomb: Yellowstone

From Grand Teton National Park, the John D. Rockefeller, Jr. Memorial Parkway slowly ascends towards Yellowstone National Park. The parkway bears the name of John D. Rockefeller, Jr. in honor of 30,000 acres/12,000 ha of land he deeded to the government as gift. Adjacent to where the Yellowstone Plateau swallows the Teton Range, you enter the world's first national park. As you travel through this global treasure, look beyond the traffic and crowds; remember the words of John Muir, "A thousand Yellowstone wonders are calling, 'Look up and down and round about you!'"

With more than 300 geysers and nearly 10,000 other thermal features contained in the 2.2 million acres set aside by the United States Congress in 1872, more thermal activity bubbles, spouts, and sprays in Yellowstone National Park than anywhere else in the world. No where in the "lower 48" is the variety and numbers of wildlife greater than in Yellowstone. This is the southernmost habitat of the grizzly bear. The Trail of the Great Bear begins here. On a typical summer day, 29,000 people enter the park. Each year, more than 972,809 vehicles containing 2.85 million people from around the world visit Yellowstone, an area so unique that the United Nations Educational, Social, and Cultural Organization (UNESCO) designated it a World Heritage Site and a World Biosphere Reserve. The United Nations bestows the World Heritage Site designation upon an area to recognize it as a unique global treasure. Two others exist along the Trail of the Great Bear: Banff National Park in the Four Mountain National Park and Head-Smashed-In Buffalo Jump Interpretive Center. Here are some of the world's treasures included in the exclusive club of World Heritage Sites: the Pyramids of Egypt, Machu Picchu in Peru, India's Taj Mahal, Yosemite Valley, and Sri Lanka. As a World Biosphere Reserve, Yellowstone is recognized as an outstanding example of one of the earth's major ecosystems; there are 209 such biosphere reserves in fifty-five countries around the world, including Waterton Lakes and Glacier national parks.

Given the incredibly unique character of Yellowstone, it's difficult to imagine that anyone opposed federal protection of the area. In the 1872 debate over national park designation for Yellowstone, one Senator said, "I do not see the reason or propriety of setting apart a large tract of land . . . for a public park. There is an abundance of public park ground in the Rocky Mountains that will never be occupied. There are some places, perhaps this is one, where persons can and would go and settle and improve and cultivate the grounds. . ."

The road from the South Entrance to the West Thumb of Lake Yellowstone passes through dense stands of lodgepole pine. Forest lands cover eighty percent of Yellowstone National Park and lodgepole dominates two-thirds of this area. The red colored lodgepole are the result of mountain pine beetles. In *"Greater Yellowstone,"* Rick Reese wrote, "the beetle infestation is highly selec-

Interior of Old Faithful Inn.

tive, affecting primarily older, mature trees and ignoring the younger ones. Beetle-killed trees are not wasted. Their snags provide perching and nesting sites for hawks and eagles and for cavity-nesting birds such as the mountain bluebird."

The fires of '88

The South Entrance Road skirts the confines of Lewis Canyon; along this section you'll see charred remnants of a major conflagration. Every society tells the story of how fire came into their control. For many Western Native People, coyote stole fire from the Gods and gave it to The People; Prometheus pilfered fire from Olympus and presented it to Europeans. Ever since humans received the gift of fire, we've maintained a love-hate relationship with the elemental force. The Yellowstone fires of 1988 sparked controversy over the Park Service's "let-it-burn" policy. This is ironic as the fires could not be stopped despite the efforts of the largest firefighting force in the United States' history. Another irony is that the effects of firefighting, the fire crew campsites, helipads, trails, and over 850 miles of firelines, will take longer to heal than the burned forests. The fires resulted from a unique combination of drought (the driest summer recorded in Yellowstone), high winds, and unusually warm temperatures (the moisture content in most of the forests was lower than kiln-dried lumber). These conditions fueled powerful firestorms in which convection currents intensified the fire's movement and lifted sparks, embers, and burning branches aloft where the wind carried them miles ahead of the main fire. Man-made and natural barriers proved incapable of stopping the conflagration and in the end, Nature dosed the fires with a blanket of snow. Immense fires such as those experienced in the summer of 1988, sweep through Yellowstone about once a century due to drought; the last major fires occurred in the early-1700s and mid-1800s. Though the fire burned 1.4 million acres in the Greater Yellowstone area and 989,000 acres of parkland, wildlife escaped surprisingly unscathed. Deaths in the park were: 257 elk (less than one percent of the population), nine bison, four deer, two black bear, two moose, and no grizzlies.

Some people, influenced by Smoky the Bear, feel that the fire was bad. Many other people however, realize that the fire was a natural occurrence, a powerful and elemental force that humbled the human efforts to control, let alone dominate it.

Yellowstone Lake

The turnoff to Lewis Lake provides access to a campground, picnic area, boat ramp, and ranger station. The lush meadows above Lewis Lake provide a moist habitat favored by moose. A short ways beyond the meadows, the road crosses over to the east side of the Continental Divide; before reaching Old Faithful, you'll cross it two more times. There is a campground in the Grant Village area.

At West Thumb, the road joins the Grand Loop. A turn to the right provides access to Yellowstone Lake that, with a surface area of 136 sq mi/328 sq km, a depth of 320 ft/98 m, and a shoreline of 110 mi/177 km, is the largest mountain lake in North America. For half of the year, the lake is locked in ice.

The road to Old Faithful ascends to Craig Pass; just below the pass, the Shoshone Overlook takes in Shoshone Lake and one last view of the Tetons. Up on Craig Pass (8,262 ft/2,518 m), Isla Lake, covered with lily pads, looks like a scene Monet would've painted. Because the lake sits astride the Continental Divide, when it overflows in the winter, the water flowing west eventually finds it way to the Gulf of Mexico and the water that flows east ends up in the Pacific.

Old Faithful and how it works

If you've never seen it erupt, Old Faithful Geyser is a must; just don't judge Yellowstone National Park by the atmosphere that prevails there. The geyser blasts thousands of gallons of steaming water with a regularity that it has maintained over 120 years of observation; currently the geyser faithfully awakens about every eighty minutes. The scalding column of water is evidence of the fiery forces that set Yellowstone's thermal features in motion and will eventually send the plateau, upon which you're standing, skyward in an explosion of pulverized dust and incandescent gas.

On a brisk day, it may be hard to believe that Yellowstone is one of the hottest spots in the world. The molten rock, known as magma, is usually 20 mi/35 km beneath the earth's surface; it may be as close as 2 mi/3 km beneath Yellowstone in certain places. As a consequence, the amount of heat emitted by the Yellowstone area is twenty times higher than most anywhere else on earth. The cause of this heat flow, a subterranean caldron of magma, has been cooling ever since the last explosion (600,000 years ago) blew tons of material more than 1,000 mi/1,613 km away. The pre-historic Yellowstone explosion made the 1980 eruption of Mount St. Helens look like a firecracker; it was at least a thousand times greater.

Like a thin shell unable to support itself, the earth's crust collapsed after the enormous pool of molten rock had been discharged. The 30 x 40 mi/

48 x 65 km region that collapsed, known as a caldera, sank several thousand feet. Most of Yellowstone's hot springs, mud pots, fumaroles, and geysers exist above the fractured rock that coincides with the rim of the caldera.

When Old Faithful erupts, here's what happens; water from the Firehole River seeps down through cracks deep into the earth until it reaches hot rocks. The water is superheated and would boil except that the weight of the upper water prevents boiling. Instead, the lower water expands and pushes the cooler upper water from the surface vent, which relieves pressure, and in a flash the superheated water boils, sending a column of water and steam into the air.

The Old Faithful Inn was built in 1904 entirely of native material. A National Historic Landmark, it was originally advertised as the largest log building in the world (and who knows, maybe it is). From inside the immense lobby, the unique construction with branching logs makes it look as if the inn grew out of the ground instead from the hands of skilled craftsmen. In the winter, the Old Faithful Snow Lodge makes an excellent base for cross-country ski trips into the surrounding country. (TW Recreational Services operates the park's lodging facilities, sightseeing services, Yellowstone Lake Marina, and snowcoach service to and from Old Faithful; for more information call 307-344-7311.) A particularly pleasant ski trip, with just the right amount of uphill and a fun downhill run, is the 3 mi/5 km Fern Cascade Loop which passes through the burned remains of a lodgepole forest. Some people might think that skiing past burned trees would be unpleasant. Actually, it's quite beautiful; the contrast between blackened trees and white snow makes it like skiing in an Ansel Adams photograph.

The road from Old Faithful passes the Black Sand Geyser Basin, Biscuit Basin,

Tourists getting too close to a bison in Yellowstone National Park.

The Grand Canyon of the Yellowstone.

and the Lower Geyser Basin as it rolls along beside the Firehold River towards Madison Junction. Elk, bison, and coyotes are commonly seen throughout this area. Don't feed the coyotes; it only makes them expect food from humans and this can lead to aggressive behavior when their expectations aren't met. Aggressive coyotes are killed. So, feeding coyotes only leads to their destruction. Another service that you can do for wildlife is remain a respectful distance away when photographing them. If your presence causes an animal to move, then you're too close. For your safety and that of other travelers, find a suitable turnout before stopping to view wildlife or scenic wonders. Please, don't imitate some people who stop in the middle of narrow roads on a blind corner in order to take a snapshot from the car window. Park the car, get out of it, and walk around—you'll get better pictures and a little exercise as well. But, again, keep your distance from wildlife.

Just before the Firehole River flows into the Madison River, it plunges over Firehole Falls which is an especially beautiful sight in the winter. Both rivers provide excellent fishing. A fishing permit is required for anyone twelve years of age and older. There is no charge for the permit and it can be picked up at entrance gates, ranger stations, visitor centers, and Hamilton General Stores along with fishing regulations.

The Madison Explorer's Museum near Madison Junction, takes a look back to the early explorers and the establishment of Yellowstone National Park. From the junction, a left turn leads to the West Entrance and the town of West Yellowstone (or continue straight ahead to follow Route 1C to Mammoth Hot

Springs). The road descends with the Madison River past dramatic cliffs and the blackened remains of lodgepole forests burned in 1988. West Yellowstone marks the end of Access Route 1A and the beginning of Route 2. Hopefully, after touring the world's first national park, you'll feel as renewed as John Muir, who wrote, "Stay on this good fire-mountain and spend the nights among the stars. Watch their glorious bloom until the dawn, and get one more baptism of light. Then with a fresh heart, go down to your work, and whatever your fate, you will remember these fine, wild views, and look back with joy to your wanderings in the blessed old Yellowstone Wonderland."

ACCESS ROUTE 1A: CODY TO MAMMOTH HOT SPRINGS
62mi/100km

Travel season: Cody to Red Lodge is open year-round. The Beartooth Scenic Highway is closed from October 16 to May 30; from Cooke City to Mammoth Hot Springs is open year-round.

Road conditions and route description: From Cody, follow Highway 120, a good two-lane, all-season road, for 37 mi/60 km to the Montana border where it becomes Highway 72. Continue 10 mi/16 km to the little town of Belfry, turn left on Highway 308 and follow this good, two-lane road for 15 mi/24 km to Red Lodge. Turn left onto Highway 212, the well maintained and two-lane Beartooth Scenic Highway (closed from mid-Oct. to late May), which switchbacks up Rock Creek Canyon, over the Beartooth Pass at 10,947 ft/3,338 m, across the Beartooth Plateau, down to Cooke City, and on through the Northeast Entrance of Yellowstone National Park. Here the road loses its numerical label and proceeds to Mammoth Hot Springs.

The route: The spirit of the West found in the Buffalo Bill Historical Center makes Cody, Wyoming, an excellent starting point for the Trail of the Great Bear. Cody, with its western hospitality and friendly people, has played host to world travelers ever since Colonel William F. "Buffalo Bill" Cody first envisioned the area as a hospitality center in the late 1800s. The town of Cody offers today's travelers fine art galleries, shops for the visitor's every need, dining, and plenty of lodging from which to base exploration of the surrounding Cody Country. The Buffalo Bill Museum displays thousands of artifacts from the famous Pony Express rider, buffalo hunter, scout, civil war soldier, actor, and showman for which the museum is named. The admission ticket permits two days worth of viewing, which should give you an idea of how much there is to see in the Center's four museums. The Cody Firearms Museum is the ultimate resource for anyone interested in the evolution of projectile weapons; from the cross-bow to the uzi, over 6,000 weapons are exhibited, some dating back 2,000 years.

The Plains Indian Museum profiles the history, culture, and art of the Plains Indian tribes. The Whitney Gallery of Western Art contains an outstanding collection of western art that ranges from the work of explorer artists such as Catlin, Bierstadt, and Moran to the display of two mammoth paintings by Jackson (a contemporary western artist), to special wings devoted to Remington and Russell. The Center operates March through November, 9 a.m. to 5 p.m., with extended hours of 7 a.m. to 10 p.m. for the months of June, July, and August. For more information write to the Buffalo Bill Historical Center, Box 1000, Cody, Wyoming 82414, or call 307-587-4771.

Also in Cody, during the second weekend of April, cowboys entertain the

Undine Falls in Yellowstone National Park.

town with music, humor, poetry, and tall tales at a gathering called the Cowboy Songs and Range Ballads. One of the largest gatherings of Native People from the Plains, the Plains Indian Powwow features a day-long singing and dance competition on the last weekend of June. Over the Fourth of July weekend, attend rodeos, street dances, parades, and fireworks at the Cody Stampede. (Cody Country Chamber of Commerce: Box 2777, Cody, Wyoming 82414; 307-527-6228.)

From Cody, Highway 120 leads north towards the distinctive Heart Mountain. Due to the Yellowstone Plateau, that rises on the left and creates a rainshadow, this initial section of Route 1A traverses arid land dotted with sagebrush and, up in the rocky heights, some juniper. Atop a low pass, the Beartooth Plateau comes into view, a sight all the more dramatic following a fresh snow fall in the high country. After the road levels out, watch for antelope. North of Cody, 17 mi/27 km, it's time to flip a coin or consult the *I Ching* because you're faced with a difficult decision—turn left (west) on Highway 296 and follow the Chief Joseph Scenic Highway or continue on to Red Lodge and over the Beartooth Scenic Highway.

Trail of Tears—Chief Joseph Scenic Highway

Highway 296 follows the Clark's Fork of the Yellowstone River up a spectacular 1,200-ft-/366-m-deep gorge between the granite Beartooth Plateau on the right and the volcanic Absaroka Mountains to the left. Highway 296 also traverses a portion of the Trail of Tears, the route taken by Chief Joseph and the Nez Perce in 1872 during the 1,700-mi/2,720-km exodus from their homeland in Eastern Oregon. The tragic story began in 1855 after the Nez Perce signed a treaty to remain on a reservation, which at that time included most of their ancestral land.

Only eight years later, due to pressure from white ranchers and farmers, the reservation was reduced to a quarter of its original size. A third of the Nez Perce lived off the new reservation; natives and whites co-existed for fourteen years until the Indian Bureau, ordered all Nez Perce onto the reservation within thirty days. Joseph and his band had almost met this ridiculous deadline when a group of young warriors, seeking revenge, killed four settlers. Two days later, General Howard's soldiers attacked Joseph's camp. Five bands of Nez Perce reasoned that if they abandoned their ancestral land to the settlers, then they could go where they pleased as long as they stayed away from whites. They were wrong. "Driven out of their ancestral homelands, and pursued at times by three separate U.S. armies," wrote historian Harry Fritz in *Montana: Land of Contrast*, "the Nez Perces practically invented the successful tactics of flight and evasion." They crossed Yellowstone National Park from, what is now, West Yellowstone to Cooke City, followed the Clark's Fork River (Highway 296) out onto the plains, and headed for Canada. Just 30 mi/48 km shy of the border, Col. Nelson Miles intercepted the Nez Perce with a surprise howitzer attack. In early October, with snow on the ground, and only 480 Nez Perce alive of the 800 that started the journey, Chief Joseph spoke for his people when he said, "I am tired of fighting. Our chiefs are killed. The

Looking down at Twin Lakes from atop the Headwall.

What Good is the Grizzly Bear?
by Charles Jonkel—Bear Biologist

Some people ask, "What good are grizzly bears? Extinction is natural, look what happened to the dinosaurs." In Montana, more and more, our grizzlies are a sign of what's right with the world. Grizzlies are a measure of our quality of life. They are a symbol of whether or not we are being good stewards of the land. Good grizzly habitat is good people habitat; when we lose the grizzly, we lose those qualities of the land that people prize most—open space, unpolluted water and air, low population densities, the Big Sky.

Before humans came to North America, the grizzly filled our niche. So far as the grizzly is concerned, we are a somewhat superior, two-legged bear. We compete for the same space. As people take more of the good *habitat and change it, grizzlies decline. This process has eliminated the grizzly from most of its range in the past 100 years—an exceedingly rapid loss for one species when viewed in terms of evolutionary time. We are just too much alike, which is also one of the reasons that grizzlies fascinate people so much.*

Habitat is the key limiting factor for the grizzly. We humans can adapt, it seems, to almost any bizarre condition of living— the grizzly isn't that flexible. So we hurt the bear, unknowingly or not. An example is the saucer and marbles *model, the saucer being the habitat. When the saucer is full of marbles, you cannot add even one more—no matter what color that marble might be. People-colored marbles and grizzly-colored marbles exclude each other. We do it by shooting grizzly bears or destroying their food; they do it by being big and scary, making bluff charges, or worse.*

To the nation, to the world, Montana is John Wayne *country, the place where you can ride a horse through the old growth or yellow pine forest, hunt elk, climb beautiful mountains, or watch the* antelope play. *Montana, itself, is important to the world as the place where things are still right—the* last, best place. *The grizzly is our* canary in the mine, *and Montana is the canary for the entire planet. The way we do things has a lot to do with why we have that role. Life in the slow lane, protecting wilderness, moving over to give the grizzly room to live, and understanding why we are here in the first place is what the wild Rockies and the Trail of the Great Bear is all about.*

Site of the Smith Mine Disaster east of Red Lodge.

old men are all dead. It is cold and we have no blankets. The little children are freezing to death. My people, some of them, have run away to the hills, and have no blankets, no food; no one knows where they are—perhaps freezing to death. I want to have time to look for my children and see how many of them I can find. Maybe I shall find them among the dead. Hear me, my chiefs. I am tired; my heart is sick and sad. From where the sun now stands I will fight no more forever."

On to Red Lodge

Twenty mi/32 km beyond the Highway 296 junction, Highway 120 becomes Highway 72 as it enters Montana. At the little town of Belfry (10 mi/16 km from the border), Highway 308 begins climbing into arid foothills on its way to Red Lodge. Just outside the tiny town of Bear Creek, the road passes the site of the 1943 Smith Mine Disaster where seventy-four men died. An explosion, due to inadequate safety measures, sealed the mine. Two trapped miners, who knew methane gas would soon kill them, wrote a simple and sad farewell, "Good-bye wives and daughters. We died an easy death. Love from us both. Be good."

"A ton of welcome and good spirit awaits visitors to Red Lodge," wrote the mayor of this "historic mining and friendly town of nearly 2,000 people." The name of Red Lodge originated from a band of Crow that separated with the main tribe and moved west into the foothills of the Beartooth Range. They colored their council tepee with red clay and from this came the name, Red Lodge. Hundreds of Finn, Scottish, Irish, Italian, Yugoslavian, and Scandinavian miners flocked to the area after the discovery of coal interested the Northern Pacific Railroad, and so began the town of Red Lodge. An international atmosphere still prevails in this unique mountain village. John Johnston, popularly known as Jeremiah Johnson or "Live Eatin' Johnson," served as the town's first constable; his old homestead cabin still stands on the grounds of the Carbon County Historical Museum at the south end of town.

Today, a great deal of the town's economy revolves around tourism. Many of the buildings in the Red Lodge Commercial Historic District date back to the late 1880s and are listed on the National Register of Historic Places. Red Lodge Mountain (406-446-2610), a downhill ski resort, boasts low prices, short lift lines, and uncrowded slopes covered with fresh powder. Cross-country skiing opportunities abound; a popular 2 mi/3 km trip, the Palisades Trail, extends from the ski area to Palisades Campground with the rugged Limestone Palisades of the Beartooth Mountains overlooking the route.

One of the country's more popular rodeos, Home of the Champions Rodeo, is held on the July Fourth weekend and attended by thousands of people. In addition to traditional rodeo events there is also a parade, the Kid's Sheep Riding Contest, and a wild horse race; this is more of a contest between a three-man team and an unwilling horse. The annual Mountain Man Rendezvous, on the last week of July, attracts mountain man wanna-be's from all over the country. Besides the authentic costumes and nineteenth-century paraphernalia, there are blackpowder shoots and entertainment, every evening at 7 p.m., that includes music, dance, and old-fashioned melodrama. The Festival of Nations, a nine-day extravaganza held in early August, celebrates the ethnic diversity of Red Lodge. Each day a different nation is singled out to honor that country's customs, food, and crafts. For more information about these and other events, write to the Red Lodge Chamber of Commerce at Box 988, Red Lodge, Montana 59068; or call 406-446-1718.

The Beartooth Scenic Highway

The Beartooth Scenic Highway, one of the three most stunning mountain roads on the Trail of the Great Bear corridor, begins at the south end of Red Lodge on Highway 212. A little ways up this road and on the left, there are two campgrounds, Ratine and Sheridan. Beyond Red Lodge, 11 mi/18 km, a right turn, on Forest Road 421, leads to four more campgrounds. The road clings to the south side of Rock Creek Canyon as it switchbacks up to an alpine world.

The Beartooth Plateau formed when a block of Precambrian igneous and metamorphic basement rock (rocks don't get any older than this) rose between faults some seventy million years ago. Originally, sedimentary rock sat on top of this block; nearly all of it eroded away and exposed a relatively flat surface almost 2mi/3 km above sea level. Throughout the last ice age, 12,000 years ago, an ice cap enveloped the plateau. It gouged the lake basins found atop, and at the edges of, the plateau and then spilled over sculpting the surrounding valleys. The u-shaped bottom and steep side-walls of Rock Creek Canyon provide an excellent example of glacial erosion that can be observed from the Rock Creek Vista. Please, don't act like some travelers who jump out of their car and shoot a snapshot from the guardrail; walk the short distance to the true vista point— you'll be rewarded.

Atop the Beartooth Plateau, you'll find a "landscape similar to that found in arctic regions," wrote Beverly Magley in *Scenic Byways*. "Growing conditions are severe, and plants have evolved unique adaptive abilities, such as remaining

Arid rolling hills north of Cody and the distant Beartooth Plateau in the background.

small and low to the ground or having hairy or waxy surfaces. It can take a plant as long as fifteen years to produce a single blossom."

Just after topping out on the plateau, a turn to the right leads a short ways to a parking area. Here's a good place to enjoy alpine wildflowers in bloom and take in a little ART (attitude readjustment time). Walk over to the plateau rim that overlooks the Twin Lakes Headwall, a fifty-eight degree slope where Olympic hopefuls come to test their downhill ski skills from early June until late July. Down below, you'll see two alpine gems, the Twin Lakes. The road crosses the Beartooth Pass at 10,947 ft/3,338 m, the highest driveable point on the Trail of the Great Bear. On an unspecified date, the Red Lodge Chamber of Commerce sets up a "snow bar" of soft drinks that they serve to unsuspecting travelers. If you're a cross-country skier with plans to travel this route anytime from spring through mid-summer, by all means, pack your skies. Highway 212 flanks the southeastern end of Montana's third largest wilderness, the 934,377-acre Absaroka-Beartooth Wilderness Area. The wildlands atop the Beartooth Plateau are a hiker's paradise. (For more information contact the U.S. Forest Service, Route 2, Box 3420, Red Lodge, MT 59068; 406-446-2103.)

The Island Lake and Beartooth Lake campgrounds provide a chance to spend the night in this alpine world. Fishing up on the plateau is excellent but, as the road weaves from Montana to Wyoming to Montana, be sure you possess the appropriate fishing license. A turn at the Clay Butte Fire Tower provides access to a panoramic view of the Absaroka Wilderness, Yellowstone National Park, the Clark's Fork Valley, Absaroka and Bighorn Mountains, and the 12,799 ft/3,902 m Granite Peak (to the northwest), Montana's highest mountain. The road descends through stands of Engelmann spruce, lodgepole pine, alpine fir, and aspen with views of two prominent landmarks, Pilot and Index Peaks. From the Clark's Fork Overlook, where the Chief Joseph Scenic Highway branches off, the north-facing flanks of the mountains across the valley bear evidence of the fires of 1988.

The route continues to Cooke City with four campgrounds along the way, Crazy Creek and Fox Creek Shoshone National Forest Campgrounds in Wyoming and on the other side of Colter Pass (8,000 ft/2,439 m) in Montana, the Chief Joseph and Soda Butte Gallatin National Forest Campgrounds. Cooke City got its start as a mining settlement in 1876. Today, the communities of Cooke City and Silver Gate deserve positive recognition for successfully shifting their economic base from the boom and busts that accompanied the early mining era to taking advantage of the aesthetic resources that attract tourists, hunters, and snowmobilers.

Into the park—The Lamar Valley

The road from Cooke City to Mammoth Hot Springs is open year-round. From the Northeast Entrance of Yellowstone National Park, the route follows Soda Butte Creek, and the rugged canyon it flows through, to the more spacious Lamar Valley, which some people refer to as the Serengeti of America. "On a knoll in the Lamar Valley," wrote Rick Reese in *Greater Yellowstone*, "a small group of Yellowstone Institute participants gathered on a June evening to observe wildlife. In little more than an hour from one location the group spotted elk, moose, mule deer, pronghorn antelope, bison, bighorn sheep, black bears, and grizzlies. It may be the only place on the face of the planet where this could be done, for where else does such a variety of animals share a common home except in this one valley of Yellowstone?" The Yellowstone Institute conducts outdoor courses that focus on Yellowstone's natural history. It is based at the old Lamar Buffalo Ranch in the Lamar Valley; for more information write to Box 117, Yellowstone National Park, Wyoming 82190; or call 307-344-7381, extension 2384.

On the south side of the valley, up on Specimen Ridge, trees of stone stand in silent testimony of ancient climatic changes and volcanic activity. The petrified forest, one of the most extensive on earth, formed fifty million years ago when vast clouds of volcanic debris settled upon living conifers. The cycle of forest growth and volcanic burial probably repeated itself twenty-seven times. Water percolated down through the beds of ash and released minerals into wood fiber, transforming trees into stone.

Beyond Tower Junction, the road traverses a hillside and provides spectacular views of the Yellowstone River Valley below. This stretch of road, from Tower Junction to Mammoth Hot Springs, would be a good bike route, especially after Labor Day when visitation tapers off and fewer vehicles occupy Yellowstone roads. The Yellowstone Park Headquarters are located at Mammoth Hot Springs. Though the United States Congress created the world's first national park in 1872, it didn't designate anyone to look after it. As a consequence, poachers proliferated as did outlaws, stagecoach robbers, and unscrupulous entrepreneurs who also exploited travelers, wildlife, and the land.

Roaring Mountain.

Mammoth Hot Springs

In 1886, a fifty-man contingent of the United States Army arrived at Mammoth where they based operations. Their duties included law enforcement, firefighting, the protection of "good" animals such as deer, elk, antelope, and moose. The Army exterminated "bad" predators—wolves, coyotes, cougars, and wolverines. With the creation of the National Park Service in 1916, Park Rangers replaced a 200-man Army detachment. The new park guardians, while more experienced in woodcraft and the duties necessary to administering a national park, still continued the extermination campaign on "bad" predators. They succeeded; by the 1920s, no more wolves existed in Yellowstone. Today, Park Service attitudes have changed. Based on the original mandate to "conserve, perpetuate, and portray as a composite whole the indigenous. . . terrestrial fauna," Yellowstone National Park desires the recovery of wolves. In 1980, the U.S. Fish and Wildlife Service approved a plan to reestablish two viable populations of wolves in the

Northern Rockies. In over a decade, little has happened with wolf recovery. Wolves remain extinct in the world's first national park.

Mammoth Hot Springs is best known for the steaming travertine terraces for which the settlement is named. These colorful formations owe their existence, as do all the thermal features in the area, to precipitation finding its way down towards the massive chamber of magma underlying Yellowstone. The hot rocks super-heat the water and propel it back to the surface via fissures, faults, and vents. While the water is in contact with the magma chamber, it is charged with carbon dioxide. This hot, acidic liquid rapidly dissolves subterranean limestone, carries it to the surface where exposure to open air allows carbon dioxide to escape. The lime, no longer able to be carried in solution, solidifies and forms travertine terraces. Each day, more than two tons of dissolved limestone surface and flow down Mammoth Terrace. The white and yellow colors on the terraces are thermal bacteria, descendants of the primordial soup from which more complex life evolved. The orange, brown, and green are algaes that enjoy cooler water.

The Albright Visitor Center, at Mammoth Hot Springs, displays natural and human history related to the park as well as changing exhibits. The Center also exhibits some of Thomas Moran's watercolor sketches and William Henry Jackson's photographs from the historic Hayden Expedition that was instrumental in inspiring Congress to protect Yellowstone. A word of advice, if you spend the night at Mammoth Hot Springs Campground, take earplugs; throughout the night, vehicles roar up and down the steep North Entrance Road above which the camp is situated. In the fall, however, the camp is a good place

Bull elk and his harem in Norris Meadows.

Gibbon Falls.

to hear elk bugle. Mammoth marks the end of Route 1B and the beginning of either Route 1C to West Yellowstone or Route 3 out the Paradise Valley and on to Livingston and Bozeman.

ROUTE 1B: MAMMOTH HOT SPRINGS TO WEST YELLOWSTONE
48 mi/77 km

Travel season: Closed from about November 1 to April 30.
Road conditions and route description: From Mammoth Hot Springs, follow the park road, which is windy, narrow, and in somewhat poor condition, to Madison Junction; turn right (west) and continue to West Yellowstone.

The route: From Mammoth the Park Service road becomes more sinuous and narrow as it traverses rolling terrain forested with lodgepole pine, some of it burned in the fires of 1988. The route passes two sites significant to prehistoric native people, Sheepeater Cliff and Obsidian Cliff. Sheepeater Cliff is named for the hunters of mountain sheep, a branch of the Shoshone that, according to Ake Hultkrantz in *The Shoshones in the Rocky Mountains,* "retained the old way of living from the time before horses were introduced and who established a specialized mountain culture." For travelers interested in geology, this is a good place to see columns of basalt that exhibit columnar jointing. Obsidian Cliff is probably the "Mountain of Glass" that mountain man Jim Bridger told tall tales about. Molten magma takes on different forms depending on how it cools; if cooled slowly beneath the earth's surface, it becomes granite (like the rock found on the Beartooth Plateau), whereas cooling above ground results in rhyolite (a predominate rock in Yellowstone). Rapid cooling above ground results in the black and glass-like obsidian. Contact with ice, 150,000 years ago, cooled the magma rapidly and produced Obsidian Cliff. Ancient inhabitants of Yellowstone fashioned the volcanic glass into arrow and spear points, knives, and scraping tools. The hunters traded these products, which show up as far away as the burial mounds in Ohio (1,500 mi/2,420 km to the east). Willow Park, located between these two native sites, is a good area to observe moose in the early morning.

Farther down the road, you come to Roaring Mountain. If you sit for awhile before this scorched-earth landscape with steam hovering over dead trees, it is easy to imagine our planet in its infancy. This thermal area, though on the wane, is still quite dramatic and best viewed when back-lighted by the morning sun.

Norris—The hottest spot on Earth

In the autumn, near Norris Junction, in Norris Meadows, bull elk jealously guard their harem. While this magnificent scene attracts the wildlife photographer in all of us, please maintain a respectful distance from the elk—they need to conserve all the calories they can for the winter ahead. Norris Geyser Basin is not only the oldest geyser basin in Yellowstone, it's also the hottest and most volatile geyser basin in North America, if not the world. The hottest temperature recorded at a Yellowstone thermal area was measured here at Norris, 459 degrees F/237 degrees C (more than twice the temperature of boiling water) only .25 mi/.5 km beneath the surface. The world's highest-reaching geyser—Steamboat Geyser, which spouts steam and water over 300 ft/91 km into the air—and the most colorful thermal area are but two reasons to visit Norris Geyser Basin.

The area is named in honor of Philetus W. Norris, Yellowstone's second superintendent (1877-1882). Norris, a self-taught historian, archaeologist, and scientist, documented the park's natural and human history in addition to constructing roads to the park's major attractions and drafting recommendations that resulted in the first wildlife management program on federal lands. The Norris Soldier Station is a relic of the days when the U.S. Army protected the park. Though the Park Service, newly formed in 1916, based its duties on precedents set by the Army, a major departure was the establishment of educational exhibits to interpret the park's wonders. The Norris Museum, one of the original trailside interpretive exhibits, opened in 1930.

The United States National Park visitor centers and interpretive exhibits are part of a series of interpretive facilities found along the Trail of the Great Bear at Frank Slide, Head-Smashed-In, and Peter Lougheed Provincial Park; they are interesting and informative.

Beyond Norris, Paint Pot Hill is an example of the bulges that continue to rise above the Yellowstone Plateau like primordial bread dough. This dome also lends prophetic testimony to the subterranean time bomb that will, at some future and unknown date, launch much of Yellowstone into the upper atmosphere as it did a half-million years ago. Route 1C continues down

Gibbon Canyon where the Gibbon River cuts through deposits of ancient volcanic ash and cascades over the beautiful Gibbon Falls. From Gibbon Falls, the road leads to Madison Junction and the end of Route 1C.

For More Information About Route 1:

The Yellowstone Story, Aubrey L. Haines.
The Hiker's Guide to Wyoming, Bill Hunger.
Yellowstone Trails, Mark C. Marshall.
Greater Yellowstone, Rick Reese.

Events and Services

Yellowstone Country: P.O. Box 1107, Red Lodge, Montana 59068; 1-800-736-5276; 406-446-1005.

Cody Country Chamber of Commerce: Box 2777, Cody, Wyoming 82414; 307-527-6228.

Red Lodge Chamber of Commerce: Box 988, Red Lodge, Montana 59068; 406-446-1718.

Jackson Hole Visitors Council: P.O. Box 982, Department 8, Jackson Hole, Wyoming, 83001; 1-800-782-0011, extension 8.

Snake River Institute: 307-733-2214.

Teton Science School: Box 68P, Kelly, Wyoming, 83011; 307-733-4765.

Buffalo Bill Historical Center: Box 1000, Cody, Wyoming 82414; 307-587-4771.

Yellowstone Institute: Box 117, Yellowstone National Park, Wyoming 82190; 307-344-7381, extension 2384.

Wildlife Viewing

National Elk Refuge: 307-733-8084.

National Parks

Grand Teton National Park: Superintendent, Grand Teton National Park, P.O. Drawer 170, Moose, Wyoming 83012; 307-733-2880; telecommunications device for the deaf (TDD) number is 307-733- 2053.

Yellowstone National Park: Superintendent, Yellowstone National Park, Yellowstone National Park, Wyoming 82190; 307-344-7381.

Handicap Access Coordinator: Yellowstone National Park, Wyoming 82190; 307-344-7381.

National Forests and Wilderness Areas

Absaroka-Beartooth Wilderness Area: U.S. Forest Service, Route 2, Box 3420, Red Lodge, Montana 59068; 406-446-2103.

Gallatin National Forest: Federal Building, P.O. Box 130, Bozeman, MT 59771; 406-587-6701.

Mammoth Hot Springs

Plateau to Pit

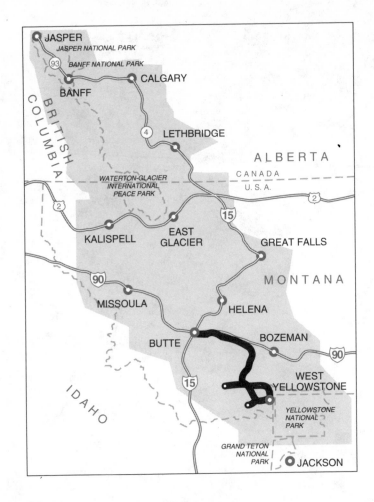

"In our family, there was no clear line between religion and fly fishing. We lived at the junction of great trout rivers in western Montana, and our father was a Presbyterian minister and a fly fisherman who tied his own flies and taught others. He told us about Christ's disciples being fishermen, and we were left to assume, as my brother and I did, that all first-class fishermen on the Sea of Galilee were fly fishermen and that John, the favorite, was a dry-fly fisherman."

Norman Maclean—*A River Runs Through It.*

ROUTE 2

WEST YELLOWSTONE to BUTTE   150 miles/241 kilometers

General description: From dark dog-hair forests to narrow canyons, from strange rock formations on a mountain pass to broad sagebrush valleys backed by snowcapped mountains, Route 2 contains the greatest variety of landscapes, and some of the best fishing found along the Trail of the Great Bear. Beginning in the dense lodgepole forests that surround West Yellowstone, Route 2 passes Hebgen Lake, situated in an open basin vegetated with aspen and sagebrush, and then descends Madison Canyon to the site of a 1959 earthquake that caused the entire side of a mountain to slide. Beyond the Earthquake Site, the route follows the Madison River down the wide, open, and remarkably undeveloped Madison Valley to the town of Ennis. From Ennis, you ascend to a low, broad saddle and then descend through open grasslands and past rocky ridges to Norris. The route continues through broad valleys of open grassland and sagebrush until it enters the scenic Jefferson Canyon and provides access to the beautifully sculpted limestone features found in the Lewis and Clark Caverns.

At Cardwell, the route follows Interstate 90 West across cultivated bottomland interspersed with open areas of sagebrush and surrounded by gentle mountains. The highway ascends past junipers and mountain mahogany to forests of Douglas-fir and lodgepole pine that grow among intriguing formations of granite found on Homestake Pass. From the pass, the route descends the west side of the Continental Divide to Butte.

Unique features: Museum of the Yellowstone, International Fly Fishing Center, Madison Earthquake Site Visitor Center, Lionhead Mountain Roadless Area, Madison and Jefferson Rivers—"legendary" blue-ribbon trout streams— Lee Metcalf Wilderness Area, Middle Mountains/Tobacco Roots Roadless Area, Lewis and Clark Caverns, Whitetail/Haystack Roadless Area.

Wildlife viewing opportunities: Red Rock Lakes National Wildlife Refuge, Cliff and Wade Lakes, Lewis and Clark Caverns.

Activities: Fishing, hiking, backpacking, mountain biking, snowmobiling, cross-country skiing.

Events: Cross Country Fall Ski Camp, Rendezvous Cross Country Ski Race, World Snowmobile Expo.

Travel season: Year-round access.

Services: Services are readily available in Butte, West Yellowstone, and in Ennis. Butte and West Yellowstone have commercial airports.

Road conditions and route description: From West Yellowstone, drive 8 mi/13 km north to where a left turn keeps you on Highway 287 which passes through Ennis and Norris. At the Highway 2 junction, 106 mi/171 km beyond West Yellowstone, turn left and continue 13 mi/21 km on a road that winds through Jefferson Canyon to Interstate 90. Take the Butte/West on-ramp and remain on the Interstate for 29 mi/47 km, over Homestake Pass (elevation 6,375 ft/1,944 m) to Butte. Highways 2 and 287 are well-maintained, two-lane, four-season roads.

The route: People from West Yellowstone insist that their town, situated at 6,666 ft/2,032 m, experiences three seasons; July, August, and winter. Long winters and abundant snow is why West Yellowstone claims the title, "Snowmobile Capitol of the World." Though people have settled in the area since the 1880s, the town of West Yellowstone owes its existence to the arrival of the railroad in 1908. From the start, West Yellowstone relied on Yellowstone National park and tourism.

"The influence of the Northern Pacific Railroad Company was not always readily apparent in the commercial affairs of the Park," wrote Aubrey L. Haines in *The Yellowstone Story*, "yet it was always there—sometimes guiding, sometimes cajoling, and sometimes threatening the concessionaires to create what the railroad management desired: a summer resort attractive to large numbers of tourists. Tourism was the goal of the Northern Pacific, and interest in the Park lasted just as long as tourism was profitable."

Following World War II, America's love affair with automobiles spelled the end of rail service to gateway communities outside the park. Summer traffic passed through West Yellowstone, but the town slumbered through long winters until the mid '60s. With the spread of a new adult toy, snowmobiles, the town welcomed snow; it was like white-gold. Now, snowmobilers from all over the country flock to West Yellowstone where they base snowmobile trips into the park or the surrounding National Forest Service land. Yellowstone is the only national park along the Trail of the Great Bear that allows snowmobiling (which is restricted to designated routes on the main roads). The World Snowmobile Expo, with exhibits, races, food vendors, and musical entertainment, is held on the third weekend of March; 2,500 snowmobiles buzzed around town during the 1991 Expo. (For more information contact the West Yellowstone Chamber of Commerce at 406-646-7701.)

In the past decade, West Yellowstone has also become a favored destination to cross-country skiers. The park, of course, is one reason. Another reason are the Rendezvous Ski Trails, located right on the edge of town. The tracks at Rendezvous are well maintained (sometimes groomed twice a day) and offers diagonal-stride tracks and twelve-foot-wide skating trails. Rendezvous Ski Trails is supported by the local merchants, inn keepers, and restaurant owners through the Chamber of Commerce Fair Share Grooming Fund.

For the entire month of November the Cross-Country Fall Ski Camp attracts international racers for intense training on the Rendezvous ski trails. There are also workshops and clinics for the general skier. (Contact Drew Barney, P.O. Box 104, West Yellowstone, Montana 59758; 406-646-9379.) The Yellowstone Rendezvous Nordic Ski Race takes place on the first or second weekend of March and features twenty-five and fifty-kilometer races and a ten-kilometer race for skiers under the age of thirteen. (Contact the West Yellowstone Chamber of Commerce or Yellowstone Rendezvous, P.O. Box 65, West Yellowstone, Montana 59758.)

After the snows melt, it's time to fly fish and there's plenty of "blue-ribbon" trout fishing found along Route 2. According to a handout from the International Fly Fishing Center, "fly fishing has been traced back to early Greece and the year 200 A.D." Conspicuously located in West Yellowstone in the Union Pacific Dining Lodge (built in 1925) the Center carries out the mandate of its sponsor organization, The Federation of Fly Fishers; "Conserving-Restoring-Educating Through Fly Fishing." The Center conducts fly tying and casting workshops and exhibits historic rods and reels, fly plates, antique memorabilia,

Earthquake Lake.

two aquariums that display aquatic insects, and a Whitlock Vikert (hatching) Box. The Pat Lilly Gallery of Angling Art maintains a permanent collection, as well as changing exhibits, of art concerned with fish, streams, and fly fishing. The International Fly Fishing Center charges no admission and is open from Memorial Day to Labor Day. (Box 1088, West Yellowstone, Montana 59758; 406-646-9541.)

Next door, in the Union Pacific Depot (built between 1907 and 1909), the private Museum of the Yellowstone houses exhibits of U.S. Cavalry, mountain man and rare Indian artifacts, wildlife dioramas, and a theatre. Fires of Yellowstone and Bears of Yellowstone are two of the Museum's special exhibits. Ironically, this private museum offers the only bear exhibit found on the entire Trail of the Great Bear. The Museum charges admission and is open 8 a.m. to 10 p.m. daily, May through October. (For more information write to Joel Janetski, Ph.D., Director, Museum of the Yellowstone, West Yellowstone, Montana 59758; 406-646-7814.) The West Yellowstone Airport is closed in the winter except to bushplanes with skis.

From West Yellowstone, Highway 287 passes from the dog-hair forests of lodgepole pine into an open basin that contains Hebgen Lake. If you couldn't find a camping spot in Yellowstone National Park or desire an escape from crowds, there are two National Forest Service Campgrounds close to West Yellowstone. The turnoff of Highway 287 to Rainbow Point Campground and Boatdock is 5 mi/8 km north of West Yellowstone and Baker's Hole Campground is only 3 mi/5 km out of town.

Earthquake slide

Eight mi/13 km beyond West Yellowstone, you must make a left-hand turn in order to remain on Highway 287. The road skirts the north shore of Hebgen Lake; in the distance (to the west) you can see where the mountains constrict and the Madison Canyon begins. At the end of Hebgen Lake, just before the road enters the narrow confines of Madison Canyon, look back because that's the last view of the Yellowstone Plateau. Across the lake (to the south), the Lionhead Mountain Roadless Area rises up to meet the Continental Divide. This relatively small area, which is important to grizzlies, is proposed for wilderness designation. The best access to the Lionhead Mountain Roadless Area is reached from West Yellowstone by turning off Highway 20 and onto Forest Service Road 167.

Even if you don't intend to spend the night at the Cabin Creek Campground, it's a good place to stretch your legs on a short walk along the Hebgen Earthquake Scarp. For those who think that the business of geology is a slow and boring process, the 15-ft-/5-m-high displacement scarp is evidence of geology in action.

This 18-mi-/29-km-long scarp, which looks like an abrupt abutment, appeared on August 17, 1959, when an earthquake suddenly tilted the Hebgen Lake Fault Block (a 125-square-mile chunk of earth). A short ways down the road, past the Beaver Creek National Forest Service Campground, there's more dramatic documentation of geology in action at the Madison Earthquake Visitor Center. The road to the Earthquake Center skirts the shores of Earthquake Lake (watch for double-crested cormorants and nesting osprey) formed by an earth dam created when the side of a mountain roared down into Madison Canyon. The Madison Slide was triggered by an earthquake, with a magnitude of 7.5 on the Richter scale (the 1964 Alaska earthquake measured 8.5), that produced a boulder field over 300 ft/91 m deep, and enough rock rubble to build a two-lane, 3-ft-/1-m-deep highway from the visitor center to New York City. Of the twenty-eight people who died that night, nineteen remain buried beneath eighty million tons of rock. The Madison Earth Quake Visitor Center (Hebgen Lake Ranger District, Box 520, West Yellowstone, Montana 59758; 406-646-7369) displays more information about the quake, a good before-and-after aerial photograph, and a working seismograph.

The Madison Valley

From the visitor center, the road leaves Madison Canyon and enters the broad and relatively undeveloped southern end of the Madison Valley with the Gravelly Range forming the western skyline and the more rugged Madison Range on the east side. The two mountain ranges are blocks of earth that rose when the Rockies formed, whereas the Madison Valley is a fault-block that sank. A short ways beyond the Highway 287 and 87 junction, a left turn on the gravel Forest Service Road 8381 leads (6 mi/10 km) to Cliff and Wade lakes (U.S. Forest Service 406-682-4253). Carol Fischer described the area in the *Montana Wildlife Viewing Guide* as, "two unique lakes [that] sit on a geologic fault, forming a chasm with cliffs surrounding much of the lakes. Both lakes support many nesting raptors,...waterfowl and beaver,...elk and moose...and occasionally trumpeter swans."

There's a public boat ramp at Cliff Lake and canoe rentals are available at Wade Lake Resort. In the winter, the Wade Lake Resort grooms 28 mi/45 km of cross-country ski trails (some for skating). For more information write

Wade Lake Resort, Box 107, Cameron, Montana 59720; 406-682-7560. Cliff Lake Lodge provides access to forty-five kilometers of groomed cross-country ski track in remote surroundings; write to Box 573, Cameron, Montana 59720; 406-682-4982.

Between the Earthquake Center and the town of Ennis there are four campgrounds and two river access points. The campgrounds from south to north are: Madison, West Fork, South Madison, and West Madison-Lyon Bridge. McAtee Bridge Fishing Access point provides passage onto the Madison River, one of Montana's legendary "blue-ribbon" trout streams.

The Montana Department of Fish, Wildlife and Parks conducted research to assess the effects of restocking the Madison with hatchery trout. The study revealed ironic results. As Michael Sample wrote in *The Angler's Guide to Montana*, "The addition of thousands of hatchery-reared trout each spring was actually reducing the number of fish in the river. . . the influx of hatchery fish was displacing the resident population. . . but the hatchery fish were unable to survive more than a short time in the demanding river environment."

A left turn at McAtee Bridge leads to the Wall Creek Wildlife Management Area. Winter is a good time to view elk here as the area provides important winter range for over 1,000 elk. The skyline of the Madison Mountains, on the right (eastern) side of the valley, forms the outer boundary of the Lee Metcalf Wilderness which encompasses 259,000 rugged acres in four separate locations: the monolithic Sphinx Mountain and other alpine peaks rise from the Taylor-Hilgard Unit before you; the Bear Trap Canyon Unit, along the Madison River, contains a 10 mi/16 km stretch of class IV and V whitewater flanked by thousand-foot cliffs; and glaciated mountains crown the Monument Mountain Unit northwest of Yellowstone National Park and the Spanish Peaks Unit southeast of Ennis.

At Ennis, the Madison River flows away from the highway to cut a narrow slot through the Madison Range. How did the river cut a channel through a mountain range; shouldn't water follow the easiest course? The Madison River did travel the easiest course, a channel that existed prior to the appearance of the Madison Range. As the mountains rose, the river continued in its original direction, carving a narrow gorge that is known today as the Bear Trap Canyon. From Ennis, a right turn (east) onto the gravel Forest Service Road 166 offers access to the northern end of Taylor-Hilgard Unit and southern end of the Spanish Peaks Unit of the Lee Metcalf Wilderness. The town of Ennis provides a good base for fishing expeditions, as evidenced by the sign at the edge of town; "Ennis, 660 people and 11 million trout." Highway 287 out of Ennis ascends to a saddle where you can see remnants of the Bozeman Trail (see Route 3), scouted by John Bozeman and used from 1863-68 as the quickest route to the gold mining boom town of Virginia City.

As Highway 287 continues north through the town of Norris and into the Jefferson Canyon, you pass through an open and broad, grassy valley, rimmed by rocky ridges with conifers, and backed by the Tobacco Roots Mountains to the left (west). These mountains form the backbone of the 90,000-acre Middle Mountains-Tobacco Roots Roadless Area. Glaciers from the most recent ice age left behind a rugged terrain, frequented by mountain goats, where numerous peaks rise above 10,000 ft/3,049 m. The term *Roadless Area* means just that; lacking roads the area is wild and pristine, however it lacks the formal protection of wilderness designation. This seldom-used area can

ROUTE 2 *WEST YELLOWSTONE TO BUTTE*

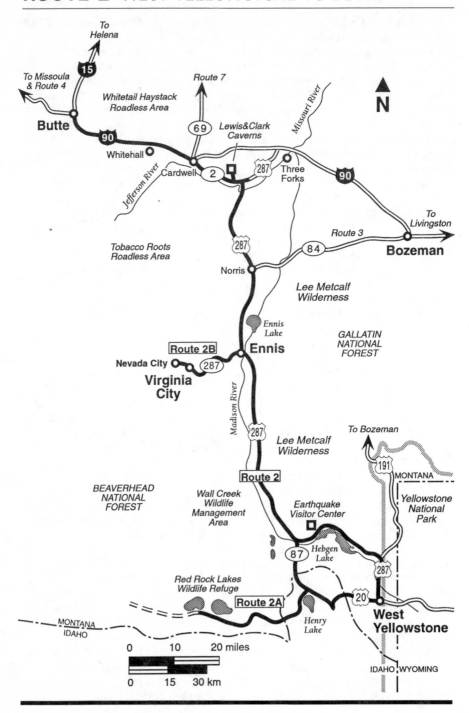

be reached by turning left off Highway 287 onto the road of the town of Pony followed by a (Beaverhead National) Forest Service Road to a campground.

Lewis and Clark Caverns

Just before the junction of Highways 287 and 2, the road crosses another legendary "blue-ribbon" trout stream, the Jefferson River. The Sappington Bridge Fishing Access permits public entry to this part of the Jefferson River. From here you can see the Sappington Water Gap (on private land), an impressive canyon, where the Jefferson continued on its course and cut down through limestone as the region rose. At the junction, turn left (west) and follow Highway 2 into the narrow confines of the Jefferson Canyon; watch for antelope. The 2,700-acre Lewis and Clark Caverns State Park is 5 mi/8 km beyond the junction. "These are truly spectacular caverns," wrote geologists Alt and Hyndman in *Roadside Geology of the Northern Rockies*, "fully equal of many better known ones in other parts of the country." Watch for golden eagles, mule deer, and red-tailed hawks along the 3 mi/5 km road that ascends from grassland along the Jefferson River to open forests of Douglas fir, limber pine, and Rocky Mountain juniper, and dense thickets of mountain mahogany surrounding the visitor center. Though Lewis and Clark traveled along the Jefferson River, they passed through oblivious to the caves that would later be named in their honor.

The labyrinth formed in 300-million-year-old limestone that once composed the floor of a shallow inland sea. Geologically speaking, the caverns are quite young, only a million years old. Groundwater penetrated cracks in the limestone and dissolved the initial caverns. As the region experienced more uplift and the Jefferson River cut its canyon deeper, the caves drained of water. That's when work on the elegant final touches began, finish-work that continues today. Rainwater percolates through and dissolves limestone above the caverns. As rainwater falls, it picks up carbon dioxide which renders it slightly acidic. When the water with dissolved limestone reaches the ceiling of a cavern and forms a drip, the water unloads some of the limestone it carried in solution and a stalactite gradually forms. When the drop splashes on the cave floor, it deposits more of its limestone load and a stalagmite starts up. Here's a good way to remember the difference between stalactites (the ones that hang down) and stalagmites (the ones that point up); stalactites hang tight (from the ceiling) and stalagmites might grow (up from the ground).

The park is open and guided tours are conducted through the caverns from May 1 through September 30. Tickets are available: May 1 to June 14 and Labor Day to September 30 from 9 a.m. to 5 p.m., June 15 to Labor Day from 9 a.m. to 7 p.m. The tour takes two hours and starts with a short, self-guided, interpretive trail to the cavern entrance. Carry a jacket for the cool walk through the caves, which are the only known maternity colony of western big-eared bats in Montana. Fear of bats is unfounded as they're not aggressive towards humans. The park also contains a campground. For more information, write to Lewis and Clark Caverns, Box 949, Three Forks, Montana 59752 or call 406-287-3541.

Madison River.

Up and over Homestake Pass

From the Lewis and Clark Caverns, Highway 2 follows the Jefferson River through the rugged and picturesque canyon named after the river that eroded it. Just beyond the town of Cardwell, Highway 2 connects with Interstate 90; take the westbound lanes towards Butte. North of the Interstate, opposite the town of Whitehall, the Golden Sunlight mining operation sits atop the remains of a mountain. Gold mining continues today; the Golden Sunlight Mine employs 170 people who remove 7,000 tons of ore each day that yields over 250 ounces of gold.

Interstate 90 ascends to the top of Homestake Pass (6,375 ft/1,944 m) where granite outcrops of the Boulder Batholith protrude from sandy soil. These spires, ridges, boulders, and pinnacles, surrounded by Rocky Mountain juniper, conifers, and mountain mahogany, look like a Japanese rock garden. The Boulder Batholith (extending clear up to Helena) was once a molten mass of igneous rock that, like a boil, swelled up beneath the earth's surface. Instead of blowing up as the molten mass below Yellowstone did, this magma cooled slowly and formed granite which cracked at fairly regular intervals. While still below the surface, water filtered down and rounded the granite blocks. Later, erosion removed loose soil and exposed this distinctive landscape.

The Whitetail-Haystack Roadless Area, north of Homestake Pass, encompasses over 70,000 acres/28,000 ha of rolling ridges covered by dense forests. This seldom-used area also contains wet meadows, grasslands, good elk habitat, and more of those intriguing boulder formations. From Homestake Pass, the Interstate descends to the colorful town of Butte, home of the 90-ft/127-m steel

Madonna, Our Lady of the Rockies, who gazes down into the Berkeley Pit.

ROUTE 2A: RED ROCK LAKES   38 mi/61 km

General description: This sidetrip ascends from West Yellowstone, through dense lodgepole forests and open meadows, over Targhee Pass (7,072 ft/2,156 m), and down to Henry Lake in Idaho. A dusty gravel road at the north end of the Lake crosses over a low saddle and leads into the important wildlife habitats found among Montana's Centennial Mountains and the Red Rock Lakes National Wildlife Area.

Travel season: Year-round.

Road conditions and route description: Follow Highway 20 for 13 mi/21 km over Targhee Pass (elevation 7,072 ft/2,156 m) to the junction with Highway 87. Turn right (north) and drive 5 mi/8 km, then turn left (west) on Red Rock Pass Road and follow this gravel road for 20 mi/32 km over Red Rock Pass (elevation 7,120 ft/2,171 m) to the refuge entrance.

The route: Many people have called the Red Rock Lakes National Wildlife Refuge the most beautiful refuge in the United States. Whatever it's called, the area definitely provides an incredibly easy opportunity to view a wide range of wildlife. The 13,000 acre/10,400 ha refuge varies from 9,000 ft/ 2,750 m peaks to extensive wetlands that provide a home to thousands of migratory waterfowl, sandhill cranes, whooping cranes, golden eagles, ferruginous hawks, and the largest breeding population of trumpeter swans in the lower United States. Sagebrush, aspen, Douglas-fir, and limber pine flank the lakes as well as a variety of wildflowers. The Red Rock area is critical wildlife habitat and an integral component of Greater Yellowstone; pronghorn antelope, deer, and elk also make their homes here. The Upper Lake Campground is a good place to watch swans; keep an eye on the willows where moose like to hang out. While most of the refuge can be seen from a car, Odell and Red Rock creeks are good places to get out and hike. The unimproved roads provide fun mountain biking.

Along a fault zone south of the refuge, the Centennial Mountains rise like an abrupt 3,000 ft/915 m wall to form part of the Continental Divide. Immediately adjacent to the Red Rocks Lakes area, 90,000 acres/36,000 ha of the Centennial Mountains are designated a Wilderness Study Area, an area that meets all the criteria for official wilderness designation but has yet to receive such protection.

ROUTE 2B: HIGHWAY 287, VIRGINIA CITY   15 mi/25km

General description: From Ennis, this sidetrip ascends through grassland and sagebrush dotted with juniper, limber pine, and Douglas-fir to a pass between the Gravelly Range and the Tobacco Roots Mountains. Near the summit, there are excellent views of the Madison Valley and the Lee Metcalf Wilderness. The road drops down to the historic gold-mining towns of Virginia City and Nevada City.

Travel season: Year-round.

Road conditions and route description: At Ennis, turn left (west) off of U.S. Highway 287 and follow Montana Highway 287 for 14 mi/23 km over a low pass to Virginia City. Nevada City is only 1 mi/1.5 km beyond Virginia City. This stretch of Montana Highway 287 is a good, all-weather road.

The route: Travelers interested in Montana mining history may find this short side-trip interesting. From Ennis, turn left (west) onto Montana Highway 287 which climbs to a saddle through sagebrush and grassland, with juniper, limber pine, and Douglas-fir growing at the higher elevations. Scenic views of the Madison drainage and Lee Metcalf Wilderness are especially photogenic in the morning or evening when long shadows stretch across the broad valley. The saddle forms the geologic division between the Gravelly Range to the south and the Tobacco Root Mountains to the north. The road drops from the saddle right down to Alder Gulch and Virginia City, followed by Nevada City a short distance farther.

In 1867, when the people of Montana voted on the location for their state capitol, they chose Virginia City, site of the world's richest placer gold discovery. Nevertheless, seven years later, Helena ended up with the honor as it continued to prosper in contrast to the sagging mine-dependent economy of Virginia City. Today, people visit Virginia City, a National Historic Landmark, to walk the boardwalks, view historically restored shops behind frontier storefronts, and watch the Virginia City Players in the old Opera House. The town's variety of architectural styles makes it a good example of a typical, old western mining town. In its heyday, 10,000 people bustled about Alder Gulch. Today, 192 people live in Virginia City. (Virginia City Chamber of Commerce, Box 67, Virginia City, Montana 59644; 406-843-5377.)

Nevada City was an Alder Gulch mining camp located 1 mi/1.5km past Virginia City. Less than a dozen of the original buildings remain, most are a collection moved to the present site from different places in Montana. However, there is supposed to be one of the few remaining two-story outhouses somewhere around Nevada City.

Though gold was first discovered, in 1858, at Gold Creek near present-day Drummond, the 1863 strike at Alder Creek instigated Montana's mining boom that would lead to Montana becoming a territory (1864) and finally a state (1889). To the Native people however, gold spelled doom and the loss of their land. Where prospectors discovered gold, more prospectors followed their trails, tent cities sprang up, freight roads were surveyed and wagons carried in supplies, and wooden towns rose above the canvas as more and more people followed the roads that the military found it necessary to guard.

Justice was dispensed by miner's courts and, due to the lack of jails, the lawbreakers were "either flogged (which was rare), banished (which was common), or," as historian K. Ross Toole wrote in *Montana: An Uncommon Land*, "hanged (which, for a time, was predominant)." Nevada City is the sight of one such hanging that inspired the organization of the Vigilance Committee and a hanging spree unprecedented in annals of Montana history. The Vigilantes of Virginia City formed due to the cold-blooded killing and robbery of over one hundred people. The band of notorious murderers secretly called themselves "The Innocents," tied a special knot in their bandanna, and trimmed their beards in a special fashion. Their leader, Henry Plummer, was the sheriff of Bannack with Alder Gulch in his jurisdiction. "Still a young man in 1862," wrote Malone and Roeder in *Montana: A History of Two Centuries*, "the handsome Plummer combined in one unstable personality qualities of charm and intelligence, but also of psychotic viciousness." Because gold miners tended to be distrustful loners, transient, and too busy with their work to chase outlaws, it took the work-halting cold of winter and the first hanging in Nevada City before the Vigilantes organized. Within a six week period, the Vigilantes hanged twenty-four of the *Innocents*, including Henry Plummer, "leaving the corpses," as one correspondent wrote, "stiffening in the icy blast."

Going to or returning from Virginia City, campgrounds along the west banks of the Jefferson River can be reached by turning south on a road (watch for the sign) that's 2 mi/3 km out of Ennis. Continue 1 mi/1.5 km to reach the Burnt Tree Fishing Access and 2.5 mi/4 km to the Eight Mile Ford Fishing Access and (very basic) Montana State Campground.

For More Information About Route 2:

The Vigilantes of Montana, or Popular Justice in the Rockies. Thomas J. Dimsdale.
The Night the Mountain Fell: The Story of the Montana-Yellowstone Earthquake. Edmund Christopherson.

Events and Services

Yellowstone Country: P.O. Box 1107, Red Lodge, Montana 59068; 1-800-736-5276 or 406-446-1005.
Gold West Country: 1155 Main Street, Deer Lodge, Montana 59722; 406-846-1943.
West Yellowstone Chamber of Commerce: 406-646-7701.
Virginia City Chamber of Commerce: Box 67, Virginia City, Montana 59644; 406-843-5377.
Ennis Chamber of Commerce: Box 291, Ennis, Montana 59729; 406-682-4388.
Museum of the Yellowstone: West Yellowstone, Montana 59758; 406-646-7814.
Madison Earthquake Visitor Center: Hebgen Lake Ranger District, Box 520, West Yellowstone, Montana 59758; 406-646-7369.
Cliff and Wade Lakes: U.S. Forest Service, 406-682-4253.
Lewis and Clark Caverns: Box 949, Three Forks, Montana 59752; 406-287-3541.
International Fly Fishing Center: Box 1088, West Yellowstone, Montana 59758; 406-646-9541.

National Forests and Wilderness Areas

Beaverhead National Forest: 610 North Montana Street, Dillon, Montana 59725; 406-683-3900.

Down Paradise Valley and up the Bloody Bozeman

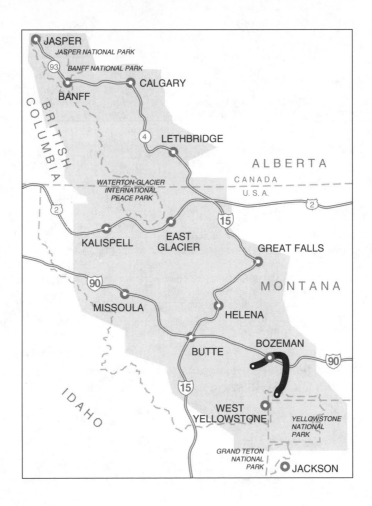

"Custer got Siouxed."

Bumpersticker on a truck traveling Route 3.

ROUTE 3

MAMMOTH to LIVINGSTON to BOZEMAN to NORRIS
116 miles/187 kilometers

General description: Flanked by the Gallatin Range and the rugged snow-capped peaks of the Absaroka-Beartooth Wilderness, Route 3 follows Highway 89, down the aptly named Paradise Valley, to the town of Livingston. Along the way, there are numerous public access points to the upper Yellowstone River, one of the last major (and pristine) rivers in the American West. From Livingston, the route follows a portion of the historic Bozeman Trail, over Bozeman Pass, and down past massive outcrops of white limestone to the city of Bozeman, home to the Museum of the Rockies. The final leg of Route 3 traverses rolling agricultural land until it drops into the sheer-walled Bear Trap Canyon to cross the Jefferson River. From the Jefferson, Highway 84 ascends to, and traverses, rolling grassland until it reaches the Highway 287 junction at the town of Norris. A side-trip from Bozeman leads, via Interstate 90, to the Madison Buffalo Jump State Park.

Unique features: Yellowstone River, Absaroka-Beartooth Wilderness, Devil's Slide, Yellowstone River, Livingston Depot Center with a commercial airport, Bridger Range Roadless Area, Museum of the Rockies, Hyalite Canyon Recreation Area.

Wildlife viewing opportunities: Absaroka-Beartooth Wilderness, Northern Yellowstone Winter Range.

Activities: Fishing, cross-country skiing, snowmobiling, golf, river float trips, mountain biking, downhill skiing.

Events: Park County Fair, Montana Winter Fair, Gallatin County Fair, Sweet Pea Festival of the Arts.

Travel season: Year-round.

Services: While Bozeman is a major service center, all services can also be found in Livingston and Gardiner.

Road conditions and route description: From Mammoth Hot Springs, Route 3 makes a rapid descent to Gardiner via 5 mi/8 km of windy, narrow Park Service road which is open year-round. (The road from Mammoth to Cooke City is also open year-round; this is the only Yellowstone National Park entrance open during the winter.) After Gardiner, Highway 89 gradually descends to Livingston on a well-maintained, two-lane, four-season road. From Livingston, Interstate 90 crosses Bozeman Pass (5760 ft/1756 m) to Bozeman and Highway 84, a good, all-weather, two-lane road to Norris, where you connect with Highway 287 and Route 2.

The route: While riding the brakes on the 1,000-ft/305-m descent from Mammoth Hot Springs to the head of the Paradise Valley, you pass the forty-fifth parallel (the half-way point between the equator and the North Pole). The Roosevelt arch, dedicated by Teddy Roosevelt in 1903, marks the original entrance to Yellowstone. The creation of the world's first national park also marked the beginning of the first national park bordertown, which served adventurous tourists and soldiers stationed at Camp Sheridan next to Mammoth Hot Springs. Gardiner turned into a real town a decade later, after the Northern

Pacific Railroad began transporting tourists from Livingston to the park via its Park Branch Line. Despite being the first national park bordertown, and therefore likely to be the most developed, Gardiner is the least pretentious of any found along the Trail of the Great Bear. The town retains much of its rustic and original character. (Gardiner Chamber of Commerce: 406-848-7971.)

There is a small airport just north of town. Northeast of Gardiner and 5 mi/8 km up Bear Gulch on Forest Service Road 493, one of Montana's outstanding ghost towns survives. Starting in 1866, Jardine became another one-resource town dependent on mining. Operations halted at the turn of the century followed by a surge of activity, centered on arsenic mining, from the 1920s to the end of World War II. The Revenue Mining Company bunk houses, stamp mill, and ore washers still stand.

About 5 mi/8 km out of Gardiner, across from the La Duke Spring Trailhead and Campground, the Devil's Slide juts out from the flank of Cinnabar Mountain. The actual slide is composed of sandstone and shale that tilted up as the Rockies grew. The shale, a softer rock than the resistant quartz sandstone, eroded faster and formed the slides. The distinctive 75-ft/225-m high fin of rock is called a dike; after the sedimentary rock had been deposited, molten igneous rock oozed in between two sedimentary layers and formed the dike.

The Yellowstone River and Moby Trout

One of the premiere streams found along the Trail of the Great Bear, the Yellowstone River originates in the park and flows down the Paradise Valley on its way to join the Missouri River. Michael Sample, in his book *The Angler's Guide to Montana*, writes that the Yellowstone River, "commands respect and inspires devotion." The Yellowstone drains a pristine watershed. "Unlike other major rivers," writes Sample, "the Yellowstone runs its entire 678-mile course without a major dam. Running free of impounding concrete slabs, the Yellowstone evokes awe in all river lovers who honor things wild." If your soul harbors a little bit of Captain Ahab in quest of Moby Trout, the Yellowstone is the river of your dreams; especially Yankee Jim Canyon where legendary monster trout lurk in 60-ft/28 ha water. (With class IV rapids during spring runoff, Yankee Jim Canyon is also a favorite of whitewater enthusiasts.)

The area from Jardine to Gardiner to Cinnabar Mountain and down to Corwin Springs forms winter range for the largest and most diverse group of hoofed wildlife in the conterminous United States. Pronghorn antelope, bighorn sheep, elk, mule deer, and bison migrate from the park to winter in the open terrain. South of Gardiner and north of Devil's Slide, a sharp eye will pick out the mile-long bison fence, funded in part by the Fund For Animals. The purpose of the fence was to prevent bison from migrating out of the park and into the gunsights of hunters. Besides bison, the fence also prevented the migration of other animals such as bighorn sheep. As a consequence, gates had to be left open which rendered the barrier an ineffective white-elephant.

ROUTE 3 *MAMMOTH TO LIVINGSTON TO BOZEMAN TO NORRIS*

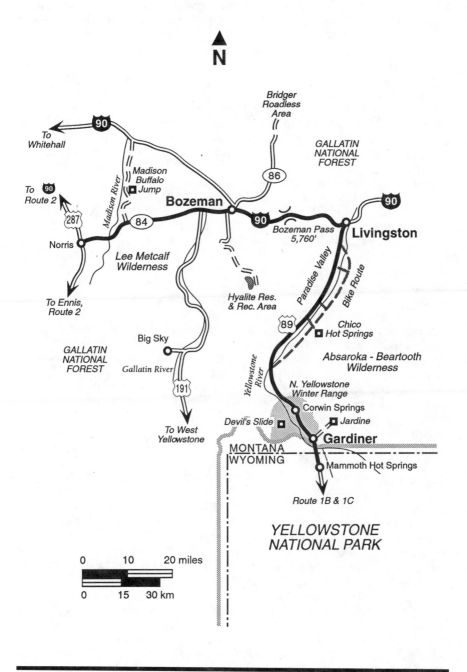

From the comfort of a car, at Corwin Spring on the dirt road across the Yellowstone River, you can watch male bighorn sheep ram into each other during the autumn rut. Bighorn sheep crossed the Bering Strait land bridge a half-million years ago. The Sheepeater Indians that lived in and around the park hunted bighorns as did their predecessors some 8,000 years ago. Market hunting, practiced by whites from 1870 to 1910, and habitat loss eliminated sheep from the Paradise Valley. Fortunately they were returned and today, 100 to 150 bighorns winter in this area from October to June. The head-butting battles determine who breeds. Eight- to ten-pound lambs are born in May or June. Both sexes possess horns; however, males have massive horns that curl while those of a female are slender and sickle-like. Bighorn sheep generally live ten to fifteen years.

The Gallatin Range rises on the left (west) side of Highway 89 as you follow the wide and grassy Paradise Valley down to the town of Livingston. These mountains crown the Gallatin National Forest, named after Albert Gallatin, the Secretary of the Treasury for Thomas Jefferson; ironically, he refused to authorize $1,500 for the Lewis and Clark Expedition because he considered it a waste of money. The Absaroka Range forms the rugged skyline on the right (west) side of the valley. The Absarokas stand within the 950,000-acre Absaroka-Beartooth Wilderness where twenty-eight peaks rise above 12,000 ft/3,660 m and more than 700 mi/1,130 km of trail await adventurous hikers. During the National Roadless and Undeveloped Area Inventory conducted in the 1970s, the Absaroka Range received the highest wilderness quality rating in the entire United States. (Information about the Gallatin National Forest and the Absaroka-Beartooth Wilderness can be obtained from the Gardiner District, 406-848-7375, and Livingston District, 406-222-1892, National Forest Service Offices.)

Nineteen mi/31 km north of Gardiner, Highway 540 branches off and runs parallel to Highway 89. This excellent bike route continues for 32 mi/52 km with three opportunities to cross the Yellowstone River and loop back around to the starting point. Road signs point the way to Chico Hot Springs (406-333-4933), a great place to soak your travel-weary body and enjoy a fine meal. Highways 540 and 89 merge 4 mi/7 km south of Livingston.

Livingston

In 1882, Livingston started off as Clark City, named by two merchants who set up their tent-stores where they sold goods to Northern Pacific Railroad construction crews. Business thrived and Clark City grew . . . until the Northern Pacific surveyed a new townsite, one that the railroad company had long before planned, platted, mapped, and named Livingston. Clark City relocated next to the tracks. So, almost from the beginning, Livingston has been a railroad town meant to house engineers, conductors, brakemen, and the crews that worked in the locomotive repairshops. The railroad work force numbered more than 1,000 until . . . .the Northern Pacific suspended passenger service in the late 1970s and finally eliminated the entire maintenance operation in 1986.

Today, Livingston (population 7,000) takes pride in preserving the historic Western atmosphere of yesteryear; the downtown area, with its decorative brickwork and ornate cornices, and two neighborhoods are listed on the National Register of Historic Places. In all, 436 building qualify for listing in the Historic Register, one of which is the Northern Pacific Depot. The

Madison Buffalo Jump State Park.

same architectural firm that designed Grand Central Station in New York designed the Livingston Depot, the most elegant example of the terra cotta Italian Renaissance Revival style used by the Northern Pacific. The showcase depot, where Yellowstone-bound tourists once transferred trains, now houses a museum. The Depot Center displays art by Russell, Picasso, Remington, and historical exhibits that range from Native beadwork to firearms to railroad memorabilia to locally made quilts. The Center is a satellite museum of the Buffalo Bill Historical Center in Cody, Wyoming. Exhibits change regularly at the Depot Center which also hosts An Evening By The Tracks, a concert series that features classical music and ballet as well as railroad songs and cowboy ballads. The Center is open from mid-May to mid-October, 9 a.m. to 5 p.m. Monday through Saturday and 1 p.m. to 5 p.m. on Sunday. (For more information write: Box 1319, Livingston, Montana 59047, or call 406-222-2300.) Also in Livingston, the Park County Fair is celebrated on the second week of August. For more information contact the Livingston Chamber of Commerce, 212 W. Park Street, Livingston, Montana 59047; 406-222-0850.

The Bloody Bozeman

From Livingston, Interstate 90 ascends to the Bozeman Pass (5,760 ft/1,756 m) situated between the Gallatin Range to the left (south) and the Bridger Range on the right (north). The Bridger Mountain Roadless Area is an isolated, though relatively narrow, block of National Forest Service land where glaciers once sculpted rugged alpine peaks from uplifted fault-blocks of sedimentary rock. On July 15, 1806, Sacajawea guided Clark over (the present-day) Bozeman Pass as they followed an old buffalo migration route and headed for the mouth of the Yellowstone River to rendezvous with Lewis.

While camped on the Yellowstone, as Bernard DeVoto wrote in *The Course of Empire*, "The Crows, honored by all Plains tribes as the most expert horse thieves, crawled up one night and got half the horses: ...The first American horses the Crows ever got."

The pass is named for John Bozeman, who led wagon trains over the saddle and on to the gold country beyond. Bozeman's route branched off the Emigrant Trail and ended at Virginia City (see Route 2B). "The Bozeman Trail," wrote Dorothy Johnson in *The Bloody Bozeman: The Perilous Trail to Montana's Gold*, "shortened the route to the rich new gold fields...But the long way was safer...The Bozeman Trail was for a kind of man who... gambled his life to better his condition, but he didn't really believe that his hair might make fringes for a Sioux or Cheyenne war shirt."

Some of the pioneers, unaffected by gold-lust, settled in the basin on the other side of the pass and established the town of Bozeman; named after, guess who?

Today, Bozeman (population 21,6500) is home to the Montana State University (406-994-2452) which is home to Montana's premier museum. The Museum of the Rockies invites people to "Be a time traveler!" The journey starts eighty-million years ago, in the company of dinosaurs; these life-size reproductions and dioramas portray dinosaur nesting colonies near present-day Choteau, Montana (on Route 9). The museum houses the skulls of a triceratops and styracosaur, an ancient nest of fossilized Maiasaurua eggs, and the largest and most complete skeleton of a Tyrannosaurus rex. The museum also exhibits Native artifacts, western art, historic photographs, and pioneer paraphernalia ranging from trapping gear to clothing to a sheepherder's wagon. The museum is especially proud of the Taylor Planetarium with its computer graphics system that propels travelers on simulated flights through space. Only five planetariums in the world can match the technical sophistication found at the Taylor. From Memorial Day to Labor Day, the museum and planetarium are open daily from 9 a.m. to 9 p.m. and during the winter, Monday through Saturday 9 a.m. to 5 p.m. and Sunday 12:30 p.m. to 5 p.m. Admission is charged to non-members. For more information write Museum of the Rockies, 600 W. Kagy Avenue, Montana State University, Bozeman, Montana 59717; 406-994-2251.

Based in Bozeman, Shakespeare In The Park is a troupe that travels throughout Montana from June to late August. Call 406-994-3901 for a summer schedule; plan to join the troupe in one of the towns along the Trail of the Great Bear where you can spread a blanket out on the grass beneath an evening summer sky and enjoy a lively performance of Shakespeare. The Gallatin County Fair (406-585-1405), featuring traditional county fair fun, is celebrated at the Fairgrounds over the fourth week of July. Also at the Fairground, draft-horse pulling contests, crafts, and other exhibits highlight the Montana Winter Fair (406-585-1397) held during the fourth week of January. The Sweet Pea Festival of the Arts, the first full weekend in August, offers a full schedule of art, music, dance, and flowers. For more information, contact the Bozeman Area Chamber of Commerce, Box B, Bozeman, Montana 59715 or call 406-586-5421 or 800-228-4224.

What makes the Hyalite Canyon Recreation Area unique from other national forest recreational areas is the special care taken to provide handicapped-access to paved trails, picnic grounds, fishing access, campgrounds, and a specially outfitted cabin. Hopefully, the Hyalite

Challenge, sponsored by the Gallatin Empire Lions Club and Gallatin National Forest, will be imitated in recreation areas across the continent. To reach the Hyalite Canyon Road, follow South 19th Avenue for 7 mi/11 km. The end of Hyalite Canyon marks a take-off point for backpack trips into the Hyalite-Porcupine-Buffalo Horn semi-wild area that contains 155,000 acres of rugged mountainous terrain dotted with alpine cirques, waterfalls, and lakes. The variety of vegetational zones, from alpine to grasslands, makes this an important habitat in the Greater Yellowstone for grizzly, bighorn sheep, and wintering elk herds. It is currently being considered for wilderness designation.

Two downhill ski areas operate within an hour of Bozeman. Bridger Bowl (406-587-2111 or 1-800-223-9606) is 16 mi/26 km northeast of town in the Bridger Mountains. Big Sky (406-995-4211) is south of Bozeman up the Gallatin Canyon and surrounded by the Spanish Peaks Wilderness Area. While cross-country skiing opportunities abound around Bozeman, two areas offer groomed track. The Bohart Ranch (406-586-9070), 16 mi/26 km up Bridger Canyon, grooms 20 mi/30 km of trail for diagonal stride and skating. forty mi/65 km up the Gallatin Canyon, Lone Mountain maintains 47 mi/75 km of groomed track and skating trails in addition to overnight accommodations (406-995-4644). Also up the Gallatin Canyon, the Big Sky Snowmobile Trail provides a 110 mi/177 km marked route for experienced snowmobilers. The Hyalite and Bridger areas also offer snowmobile trails. For more information about recreation opportunities, write to the Bozeman Ranger District Office, 601 Nikles Avenue, Bozeman, Montana 59715, or call 406-587-6920.

From Bozeman, Highway 84 heads west across farmland until it drops into the Madison River. Here the road enters the lower end of the Bear Trap Canyon Unit of the Lee Metcalf Wilderness where you pass massive rock outcrops and sheer canyon walls. (Also refer to Route 2.) Highway 84 ascends from the canyon to traverse rolling grassland to Norris and the end of Route 3.

Sidetrip—Madison Buffalo Jump State Park

For a historic sidetrip to the Madison Buffalo Jump, take the westbound on-ramp of Interstate 90 and watch for the "Madison Buffalo Jump State Park" sign at the Logan/Trident exit (number 283). Follow the signs that lead south on a gravel road for 7 mi/11 km. A small interpretive exhibit details the use of the 40 ft/12 m limestone cliff as a buffalo jump. Prior to the widespread use of horses, over a period that extended from at least 2,000 years ago until the late 1700s, Shoshone and Bannock Indians employed clever strategies to lure and then drive buffalo over the abutment. (For more information about the use of buffalo jumps, see Route 12A: Head-Smashed-In Buffalo Jump Interpretive Center.) Either reconnect with Route 3 by returning to Bozeman or continue west on Interstate 90 to the Three Forks exit and follow Highway 2 south along the Jefferson River (one of Montana's legendary "blue-ribbon" trout streams) to the junction with Highway 287 and the tail end of Route 2.

Jefferson River.

Events and Services

Yellowstone Country: P.O. Box 1107, Red Lodge, Montana 59068; 1-800-736-5276 or 406-446-1005.

Gardiner Chamber of Commerce: 406-848-7971.

Livingston Chamber of Commerce: 212 W. Park Street, Livingston, Montana 59047; 406-222-0850.

Bozeman Area Chamber of Commerce: Box B, Bozeman, Montana 59715; 406-586-5421 or 800-228-4224.

Depot Center: Box 1319, Livingston, Montana 59047; 406-222-2300.

Museum of the Rockies: 600 W. Kagy Avenue, Montana State University, Bozeman, Montana 59717; 406-994-2251.

Shakespeare In The Park: 406-994-3901.

Chico Hot Springs: 406-333-4933.

National Forests and Wilderness Areas

Gallatin National Forest and the Absaroka-Beartooth Wilderness Information: National Forest Service Offices at Gardiner District, 406-848-7375, and Livingston District, 406-222-1892. Gallatin National Forest, Bozeman Ranger District Office: 601 Nikles Avenue, Bozeman, Montana 59715; 406-587-6920.

Mountain goat can be occasionally spoted by hikers in the Absaroka Range near the Paradise Valley.

Battlefield of the Copper Kings

"Life was pretty cheap for the money that some of these companies were making. It was nothing to go into one of these miners' wards and see all the beds full. A lot of broken legs and broken backs. Some days I would just hate to go to work because I knew where I was going to be working and I knew it was going to be hot and... gassy. I'd get a pounding, pounding headache. But then you get on surface and go up to Big Butte Tavern and have a beer and a hamburger sandwich and talk it over, and you were back the next day to hate the same thing all over again. I just never could explain why I liked the mines. I never thought I'd live to see the day that one wheel wouldn't be turning. I thought there'd always be one mine. We never knew how good Anaconda was until they left us."

Oral interview with Dennis "Dinny" Murphy,
transcribed by Teresa Jordan.

ROUTE 4

BUTTE to MISSOULA   *212 miles/341 kilometers*

General description: Route 4 begins in the historically rich town of Butte after which it makes a circuitous journey through open valleys and forested canyons. The route follows Highway 1, a more picturesque and interesting alternative to Interstate 90; two wildlife viewing areas are easily accessed here. Beyond the Anaconda Smelter Stack, the road passes aspen woodlands and former mining sites, with occasional views of the rugged Anaconda-Pintler Wilderness, as it ascends to Georgetown Lake. After the lake, the route descends the Philipsburg Valley, past the town of Philipsburg, following Flint Creek, through subdued mountains with open and forested areas, and finally reentering the Deer Lodge Valley where the Clark Fork River flows.

From Drummond, another short stint on Interstate 90 connects with the lesser-traveled Highway 141 which ascends a low divide and then winds its way down Nevada Creek to the Blackfoot River. On the way to Missoula, the opportunity exists to take a side trip to the historic ghost town of Garnet and visit four wildlife viewing areas.

Unique features: Butte Historic District, World Museum of Mining and Hell Roarin' Gulch, Georgetown Lake, Lost Creek State Park, Anaconda-Pintler Wilderness, Philipsburg Historic District, Flint Creek Range-Dolus Lakes Roadless Area, Garnet "Ghost Town" Historic District, Grant-Kohrs Ranch National Historic Site, Old Montana State Prison, Fairmont Hot Springs, Towe Ford Museum, gen mines, and saphire panning.

Wildlife viewing opportunities: Sheepshead Mountain Recreation Area, Mount Haggin Wildlife Management Area, Lost Creek State Park, Nevada Lake Wildlife Management Area, Brown's Lake, Blackfoot-Clearwater Wildlife Management Area, and Babcock Mountain Bighorn Sheep Viewing Area.

Activities: Backpacking, cross-country skiing, downhill skiing, snowmobiling, sailboarding, mountain biking, fishing, golf.

Events: Butte Silver Bow County Fair, St. Patrick's Day in Butte, Winternational Sports Festival.

Travel season: Year-round.

Services: Services are readily available along the southern half of Route 4 (Interstate 90 and Highway 1) and especially concentrated in Butte (which has a commercial airport) the Deer Lodge area and Anaconda. Gas and grub can be found sporadically along Highway 141 and 200. Missoula is a major service center.

Road conditions and route description: From Butte, follow Interstate 90 (for 17 mi/27 km) and turn at the Highway 1 exit. Highway 1 is a two-lane, all-weather road that extends 64 mi/103 km, past Anaconda and Philipsburg, to Drummond. From Drummond, go south on Interstate 90 for 21 mi/34 km to the Garrison Turnoff. Follow Highway 12, a well-maintained, two-lane road, for 13 mi/21 km to Avon and turn left (north) on Highway 141. Highway 141, a two-lane, all-weather road, stretches 33 mi/53 km to its junction with Highway 200 which follows the Blackfoot River for 57 mi/92 km to Bonner. From Bonner, take Interstate 90 for 5 mi/8 km to Missoula.

The route: Butte, "the richest hill on earth," started as a gold camp in 1860s and became a center for silver production in the 1870s and 1880s. In 1893, President Cleveland abolished federal subsidization of the silver industry, a move that shook Montana's economy to its very core. Mines closed and communities like Granite (farther up Route 4) and Elkhorn (on Route 8) never recovered; they became ghost towns.

The Copper Kings

No one paid attention to copper because shipping the ore cost too much and the cost of building a smelter seemed astronomical. Marcus Daly changed all that after he bought the Anaconda Gold and Silver Mining Company. The mine ran out of silver and smackdab into a seam of copper 100 ft/30 m wide; the richest deposit of copper the world had ever seen. Daly built smelter facilities in Anaconda. Meanwhile, in Butte, William Clark utilized his position as a banker to gain control of the mines. In *Montana: Land of Contrast*, Harry Fritz wrote that Clark "displayed all the less desirable characteristics of a young man in a hurry: craft, cupidity, and lack of conscience. He ended his career as . . . one of the world's richest men. Montana, however, has little save the scars he left to remember him by."

Daly and Clark maintained a friendship until their mutual pursuit of wealth evolved into the quest for political power. This rivalry started the War of the Copper Kings; "the result," wrote Fritz, "was a donnybrook of gargantuan proportions, a political free-for-all that dominated the state for fifteen years and made Montana nationally known for political corruption." This unprincipled though colorful chapter of Montana history is part of what makes a visit to the Butte/Anaconda area so interesting.

Back when the mines operated non-stop, 70,000 people lived in Butte; today, the city, with a population of 37,200, is getting back on its feet after the economic blow that came from relying on a single non-renewable resource for its financial base. This recovery and the positive attitude that prevails in Butte earned it the title of an ALL AMERICAN city in 1988.

The World Museum of Mining (406-723-7211) features indoor and outdoor displays of historic mining equipment. Hell Roarin' Gulch, an exhibit that draws a lot of attention, is a replica of the 1900 mining camp. Admission to the museum is free; it's open daily from 9 a.m to 9 p.m. from mid-June to Labor Day and 10 a.m. to 5 p.m. the rest of the year (closed on Monday from November to March). The Neversweat and Washoe Railroad, a project of the Butte Anaconda Historic Parks, departs from the Museum and travels to the Kelly mine while the train crew delivers a running commentary about Butte's mining and social history. Tours are conducted daily from Memorial Day to Labor Day, 10 a.m. to 5 p.m., and leave on the hour; admission is charged (call 406-723-4349).

Butte played such an important role in the labor movement that it became known as the "Gibraltar of Unionism." Safety concerns, not higher wages, motivated miners to band together in unions. For instance, hardrock miners wanted a simple changing-house at the mouth of the mines so they could change into dry clothes; otherwise they walked home, in the dead of winter, soaked-to-the-bone after working an arduous shift in the mines. Pneumonia killed many miners. The 1917 Speculator Mine Fire, that claimed the lives of 168 men (more than any other mining disaster in the United States), caused a strike and inspired union activity over safety measures, for good reason.

The Berkeley Pit

At one time the mines beneath Butte extended 5,000 ft/1,524 m deep with more than 3,000 mi/4,839 km of passageways. Beginning in 1955, entire sections of Butte disappeared as the Anaconda Company commenced open-pit mining operations. The Berkeley Pit consumed 3 square mi/48 km of earth down to a depth of 1,800 ft/457 m and was laced with 2,500 mi/4,032 km of road. The pit is large enough to be visible from space. However, unless you're booked on the space shuttle, you'll have to settle for a ground-level view from an observation stand located just off Continental Drive. In 1981, Atlantic Richfield Company (ARCO) bought the ailing Anaconda Company. A year later, in April 1982, mining stopped in the Berkeley Pit and water from underground mines began to rise. Today, the Berkeley Pit is the deepest body of water in Montana (700 ft/213 m deep); it's also part of the Silver Bow Superfund Site, designated by the Environmental Protection Agency as a priority site for the cleanup of industrial wastes.

Self-guided walking tours of historic, uptown Butte are available at the Chamber of Commerce (2950 Harrison Avenue, Butte, Montana 59701; 406-494-5595 or 800-735-6814). The walk includes a visit to the Copper King Mansion, the elaborate (and a bit ostentatious), three-story, thirty-four room (including a ballroom) home of billionaire William Clark. Take a good look. This is all that Clark left to Montana. Also uptown, the Arts Chateau (406-723-7600), listed on the National Register of Historic Places, provides an opportunity to witness the exceptional craftsmanship of the 1890s as you wander through exhibitions of local, regional, and national artists. The Arts Chateau conducts workshops, lecture series, gallery talks, and art classes.

Out on "The Flats," at the south end of town, the United States High Altitude Sports Center, with its 400-meter skating rink and 22,000 square-foot training center, furnishes professional facilities to U.S. Winter-Olympic athletes. The Winternational Sports Festival, held for nine weekends beginning in February, is open to all comers; competition includes cross-country and downhill skiing, speedskating, hockey, and other sports such as swimming, archery, and recquetball. (For intormation on entry forms, write to Butte Silver Bow Chamber of Commerce.)

In August, Butte hosts the Silver Bow County Fair. The celebration of St. Patrick's Day is truly a Butte original with people painted green and beer flowing like there was no tomorrow. Butte has always known how to party. Steve Devitt wrote, "Butte never really attempted prohibition. Liquor continued to be served publicly . . . Eliot Ness might take on Al Capone in Chicago, but no lawman, federal or otherwise, was about the tell thousands of hardrock miners they weren't going to drink."

Our Lady of the Rockies, the massive white Madonna, that at night glows above Butte from atop Saddle Rock, was the result of a promise that Bob O'Bill (a Butte laborer) made to his God. When his wife's illness became deadly serious, Bob promised that if she was spared he would build a shrine. Private donations financed the construction of the 90 ft/27 m steel statue and U.S. military helicopters lifted it (in sections) to the ridge. As Bill said, "I don't believe a project like this would be possible anywhere except in a place like Butte."

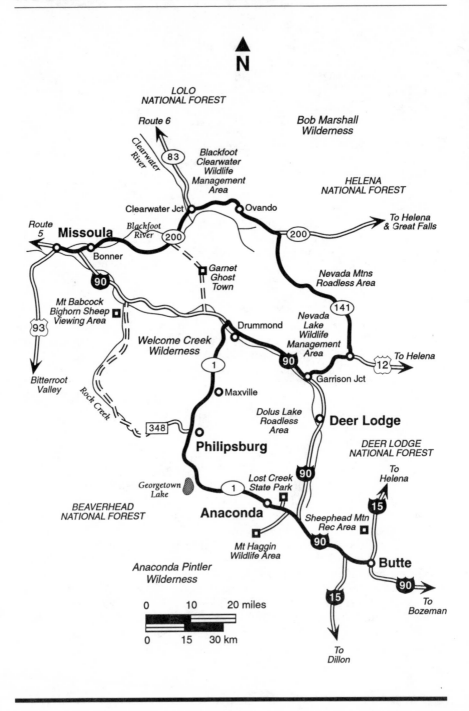

N

LOLO
NATIONAL FOREST

Route 6

Bob Marshall
Wilderness

Clearwater River

83

Blackfoot
Clearwater
Wildlife
Management
Area

HELENA
NATIONAL FOREST

Clearwater Jct

Ovando

Route
5

Missoula

Blackfoot River

200

To Helena
& Great Falls

200

Bonner

Garnet
Ghost
Town

Nevada Mtns
Roadless Area

90

Mt Babcock
Bighorn Sheep
Viewing Area

141

Nevada
Lake
Wildlife
Management
Area

93

Welcome Creek
Wilderness

Drummond

To Helena

12

1

90

Garrison Jct

Bitterroot
Valley

Rock Creek

Maxville

348

Dolus Lake
Roadless
Area

Deer Lodge

Philipsburg

DEER LODGE
NATIONAL FOREST

To
Helena

Georgetown
Lake

Lost Creek
State Park

1

90

BEAVERHEAD
NATIONAL FOREST

Anaconda

Sheephead Mtn
Rec Area

15

Mt Haggin
Wildlife Area

90

Anaconda Pintler
Wilderness

Butte

90

0   10   20 miles

15

To
Bozeman

0   15   30 km

To
Dillon

Wildlife viewing

A short ways north of Butte, the Sheepshead Mountain Recreation Area provides handicapped-access to campgrounds, trails, a picnic area, bathrooms, and a fishing area. To reach Sheepshead, follow Interstate 15 for about 8 mi/13 km out of Butte and exit at mile-sign 138 (Elk Park) and drive west following the signs. The meadows, marshes, and forest are home to deer, moose, and elk. For wildlife viewing from the car, take the 16-mi/26-km Hail Columbia Gulch (gravel) Road. (For more information, call the Deer Lodge National Forest Service at 406-494-2147.)

From Butte, Route 5 follows the broad Deer Lodge Valley through agricultural and open grassland vegetated with sage, scattered Douglas-fir, limber pine, juniper, and Ponderosa pine and dotted with granite boulders. The boulders are outcrops of the Boulder Batholith discussed in Route 2. To reach Montana's largest wildlife management area, follow Highway 1 for 3 mi/5 km after exiting Interstate 90; turn left (south) on Secondary 274; the road enters the wildlife area a short ways beyond the Continental Divide. With the Pintler Range for a dramatic backdrop, the Mount Haggin Wildlife Management Area (Montana Department of Fish, Wildlife and Parks: 406-994-4042) covers 54,137 acres situated among forested mountains, rolling hills covered with aspen, and bottomlands thick with willow. There are numerous unmarked trails, and mountain biking opportunities are excellent. Watch for moose, elk, and sandhill cranes. Mt. Haggin is also a good place for cross-country skiing.

Back on Highway 1, beneath the famous Anaconda Smelter Stack (the world's largest, though inactive, copper smelter), you pass the historic tailings ponds. Crusts of colorful blue-green copper compounds line the muddy banks with iron adding the rich red tint seen in the water. The water flowing over, through, and beneath the tailings finds its way into the Clark Fork River; a little more about that father down the road. After a mile of tailings ponds, a right turn (north) on the road to Galen leads to Lost Creek State Park where bighorn sheep and mountain goats traverse the 1,200-ft/366-m limestone cliffs. An interpretive sign situated in a pullout near the park entrance is a good place to watch for goats. Sheep can be easily spotted, during the winter and spring, in the open grassland located near the entrance; black bear also roam the open hillsides in the spring. There is a public campground in the park. In the winter, the 2-mi/ 3-km park road provides a good cross-country ski trip; watch for moose along the creek bottom. (For more information call Montana Fish, Wildlife and Parks at 406-542-5500.)

Anaconda and Georgetown Lake

Anaconda started out with the name of Copperopolis, but believe it or not, another town already sported that name. With a desire for something original, the postmastre named the town after reading about a Civil War battle where General Grant's troops encircled General Lee's and tightened their hold like an anaconda. Anaconda's courthouse and Washoe Theater are listed in the

Our Lady of the Rockies overlooks Butte.

National Register of Historic Places. The Smithsonian Institute rated the Washoe Theater building fifth due to its architectural importance. The renovated City Hall Building houses the Copper Village Museum and Art Center where cultural and historic exhibits are displayed (406-563-2422). The Chamber of Commerce provides information for a self-guided walking tour of the downtown area. (For more information write Chamber of Commerce, 36 East Park, Anaconda, Montana 59711 or call 406-563-2400.)

Spelunkers take note, access to Garrity Cave begins 4.5 mi/7 km beyond Anaconda with a right turn on a rough dirt road that leads up Olson Gulch to the top of Olson Mountain. The cave contains 602 ft/184 m of passageways and steel ladders to ease the 227-ft/70-m descent. Anaconda's visitor publication provides directions to the cave.

From Anaconda to Georgetown Lake, the road passes through a valley that was filled with glacial ice during the last ice age. The white bluffs south of the road are the remnants of former hot springs. Between Silver and Georgetown lakes, the remains of the Gold Coin stamp mill still stand just off the road. Ten campgrounds surround the 3,000-acre/1,200 ha Georgetown Lake, a popular destination for fishing in both the summer and winter and for sailboarders. Discovery Basin Ski Area (406-563-2184) with 160 acres of groomed slopes is a short ways up Highway 1 from Georgetown Lake. Rising behind the lake, the Anaconda Range crowns the lightly-visited Anaconda-Pintler Wilderness. From riparian willow to alpine meadows on the Continental Divide, this 150,000-acre/60,000 ha wilderness offers a mile of elevation difference and a wide variety of vegetation. A Deerlodge National Forest map shows dirt roads that lead to trailheads. (Write the Butte Ranger District, 1820 Meadowlark Lane, Butte, Montana 59701; 406-494-2147 or Philipsburg Ranger District, Box H, Philipsburg, Montana 59858; 406-859-3211.)

Philipsburg was a major mining center from 1866 to 1887 with another brief burst of activity in the 1890s. The town still contains a number of excellent examples of late Victorian architecture, many of which are on the National Historic Register. The ghost town of Granite, now a state monument, is 5 mi/8 km southeast of Philipsburg. After braving a dirt road, best traveled when dry, you can explore the remains of a once thriving town (population 5,000) that boasted of the richest silver mine on earth. Granite was virtually abandoned in a day when the bottom fell out of the silver market.

Near the little town of Maxville, large granite boulders cover the valley floor. They are the result of a catastrophic flood that occurred several thousand years ago when a natural dam broke and water roared down Boulder Creek carrying the large rocks in its wake. With the Flint Creek Range on the right, Highway 1 continues, past cropland and small ranches, down to Drummond and Interstate 90, where once again the route follows the Deer Lodge Valley.

Between Drummond and Gold Creek (believed to be the site of Montana's first gold discovery), flows one of the best fishing sections on the Clark Fork River (especially for brown trout).

Two-For-One Ranch and Hardtime Prison

Though Route 4 departs from Interstate 90 at the Garrison Junction (with Highway 12), by remaining on the interstate for an additional 10 mi/16 km, you can visit the Grant-Kohrs Ranch National Historic Site, Montana Law Enforcement Museum, and the Old Montana State Prison in the town of Deer Lodge (population 4,500). (Deer Lodge Chamber of Commerce: 1171 Main Street, Deer Lodge, Montana 59772, 406-846-2094.)

Operated by the National Park Service, the Grant-Kohrs Ranch is a working-demonstration ranch that commemorates the frontier cattle era. As one of Montana's first ranches, Richard Grant ran a profitable operation based on two-for-one trades with passing pioneers traveling on the Oregon Trail; they gave Grant two travel-worn cattle for one of his fattened cows. Conrad

Kohrs bought the ranch and amassed a fortune selling beef to those seeking their fortune in gold. Self-guided or ranger-guided tours of the outfit take in the bunkhouse, blacksmith shop, ice house, barns, tackhouse, and the elaborate Victorian ranch house. The ranch is open year-round; summer hours (Memorial Day to Labor Day) are 9 a.m. to 5:30 p.m. and for the rest of the year from 10 a.m. to 4 p.m. For more information, call 406-846-2070.

Prisoners constructed the grey walls of quarried sandstone that surround the Old Montana State Prison like a medieval fortress. The prison started in 1870 and closed in 1979. Listed on the National Historic Register, the ex-correctional facility is presently run by the Powell County Museum and Arts Foundation and open to the public. Guided and self-guided tours follow the grim and echoing corridors (call 406-846-3111). In the summer, Wednesday through Sunday at 8 p.m., the Old Prison Players present live theatre (406-846-314).

Back on the main route, after exiting the Interstate at the Highway 12 off-ramp, you follow the Little Blackfoot River for 13 mi/21 km to the little town of Avon and then turn left (north) onto Highway 141. Highway 141 ascends the open and broad Avon Valley that is flanked by the subdued Garnet Range on the left (west) and the rounded mountains forming the Nevada Mountain Roadless Area that straddles the Continental Divide on the right. This 100,000-acre roadless area, seldom visited except during the hunting season, provides winter range to deer and elk.

Blackfoot River

About 15 mi/24 km up Highway 141, on the left side of the road, the Nevada Lake Wildlife Management Area provides a small wetland habitat for watching migrating and nesting waterfowl. At the junction of Highways 141 and 200, the route enters the Blackfoot River drainage; this is the river that Norman Maclean wrote so eloquently about in his book *A River Runs Through It*. "It isn't the biggest river we fished, but it is the most powerful, and per pound, so are its fish. Near its headwaters on the Continental Divide (30 mi/48 km to the east) there is a mine with a thermometer that stopped at 69.7 degrees below zero, the lowest temperature ever officially recorded in the United States (Alaska omitted)...its lower twenty-five miles were made overnight when the great glacial lake covering northwestern Montana and Idaho broke its ice dam...It was the biggest flood in the world..." The Blackfoot is a good river for floaters; south of Ovando, the 30-mi/48-km stretch from Scotty Brown Bridge to Johnsrud Park is a recreational corridor (thanks to the efforts of private landowners, Champion International, Inc., and concerned individuals) with sites designated for public access, day use, and overnight camping. A pamphlet from the Montana Department of Fish, Wildlife and Parks maps these spots (Regional Office, 3201 Spurgin Road, Missoula, Montana 59801; 406-542-5500). Please follow the regulations; the Blackfoot recreation corridor is a national example of a cooperative approach to river preservation and public access.

For a chance to watch bald eagles, osprey, loons, heron, Canada geese, and sandhill cranes, turn left (south) on the unpaved road to Brown's Lake that's less than 3 mi/5 km beyond the junction of Highways 141 and 200. While many birds can be seen from the unpaved dirt road, a mountain bike or canoe provide an even better method of seeing the Brown's Lake area (the northeast corner of the lake is closed to boating during the nesting season, from April 1 to July 15).

The giant cow that stands at the Clearwater Junction marks the beginning of Route 6 up the Swan Valley. Access to the Blackfoot-Clearwater Wildlife Management Area (see Route 6) is only a short ways up Highway 83.

Garnet Ghost Town

Set back in the forested and rolling Garnet Range, the ghost town of Garnet provides historical insights into one of Montana's last gold mining boom-towns. Garnet is one of the two best preserved ghost towns in Montana (the second being Bannock). Currently, the Garnet Preservation Society, in conjunction with the BLM, is developing an interpretive plan for the town which entails restoring fifty log or wood structures that range from false-front stores to saloons to cabins. Also in this area, the BLM administers more than 55 mi/89 km of snowmobile and cross-country ski trails; for access to the Garnet National Winter Recreation Trails, turn left (east) off Highway 200 (at Greenough) and follow the Garnet Range Road; 11 mi/18 km up this gravel road is the ghost town of Garnet. This road is best traveled when dry; use by motorcoach is not advised. During the winter months, restored cabins are available for rent. (For more information contact the BLM, Garnet Resource Area, 3255 Fort Missoula Road, Missoula, Montana 59801-7923; 406-329-3914.)

Highway 200 continues down the scenic Blackfoot River to its confluence with the Clark Fork River.

For some good fishing, turn off at the Rock Creek Road exit and drive south along one of Montana's "blue-ribbon" trout streams. An interpretive sign, 4.5 mi/7 km down the road (which turns to dirt), indicates the Babcock Mountain Bighorn Sheep Viewing Area. Grassy hills and steep cliffs provide habitat to a herd of 150 sheep that are most visible in the winter and spring. Hikers can stretch their legs on the Babcock Creek Trail or the Spring Creek Trail; both trails are closed from April to mid-May during the lambing season.

For More Information About Route 4:

The War of the Copper Kings, Carl B. Glasscock.
Butte: The Town and Its People, Steve Devitt.

Events and Services

Gold West Country: 1155 Main Street, Deer Lodge, Montana 59722; 406-846-1943.
Butte Chamber of Commerce: 2950 Harrison Avenue, Butte, Montana 59701; 406-494-5595 or 800-735-6814.
Anaconda Chamber of Commerce: 36 East Park, Anaconda, Montana 59711; 406-563-2400.
Philipsburg Chamber of Commerce: Box 661, Philipsburg, Montana 59858.
Deer Lodge Chamber of Commerce: 1171 Main Street, Deer Lodge, Montana 59772, 406-846-2094.
World Museum of Mining: 406-723-7211.
Neversweat and Washoe Railroad Tour (project of the Butte/Anaconda Historic Parks): 406-723-4349.
Copper Village Museum and Art Center: 406-563-2422.
Grant-Kohrs Ranch National Historic Site: Box 790, Deer Lodge, Montana 59722; 406-846-2070.
Old Montana State Prison: Powell County Museum and Arts Foundation, 406-846-3111.
Old Prison Players: 406-846-314.

Garnet Ghost Town Historic Site: BLM Missoula Office, Garnet Resource Area, 3255 Fort Missoula Road, Missoula, Montana 59801-7923; 406-329-3914 or 406-721-4269.

Blackfoot River Recreational Corridor: Montana Department of Fish, Wildlife and Parks, Regional Office, 3201 Spurgin Road, Missoula, Montana 59801; 406-542-5500.

National Forests and Wilderness Areas

Anaconda-Pintler Wilderness: Butte Ranger District, 1820 Meadowlark Lane, Butte, Montana 59701; 406-494-2147 or Philipsburg Ranger District, Box H, Philipsburg, Montana 59858; 406-859-3211.

Deerlodge National Forest: Federal Building, P.O. Box 400, Butte, Montana 59703; 406-496-3400.

Wildlife Viewing

Sheepshead Mountain Recreation Area: Deer Lodge National Forest Service, 406-494-2147.

Mount Haggin Wildlife Management Area: Montana Department of Fish, Wildlife and Parks: 406-994-4042.

Lost Creek State Park: Montana Fish, Wildlife and Parks: 406-542-5500.

Brown's Lake Wildlife Area: Montana Fish, Wildlife and Parks, 406-542-5500.

Blackfoot-Clearwater Wildlife Management Area: Montana Fish, Wildlife and Parks, 406-542-5523.

Babcock Mountain Bighorn Sheep Viewing Area: United States Fish and Wildlife Service, 406-329-3814.

Lewis and Clark Caverns.

The Place of Encirclement

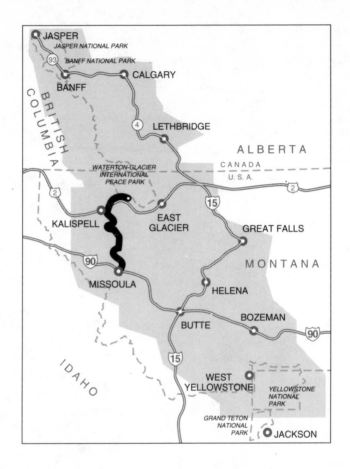

"The grizzly bear is a symbol of what's right with the world."

Charles Jonkel, bear biologist.

ROUTE 5

General description: The Rocky Mountain Trench provides the travel corridor for this route. Highway 93 traverses the Flathead Indian Reservation, situated in the Mission Valley, and affords exceptional views of the rugged Mission Mountains. From Ravalli, you can take a sidetrip to the National Bison Range. Just before Polson, choose between skirting the east or west shore of Flathead Lake. The routes merge at the lake's north end where it crosses the fertile farmlands of the Flathead Valley and then passes through Bad Rock Canyon to follow the Flathead River to West Glacier.

Unique features: Rattlesnake Wilderness, Flathead Indian Reservation, St. Ignatius Mission, Flathead Lake, Flathead River, Chief Cliff.

Wildlife viewing opportunities: National Bison Range, Ninepipe and Pablo National Wildlife Refuge.

Activities: Wildlife viewing, hiking, river rafting, climbing, fishing, golf, downhill skiing, cross-country skiing, snowmobiling.

Events: International Wildlife Film Festival, Western Montana Fair and Rodeo, (Missoula), Flathead United Peoples Powwow and Festival, Northwest Montana Fair, Arlee Powwow, Standing-Arrow Powwow, Annual Whitewater Festival and Celebration, The Gathering At Bigfork, Bigfork Summer Theater, North American Indian Days.

Travel season: Year-round.

Services: Services are readily available and especially concentrated in Missoula, Bigfork, Polson, Kalispell, and Whitefish. Commercial airports are located in Missoula and Kalispell.

Road conditions and route description: For this entire segment, travel is on good-quality, all-weather, well maintained roads. Ten mi/16 km from Missoula, turn off of Interstate 90 and follow Highway 93 for 104 mi/168 km. At the top of Flathead Lake, past Somers, turn right on Highway 82 for 7 mi/11 km, then left on Highway 35 for 12 mi/19 km, and then right onto Highway 206 for 10 mi/ 16 km. At Highway 2, go right and continue to West Glacier for 17 mi/27 km.

The route: Missoula, the "Garden City," is the home of the University of Montana and, with a population of 42,900, western Montana's largest community. In the *Rating Guide to Life in America's Small Cities*, Missoula ranked number two in sophistication. Missoula offers numerous art galleries, professional theaters, ethnic dining, a wide array of shopping choices, a commercial international airport, two downhill ski areas, Snowbowl (406-549-9777) and Marshall (406-258-6619), and three golf courses. How many cities can boast of a wilderness area within a few miles of the city limits? The 56,000-acre Rattlesnake Wilderness north of town offers forested valleys, alpine high country, and grizzly habitat. From Missoula, Van Buren Street provides convenient access to a trailhead. For more information: Selway/Bitterroot Wilderness Area, District Ranger, Stevensville Ranger District, Bitterroot National Forest, 88 Main Street, Stevensville, Montana 58970; 406-777-5461.

Exhibits at the Fort Missoula Historical Museum, at Fort Missoula (406-728-3476), depict industry of the American West from 1880 to 1920 as well

75

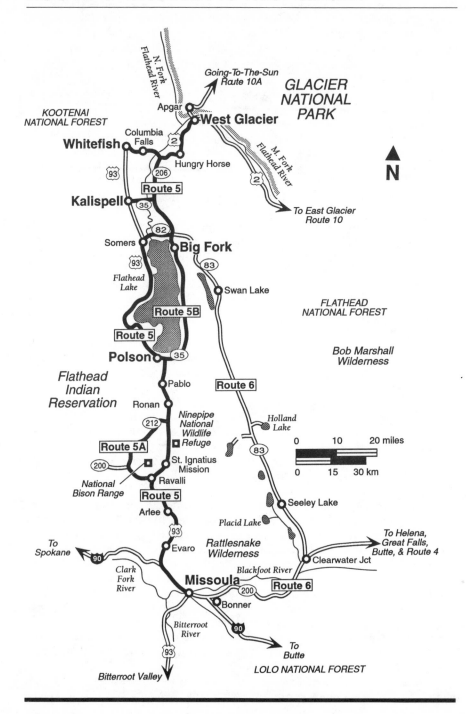

as other westernhistory exhibits that change regularly. The Missoula Museum of the Arts (406-728-0447), in the downtown area, hosts regularly changing exhibits in a variety of media, which are often community-based, and maintains a permanent collection of nineteenth and twentieth century art of the western United States. One of the fastest growing conservation organizations in the United States, the Rocky Mountain Elk Foundation (406-721-0010), is headquartered in Missoula on West Broadway. The Elk Foundation raises money for the purchase and improvement of elk habitat. The visitor center is open seven days a week and offers mounted displays of world-record elk, wildlife paintings, and documentaries about elk and other wildlife in the fifty-seat theater. The U.S. Forest Service Smoke Jumper School (406-329-4900), near the airport, features exhibits, a documentary film, and tours that describe the work of the people who parachute to remote locations and fight fires.

Noteworthy events in Missoula include Out To Lunch, the Farmer's Market, the International Wildlife Film Festival, and the Western Montana Fair and Rodeo celebrated during the third week of August. Out to Lunch occurs every Wednesday at noon from June through August at Caras Park and features music and vendors who sell a variety of foods. On Saturday mornings and Tuesday evenings, the Farmer's Market, near the old Northern Pacific train depot at the north end of Higgins Avenue, combines garden produce, baked goods, espresso, and music that ranges from country to jazz. During the first week of April, the International Wildlife Film Festival (406-728-9380) conducts filmmaking workshops and screens the best wildlife films from around the world in the historic Wilma Theater located on the north side of the Higgins Street Bridge. (Missoula Chamber of Commerce: 406-543-6623.)

The Bitterroot Valley

The Bitterroot Valley, also known as the "Banana Belt of Montana" due to the relatively mild climate, rises to the south of Missoula. There you'll find the 2,800-acre Lee Metcalf National Wildlife Refuge (406-777-5552), the Bitterroot Mountains which form the heart of the 1.3-million-acre Selway/ Bitterroot Wilderness (District Ranger, Stevensville Ranger District, Bitterroot National Forest, 88 Main Street, Stevensville, Montana 58970; 406-777-5461), and "blue-ribbon" trout fishing on the Bitterroot River and its many feeder streams. The Bitterroot Mountains offer some fine rock and ice climbing, hiking, and ski-mountaineering.

Flathead Reservation

To continue your journey northward on the Trail of the Great Bear, follow Interstate 90 for 10 mi/16 km west of Missoula and turn right (north) on Highway 93. From rolling grasslands, the route ascends for 1,000 feet to forests of Douglas-fir and Ponderosa pine. At the little town of Evaro, you enter the Flathead Reservation, home to the Confederated Salish and Kootenai tribes. For the next 80 mi/129 km, the route traverses tribal land.

Formation of the Flathead Reservation resulted from the 1855 Hellgate Treaty in which the Pend d'Oreille and Kootenai ceded twenty-two million acres of ancestral lands to the U.S. Government in order to retain 1.2 million acres. Chief Victor, of the Salish (Flathead) tribe, also participated in the treaty negotiations but refused to sign away his people's land in the Bitterroot Valley. Fifteen years later, Victor died. Due to pressure exerted by Bitterroot settlers, President Grant ordered the Salish to move north to the Flathead Reservation. Arlee, a war chief,

St. Ignatius and the Mission Mountains.

signed the treaty and moved, along with eight families. As a result of his cooperation, the U.S. Government recognized Arlee as the head chief of the Salish people. Most of the Salish however, remained in the Bitterroot with Chief Charlo, Victor's son, who also refused to sign the treaty. Finally, in 1891, with the wild game destroyed by whites and his people starving, Charlo capitulated and a mile-long procession of Salish journeyed north to the Flathead Reservation.

In the years that followed, the Confederated Salish and Kootenai peoples struggled to preserve their cultural heritage and resisted total assimilation into white culture. Today, the economic mainstays of the Flathead Reservation include farming, cattle ranching, timber harvesting, and some light industry; unemployment, however, is a significant problem as it is on most reservations.

A little north of Evaro, you pass the Mule Palace, site of the annual Fourth of July Mule Marathon, a twenty-six mile cross-country mule race followed by a ten-hour country-western music concert (406-726-3828). Beyond the Mule Palace, you catch a glimpse of the Mission Mountains, the rugged backbone of a 159,000-acre alpine wilderness area. In Arlee, with its distinctive red water tower, during the Fourth of July weekend, you can attend the Arlee Powwow (406-675-2700). This powwow, one of the largest in the Northwest, features dancing, stick games, rodeo, and arts and crafts. (Alcohol is strictly prohibited.)

The Mission Mountains

As you near the little town of Ravalli, watch for fine-grained, light-colored dirt along road cuts; these 10,000-year-old glacial silt deposits settled to the floor of an immense lake known as ancient Lake Missoula. (See sidebar for more information.) If you want to see a place where the buffalo still roam, turn left (west) at Ravalli onto Highway 200, and then right on Secondary 212 to Moise and to the National Bison Range.

Just before St. Ignatius, you're treated to a fantastic panorama of the Mission Mountains. Up to the left of the frothy white waters of Mission Falls, McDonald Peak (9,820 ft/2993 m) dominates the Mission Range. The road descends into the Rocky Mountain Trench, a fault-block valley that extends for more than 800 mi/1,290 km beyond the U.S.-Canadian border. The southern end of this depression, bounded by the Mission Mountains on the east and the Salish Mountains on the west, is known as the Mission Valley. The original inhabitants, the Pen d'Oreille and Kootenai, called this area the "Place of Encirclement." Imagine it before the advent of roads, fences, tractors, and cars. Back when people traveled on foot or by horse, this broad valley, so rich in wildlife, was a world unto itself.

The 89,000-acre Mission Mountain Wilderness is the first Native American land designated as a wilderness preserve. (An additional 70,000 acres/29,000 ha of wilderness in the Bob Marshall Wilderness Area lays on the other side of the Mission crest and is best reached via the Swan Valley.) Carlence Woodcock, cultural director for the Flathead Reservation, described the wilderness as, "lands where our people walked and lived. Lands and landmarks carved into the minds of our ancestors through Coyote stories and actual experiences. Lands, landmarks, trees, mountain tops, crevices that we should look up to with respect." A Tribal Recreation permit is needed for use of the wilderness area as well as for hunting, fishing, and other activities on the Flathead Reservation. (For more information contact the Wilderness Manager, Confederated Salish and Kootenai Tribes, Wildlands Recreation Department, Box 98, Pablo, Montana, 59855; 406-675-2700.)

The Mission Mountain Wilderness provides habitat for a small population of ten to thirty grizzly bears. In recent years, no female grizzlies with cubs have been sighted in the Mission Range. This stagnation of the grizzly population is the result of habitat fragmentation that has cut the Mission Mountains grizzlies off from a larger grizzly population in the Continental Divide ecosystem.

St. Ignatius Mission

To visit the historic St. Ignatius Mission, take the right-hand turn to the town of St. Ignatius. For some reason, in the 1830s, the Bitterroot Salish sent a delegation east in search of Black Robes. Jesuit missionaries answered the call and arrived eleven years later. In addition to supervising construction of the St. Ignatius Mission, the Jesuits taught the Pen d'Oreille farming, Christianity, and domestic skills. After the old mission burned, Native American craftsmen built the current brick structure; it's open to the public for self-guided tours. (An interesting note: a mission cook painted frescos, the illustrations of Bible stories that adorn the walls and ceiling. These have been refurbished and are well worth a look.)

Pablo and Ninepipe National Wildlife Refuges

Between St. Ignatius and Ronan, a 5,037-acre/2,090-ha complex of wetlands, glacial potholes, and a 1,770-acre/737-ha reservoir forms the Pablo and Ninepipe National Wildlife Refuges (406-644-2211). This superb birding area offers habitat to more than 180 species and includes cormorants and great blue herons; for access, turn off at the Watchable Wildlife signs along Highway 93. Throughout most of the United States, duck populations have plummeted as wetlands are drained. Conservation efforts by organizations like Ducks Unlimited are addressing these problems. In the Mission Valley, however, due to habitat acquisition, restoration, and preservation, populations are increasing. According to the *Montana Wildlife Viewing Guide*, "One of the best viewing places is the picnic area; follow Secondary 212 for about two miles, and then take Ninepipe Road across the dike." Pablo and Roman provide services near the wildlife refuge.

Flathead Lake

The first view of Flathead Lake occurs atop a rise just south of Polson. The lake resulted from a massive glacier that bulldozed its way down from British Columbia during the last ice age, 12,000 years ago. After the glacier melted, the rocks and earth that were pushed ahead of the glacier (now known as the Polson Moraine) acted like an earthen dam and impounded the waters of Flathead Lake. The lake is about 28 mi/45 km long, 6 mi/10 km wide, and 340 ft/103 m deep. Occupying over 200 sq mi/512 sq km, it is the largest natural lake in the western United States. The Kootenai-Salish tribe regulates the south

Flathead Lake, the domain of the KSANKA-Dayton/Elmo band of the Kootenai.

half of the lake and river. For more information contact the tribe's shoreline office, 406-675-2700. In addition to fishing for cutthroat, lake trout, kokanee salmon, whitefish, and largemouth bass, you can indulge in watersports that range from a simple swim to water-skiing to sailing a yacht.

With its unique nautical atmosphere, the post town of Polson (population 2,800) just beyond the turnoff for Great Bear Route 5B offers full services as well as an eighteen-hole golf course and summer theater from early-July through late-August (Polson Chamber of Commerce: 406-883-5969). Class III whitewater can be found southwest of Polson, below the Kerr Dam, on a 6 mi/10 km stretch of the Flathead River called the Buffalo Rapids. As this portion of the river flows through the Flathead Indian Reservation, a Tribal Recreation permit is needed to float it. (Confederated Salish and Kootenai Tribes, Tribal Fish and Game Office, Pablo, Montana 59855; 406-675-2700.)

Highway 93 continues north through meadows and coniferous forests along the west side of the lake. The Mission Mountains rise behind the southern end of Flathead Lake and the Swan Range serves as a backdrop at the northern end. The majestic Chief Cliff in the area is the subject of many Kootenai legends. During the third weekend in July, the Kootenai Nation hosts the Stand Arrow Powwow in Elmo (406-844-5541). This celebration is open to the public and features ritual dance, song, and highlighted competition. (Alcohol is strictly prohibited.) Beyond the settlement of Collins, you leave the Flathead Indian Reservation.

The Montana Department of Fish, Wildlife and Parks operates three campgrounds spread out along the west shore of Flathead Lake. Big Arm State Park (406-849-5255) is a quarter of the way up the lake; Elmo State Park (406-849-5744) is a third of the way, and West Shore State Park (406-844-3901) is about halfway up the lake. All of the campgrounds offer overnight camping for a fee; there is also a boat ramp at each of them. Public boat ramps also exist at Walsted, a mile south of Big Arm State Park, and at Somers, on the northwest end of the lake. The lake's largest and least developed island, Wild Horse Island State Park (day use only, 406-752-5501), is home to a herd of bighorn sheep in addition to mule deer, eagle, osprey, endangered palouse prairie habitat, and a few coyotes, black bear, and wild horses. You'll need a boat to visit Wild Horse Island. The Polson tour boat passes the island but doesn't land. If you don't own a boat, rentals are available at private marinas in Big Arm Bay.

Flathead Valley

At Somers, turn right (east) on Highway 82 and then go left (north) on Highway 35 up the broad Flathead Valley with its farms and Christmas tree plantations. The fertile farmlands here are the result of glacial silt deposited 12,000 years ago. Watch for osprey nests atop telephone and power poles. At the colorful Gatiss Memorial Gardens (open April through September), you can turn right (east) off Highway 35 and drive one mile for a self-guided tour of the Creston National Fish Hatchery (406-755-7870). Spawning occurs between January and March with the largest fish populations between April and June. Four mi/6.5 km north of Creston, you can stay with Highway 35 to reach Kalispell or turn onto Highway 206 for access to Highway 2. The valley hosts eight spectacular golf couses. Eagle Bend in Bigfork has been rated one of the top fifty courses in America.

Glacial Lake Missoula and the World's Greatest Flood

If you could visit the area occupied by Missoula 12,000 years ago, you'd be treading water—1,400 feet of water. During the last ice age, a lobe of glacial ice crept down the Idaho Panhandle and dammed the Clark Fork River. The water of Glacial Lake Missoula inundated the Missoula Valley (which, by the way, is one of the very few intermontane basins to run east-west) and covered 3,300 square miles of western Montana, an area three times the size of Rhode Island. Climatic warming weakened the dam and when it crumbled, a 2,000-foot wall of water charged west. According to David Alt, geologist and author of Roadside Geology to the Northern Rockies, *the lake drained in a few hours and at a discharge rate of eight to ten cubic miles of water per hour, "200 times the flow rate of the Mississippi River at maximum flood. . ., more than the combined flow of all the modern rivers in the world." This cataclysmic flood raced towards the Pacific Ocean at forty-five to sixty miles-per-hour and formed the Channeled Scablands and coulees of eastern Washington. Geologists believe that the lake filled and drained thirty-six times. From Missoula, if the light is right on Mount Jumbo (the one with the "L" on it) or Mount Sentinel (the one with the "M" on it), you can see ancient shorelines stretching horizontally across the hills, evidence of a prehistoric lake and the greatest flood recorded in geologic history.*

Kalispell

Kalispell (population 10,650) is a major city with full services, a golf course, and a commercial airport. The Hockaday Center for the Arts (406-755-5268), located downtown in the historic Carnegie Library Building, maintains a permanent collection of contemporary Montana artists and changing exhibits that display the work of contemporary Northwest and Montana artists. In Depot Park, on the last weekend of July, the Hockaday Center hosts Arts in the Park, northwest Montana's largest arts and crafts fair featuring over sixty juried artists, art demonstrations, food, and entertainment. The historic Conrad Mansion, the restored home of Kalispell's founder, built in 1895, is open for public tours from May 15 through October 15. Spread out over the last two weeks of July and a variety of locations, the Flathead Festival (406-862-1780) presents eight to ten musical performances that range from classical to jazz to folk/pop to country-western. The Northwest Montana Cattledrive (406-752-8812), in mid-July, offers an opportunity to live out your cowboy fantasies by accompanying an authentic cattledrive. The Northwest Montana Fair takes place on August 15-22. (Kalispell Chamber of Commerce: 406-752-6166.)

Just 14 mi/23 km north of Kalispell the alpine resort town of Whitefish (population 3,700) offers world-class skiing at Big Mountain (406-862-3511). The

Whitefish Winter Carnival, celebrated on the second weekend in February, features contests, parades, races, feasts, and games. (For more information: Whitefish Area Chamber of Commerce, Box 1120, Whitefish, Montana 59937, 406-862-3501.) Whitefish is also a large summer activities community.

West Glacier

Highway 2, from Columbia Falls to West Glacier (15 mi/24 km), passes through a highly developed corridor with thick stands of Douglas-fir and lodgepole pine. The Flathead River provides "blue-ribbon" trout fishing and adventurous float and raft trips. The three forks of the Flathead River flow through pristine wildlands, 219 mi/353 km of which are designated as "Wild, Recreational, or Scenic." The North Fork forms the western boundary of Glacier National Park; the Middle Fork roars through the Great Bear Wilderness and then forms the park's southern boundary; and the South Fork originates in the Bob Marshall Wilderness Area. (North Fork: Glacier View Ranger District, Box W, Columbia Falls, Montana 59912; 406-892-4372. Middle Fork: Hungry Horse Ranger District, Box 340, Hungry Horse, Montana 59919; 406-387-5243. South Fork: Spotted Bear Ranger Station, Box 310, Hungry Horse, Montana 59919; 406-752-7345).

East of Columbia Falls, Highway 2 enters Bad Rock Canyon named by the Flathead after a number of warriors from the tribe met their doom in an ambush set up by a Blackfeet raiding party. Trail of the Great Bear Route 5 ends at West Glacier. Depending upon the season, the time available, and what you want to see, you can continue over Marias Pass and on to East Glacier (via Highway 2, which is a four-season road) or enter Glacier National Park.

ROUTE 5A: HIGHWAY 212, THE NATIONAL BISON RANGE
27 mi/43 km

Road conditions and route description: At Ravalli, 28 mi/45 km up Highway 93, turn left on Highway 200. Five mi/8 km later, at Secondary 212 (open year-round), turn right and continue for 5 mi/8 km to the Bison Range entrance. From the Bison Range, continue on Highway 212 for 22 mi/36 km to Highway 93.

The route: The story of the American bison is a tragedy that concludes with a triumphant note of hope. In the early 1800s, great herds of bison, some up to fifty million strong, roamed the open prairie from Canada to Mexico and Oregon to Tennessee. By 1883, after forty years of slaughter, the bison population teetered on the brink of extinction. By 1900, only twenty wild bison wandered free.

The National Bison Range (406-644-2211), one of the oldest big-game refuges in the United States, was established in 1908. With $10,000, the American Bison Society purchased thirty-four bison from the Conrad estate in Kalispell. These thirty-four animals owed their existence to a party of Pend d'Oreille that returned to the Flathead Valley with four bison calves after a hunting trip on the plains east of the divide. Today, 300 to 500 bison make their home on the rolling grasslands of the Bison Range.

A visit to the Bison Range begins at the visitor center where you'll find interpretive exhibits about bison and information to make a tour of the range more enjoyable. The visitor center, environmental education program, and nature trails are designed to accommodate people with physical disabilities.

The Flathead Indian Reservation
Homeland of the Confederated Salish and Kootenai Tribes
by Velda Shelby, Development Specialist

The Flathead Indian Reservation is the homeland of 6,675 members of the Confederated Salish and Kootenai tribes. These Tribes are often referred to as the Flathead Nation since they function politically as a unified tribal government pursuant to the Indian Reorganization Act of 1934. Ten elected officials from throughout the Reservation serve the Tribal Council which functions as the governing body. Council meetings are scheduled weekly to deal with Tribal business at the Tribal headquarters in Pablo.

The Flathead Nation is the largest employer on the Reservation. Tribal services include a spectrum of education programs, housing, health, social, economic, law enforcement, land, environmental protection, and numerous other natural resource related services. With an operating budget of over $70 million and approximately 1,200 employees, the Tribes provide a significant contribution to the quality of life enjoyed on the Flathead Reservation.

There is an eternal splendor to the 1.243 million acres that encompass the Flathead Indian Reservation extending from Rollins to the north and Evaro to the south. The Cabinet Mountains border the west side of the Reservation and the majestic Mission Mountains border the east side. In 1979, the Flathead Nation designated 95,000 acres as a Mission Mountain Wilderness Area. The wilderness and other Tribal wildlands are managed year-round to prevent environmental disturbances.

Visitors must obtain Joint Tribal Use/State Conservation permits to recreate on the Reservation. Permits can be obtained from area distributors for $5 per year. Joint bird and fishing stamps are an additional $10 apiece. All proceeds from these permits are reinvested in Tribal conservation, wildland, and recreation programs for the maintenance and improvement of Reservation resources. For more information please write or call: The Confederated Salish and Kootenai Tribes, P.O. Box 278, Pablo, Montana 59855; 406-675-2700, Fax 406-675-2806, or toll-free 1-800-634-0690.

A two-hour tour along the nineteen-mile Red Sleep Mountain Scenic Drive, with its interpretive turnouts, offers the opportunity to see bison, elk, bighorn sheep, pronghorn antelope, and mule and whitetail deer. Buffalo Prairie Drive, open all year, provides a half-hour trip. The Bison Range is open daily from 8 a.m to 8 p.m. in the summer and on weekdays from 8 a.m. to 4:30 p.m. during the winter (late October through mid-May).

Return to Highway 93 by means of the route you entered the Bison Range or continue up Secondary 212. The latter route, via the Ninepipe Road (across the dike to the picnic area), provides access to the best viewing spot on the Ninepipe National Wildlife Refuge.

ROUTE 5B: THE EAST SHORE OF FLATHEAD LAKE

34 mi/55 km

Road conditions and route description: Just below Polson, turn right (east) onto Highway 35. Thirty-four mi/55 km later, this section joins the main route 2 mi/3 km above Bigfork. While this is a good-quality, all-weather, and well maintained road, winding sections make passing a gamble.

The route: After the turnoff from Highway 93, Highway 35 crosses the Polson Moraine. Notice that the Mission Mountains become less rugged and more rounded to the north; this is the result of being workedover by a glacier so massive that it engulfed entire mountains.

Highway 35 follows the east shoreline of Flathead Lake with little elevation gain as it passes through dense stands of Douglas- and grand fir, ponderosa pine, and birch. On this side of Flathead Lake, you'll find three Montana State Recreation Areas that offer camping and boat ramps. Finley Point (406-887-2715) is located on the southern end of the lake; Yellow Bay (406-982-3291) is a third of the way up the lake; Wayfarers (406-837-4196) is on the north end near the town of Bigfork.

Beyond Finley Point, where Highway 35 hugs the shoreline for a few miles, there are three turnouts on the left side of the road. If it's a hot day and you've been driving too long, a little ART (attitude readjustment time) might help; pull over and take a refreshing dip. In this area, just beyond the shore, Flathead Lake reaches its maximum depth.

Bigfork

The resort town of Bigfork, a quaint community on the shores of Flathead Lake, is the art and creative center of the Flathead Valley. Big Fork offers boutiques, arts, galleries, and lakeside accommodations. The Bigfork Center for the Performing Arts offers year-round performances with the Northwest Repertory Theater staging plays from the last weekend of May through the final weekend of August. On the first weekend of May, during The Gathering At Bigfork, playwrights from around the world participate in seminars and attend staged readings of new plays and works-in-progress. A triathlon and competition-kayaking on class V rapids highlight the Annual Whitewater Festival and Celebration during the middle of May. (For specific information about these events, call the Bigfork Chamber of Commerce at 406-837-5888.)

Two miles beyond Bigfork, Routes 5 and 5B of the Trail of the Great Bear merge and continue to West Glacier.

For More Information About Route 5:

Events and Services

Glacier Country: 945 4th Avenue, East, Suite B, Kalispell, Montana 59901; 1-800-338-5072, 406-756-7128.

Missoula Chamber of Commerce: P.O. Box 7577, 825 E. Front, Missoula, Montana 59807; 406-543-6623.

Kalispell Chamber of Commerce: 15 Depot Loop, Kalispell, Montana 59901; 406-752-6166.

Bigfork Chamber of Commerce: Box 237, Big Fork, Montana 59911; 406-837-5888.

Whitefish Chamber of Commerce: Box 1120, Whitefish, Montana 59937; 406-862-3501.

Polson Chamber of Commerce: Box 677, Polson, Montana 59860; 406-883-5969.

Flathead Valley Convention/Visitor Association: 406-756-8091, 1-800-543-3105.

Missoula Convention and Visitor Bureau: Box 7577, Missoula, Montana, 59807; 406-543-6623.

Confederated Salish and Kootnai Tribes: Pablo, Montana 59055; 406-675-2700.

Northern Pacific Nine Mile Historic Depot and Visitor's Center: Missoula, 406-626-5261.

St. Mary's Mission: Fort Avenue, Stevensville, Montana; 406-542-5500.

National Forests and Wilderness Areas

Mission Mountains Wilderness Area: Wilderness Manager, Confederated Salish and Kootenai Tribes, Wildlands Recreation Department, Box 98, Pablo, Montana 59855; 406-675-2700.

Rattlesnake National Recreation and Wilderness Area: District Ranger, Missoula Ranger District, Lolo National Forest, Building 24-A, Fort Missoula, Montana 59801; 406-329-3750.

Selway/Bitterroot Wilderness Area: District Ranger, Stevensville Ranger District, Bitterroot National Forest, 88 Main Street, Stevensville, Montana 58970; 406-777-5461.

Bitterroot National Forest: 316 North Third Street, Hamilton, Montana 59840; 406-363-3131.

Lolo National Forest: Building 24, Fort Missoula, Missoula, Montana 59801; 406-329-3750.

Floating, Canoeing, and Kayaking on the Flathead River:

North Fork: Glacier View Ranger District, P.O. Box W, Columbia Falls, Montana 59912; 406-892-4372.

Middle Fork: Hungry Horse Ranger District, P.O. Box 340, Hungry Horse, Montana 59919; 406-387-5243.

South Fork: Spotted Bear Ranger Station, P.O. Box 310, Hungry Horse, Montana 59919; 406-752-7345.

Buffalo Rapids: Confederated Salish and Kootenai Tribes, Tribal Fish and Game Office, Pablo, Montana, 59855; 406-675-2700.

Flathead National Forest: Kalispell; 406-755-5401.

Glacier National Park: 406-888-5441.

Wildlife Viewing

Lee Metcalf National Wildlife Refuge: USFWS, 406-777-5552.

National Bison Range: USFWS, 406-644-2211.

Ninepipe National Wildlife Refuge: USFWS, 406-644-2211.

Creston National Fish Hatchery: USFWS, 406-755-7870.

Mountaineers in the Mission Mountains.

Chain Lakes & Golden Conifers

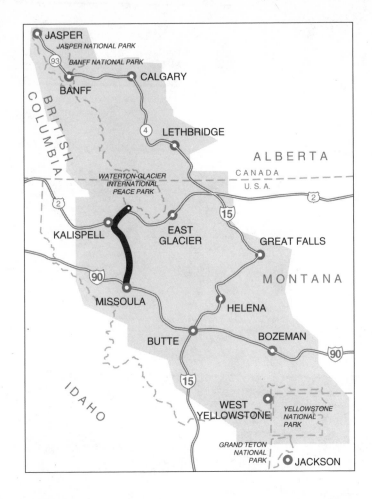

"By such a river it is impossible to believe that one will ever be tired or old."

Wallace Stegner, *The Rockies Filled With The Sound of Mountain Water.*

ROUTE 6

THE SWAN VALLEY   *91 miles/146 kilometers*

General description: Bordered by the Mission Mountains on the west and the Swan Range on the east, Route 6 follows the Clearwater and Swan River Valleys along a chain of glacially-formed lakes and provides good opportunities for wildlife viewing. The route skirts wetlands, riparian habitat, and passes through dense stands of moist coniferous forests of Ponderosa pine, Douglas-fir, Engelmann spruce, western larch, and lodgepole pine with very little elevation gain or loss.

Unique features: Jewel Basin, Mission Mountains Wilderness, Bob Marshall Wilderness Complex.

Wildlife viewing opportunities: Blackfoot-Clearwater Wildlife Management Area, Clearwater Canoe Trail, Swan River National Wildlife Refuge, Old Squeezer Loop Road.

Activities: Canoeing, hiking, biking, cross-country skiing.

Travel season: All year, especially scenic in the fall when the larch turn gold.

Services: Seeley Lake has complete services, also Condon, Swan Lake, and Holland Lake Lodge.

Road conditions and route description: From Clearwater Junction, follow Highway 83 north to its junction with Highway 35. Highway 83 is an all-weather, two-lane road.

The route: A cow the size of Babe, Paul Bunyan's legendary blue ox, marks the Clearwater Junction and the beginning of Route 6. Turn left (north) off Highway 200 and onto Highway 83. Within .5 mi/1 km, you come to a wildlife viewing site on the 50,000-acre/20,000-ha Blackfoot-Clearwater Wildlife Management Area, a good place to watch elk in the winter. (For information contact the Montana Department of Fish, Wildlife and Parks at 406-542-5523.)

In the past we primarily protected areas with obvious aesthetic qualities such as mountain ranges. Look where the boundaries were drawn for the Mission Mountains Wilderness, right at the foot of the mountains. Some people call such designations "rock and ice" preserves. The land within the boundaries provide a decent summer home for animals such as elk, bear, deer, and moose, but come winter these animals require bottomlands near a stream where it's easier to acquire food and water. Such an area is called winter habitat. The Blackfoot-Clearwater Wildlife Management Area is a good example of conservation measures that provide wildlife with much-needed winter habitat.

Except from November 30 to May 15 when the Blackfoot-Clearwater is closed, you can hike cross-country or ride mountain bikes on the network of unpaved roads east of Highway 83. Upsata Lake, a good place to see loons, can be reached by taking the first right (east) turn; follow the unpaved road for 6 mi/10 km to the end, turn left and drive 3 mi/8 km to the lake.

A little farther up Highway 83, an unpaved road on the left provides fishing access to Harper's Lake which has a campground and picnic area. This is also a good place to start a float trip down the Clearwater River.

Salmon Lake

For a short ways, the valley narrows and you pass through stands of Ponderosa pine. From here on, whitetail deer are abundant, especially during the morning and evening hours, so drive carefully. Salmon Lake is the first in a chain of lakes that provide good wildlife viewing. The lakes are home to the largest population of common loons in the western United States. Should you spot nesting loons in marshy areas or on small islands, please stay at least 200 ft/60 m away otherwise the loon may abandon its nest.

You'll find a campground and boat ramp at the Salmon Lake (406-542-5501) and Placid Lake (406-542-5500) State Recreational Areas. National Forest Service campgrounds with boat ramps are situated on Seeley Lake, Lake Inez, and Alva Lake. For Seeley Lake, Lake Inez and Alva, contact the Seeley Lake Ranger District, Seeley Lake, P.O. Box 171, Seeley Lake, Montana 59868; 406-667-2233. Above Salmon Lake, the slow-flowing Clearwater River winds its way through wetlands, marshes, and thick stands of alder; watch for beaver dams and muskrat hollows. What you see along this portion of the route is called riparian habitat. Use of the words riparian habitat is not only quicker than saying "trees and shrubs that grow along a stream," it also makes you sound like an authentic naturalist.

Seeley Lake

A few miles beyond Salmon Lake, the valley opens up and you get your first view of the Mission and Swan range. Both ranges resulted from fault-blocks that tilted eastward; in other words, blocks or chunks of earth that tilted so that the eastern edge (or fault face) rose and the western edge subsided. The Swan Valley is situated on the western edge of a fault-block and the crest of the Swan Range forms the top of the eastern edge. During the most recent ice age, some 12,000 years ago, the Swan Valley filled with glacial ice that spilled in from the Flathead Valley through a the low-lying section of the northern Missions. The glacier scooped out basins and created a chain of lakes.

A couple miles north of the town of Seeley Lake, a turn to the left leads to the National Forest Service Big Larch Campground. If you're carrying a canoe or kayaks, take advantage of an exceptional float trip on the Clearwater Canoe Trail. At the Canoe Trail sign, 4 mi/6.5 km north of the town of Seeley Lake, turn left (west) and drive a short ways to the put-in. From the take-out, a 1.5-mi/2.5-km trail leads back to the point of departure and eliminates the need for a shuttle. The take-out is behind the Seeley Lake Ranger Station; here you can obtain more information about this canoe trip where there's an excellent chance that you'll see or at least hear the melodious cry of loons. (For more information contact the U.S. Forest Service, Seeley Lake Ranger Station, Seeley Lake, Montana, 59868; 406-677-2233.)

At the ranger station, you can also learn more about access to the Mission Mountain and Bob Marshall Wilderness areas. Over 70,000 acres of rugged, snow-capped mountains, heavily forested slopes, alpine lakes, and a few small glaciers make up the Mission Mountains Wilderness Area. Should you cross the Mission crest, you enter Flathead Indian Reservation land where a Tribal permit is required. (Contact: Confederated Salish and Kootenai Tribes, Wildlands Recreation Department, Box 98, Pablo, Montana 59855; 1-800-634-0609.)

ROUTE 6 *SWAN VALLEY*

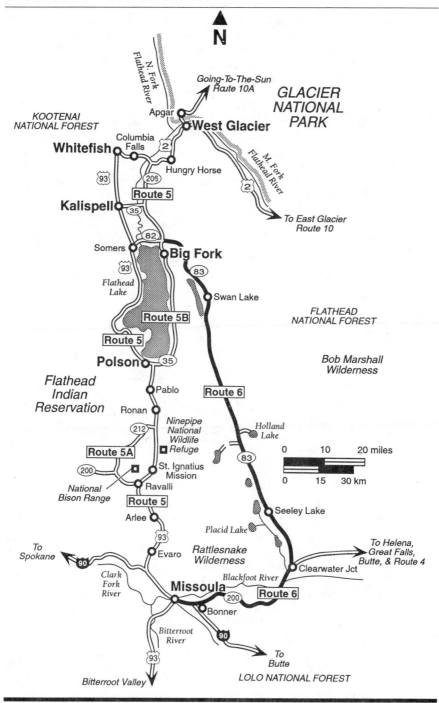

Bob Marshall Wilderness

While the grizzly population in the Mission Mountains is stagnating due to habitat fragmentation, the outlook for grizzlies is better on the east side of the Swan Valley, up in the Bob Marshall Wilderness complex. The Complex is comprised of three wilderness areas—the Bob Marshall, Scapegoat, and Great Bear—and totals over 1.5 million acres of wildland. These three areas form the largest continuous wilderness in the conterminous United States. Another unique aspect of the "Bob" is that it's one of the few wilderness areas that encompasses an entire drainage, the South Fork of the Flathead River. Most wilderness areas are made up of a mountain range with the valley bottoms reserved for human occupation. To reach trails that cross the Swan Range and descend into the heart of the Bob Marshall Wilderness, turn right on the road that leads to Morrell Falls out of Seeley Lake (Forest Service Road 4353), or the Holland Lake turnoff (Forest Service Road 44), or Forest Service Road 680 (2 mi/3 km south of Swan Lake).

At Lake Inez, western larch become more apparent. In the fall, the golden larch flank the road and turn the Swan and Clearwater valleys into a visual treasure. This stately tree is the only conifer that loses its needles after turning color in the autumn. The larch stands out from other trees for most of the year—bare in the winter but sprouting soft, electric-green needles in the spring. The bark at the base of an old-growth larch is often 6 in/15 cm thick, and 3 to 4 in/10 cm thick on second-growth trees, making it extremely fire resistant. While larch commonly live to the ripe old age of 500, in parts of western Montana some have lived 900 years.

A National Forest Service campground is located on Lake Inez. A few miles beyond Alva Lake, where there's another National Forest Service campground with a boat ramp, you pass over the inconspicuous divide between the Clearwater and Swan drainages. Behind you, water flows south, via the Clearwater, into the Blackfoot and then into the Clark Fork River. Up ahead, the Swan River drains north into Flathead Lake.

Fifteen mi/24 km beyond the town of Seeley Lake, a left turn (west) provides access to Lindbergh Lake and the Mission Mountains Wilderness beyond. There's a National Forest Service campground on Lindbergh Lake for summer use and during the winter, the lake's frozen surface is a good place to cross-country ski.

Swan Lake/Swan River National Wildlife Refuge

Towards the northern end of the Highway 83 and near the mouth of Swan Lake, the 1,568 acre/1,627 ha Swan River National Wildlife Refuge (406-755-4375) contains conifer forests and swampland. This undeveloped refuge is home to grizzly and black bears, great blue herons, eagles, and tundra swans. Nearby, at the Swan Lake National Forest Campground, a paved trail allows people confined to wheelchairs to explore the forest.

Jewel Basin is a popular hiking area and for good reason; a number of easy trails lead to a mountain basin dotted with twenty-eight lakes, swift streams full of fish, dense subalpine forests, and lush alpine meadows. The area is only open to foot travel (no pack stock or motorized vehicles). Should you think this sounds too good to be true, you're right; don't hike in expecting a wilderness experience, Jewel Basin is heavily used. If you decide on hiking Jewel Basin be sure to carry a backpacking stove, camp in previously used sites, and treat the area with tender loving care (as you would all backcountry).

Blackfoot/Clearwater Wildlife Management Area.

To reach the trailhead, go 2.5 mi/4 km beyond the turnoff to Bigfork (via Highway 209) and take the Echo Lake Road (on the right-hand side); proceed 2.5 mi/4 km to the Noisy Creek Road and follow it to the parking lot situated at road's end.

The top of Highway 83 crosses open farmlands as it enters the Flathead Valley. Within a few miles, you reach Highway 35 and once again, it's decision time— Marias Pass to East Glacier or Going-To-The-Sun Highway and Logan Pass?

For More Information About Route 6:

Events and Services

Glacier Country: 945 4th Avenue East, Suite B, Kalispell, Montana 59901; 1-800-338-5072, 406-756-7128.

Seeley Lake Chamber of Commerce: P.O. Box 865, Seeley Lake, Montana 59868; 406-677-2880.

Swan Lake Chamber of Commerce: Hwy 83, Swan Lake, Montana 59911; 406-886-2354.

Clearwater Canoe Trail: U.S. Forest Service, Seeley Lake Ranger Station, Seeley Lake, Montana 59868; 406-677-2233.

Wildlife Viewing

Blackfoot-Clearwater Wildlife Management Area: Montana Departmentof Fish, Wildlife and Parks; 406-542-5523.

Swan River National Wildlife Refuge: 406-755-4375.

National Forests and Wilderness Areas

Mission Mountains Wilderness: Confederated Salish and Kootenai Tribes, Wildlands Recreation Department, Box 98, Pablo, Montana 59855; 406-675-2700.

Bob Marshall Wilderness, Jewel Basin: District Ranger, Swan Lake Ranger District, Bigfork, Montana 59911; 406-837-5081.

Flathead National Forest: 1935 Third Avenue East, Kalispell, Montana 59901; 406-755-5401.

The Swan Valley near the north end of Swan Lake. Darrin Schreder photo.

Gold Fever Country

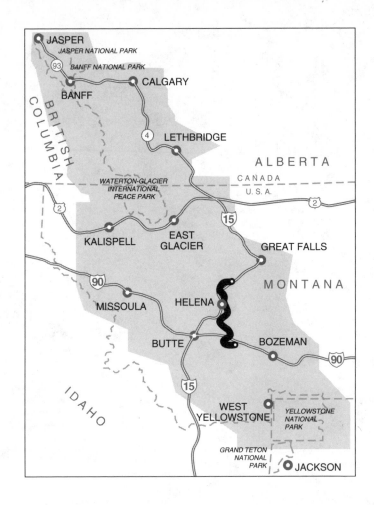

"A friend of mine went out panning in a promising creek. . . and had three little specks of gold by the end of the afternoon—the genuine article. He had them weighed and found that all he needed was 2,000 specks just like those three and he would have an ounce. He is still working at his same old job."

David Alt, geologist.

"Gold is for thieves and swindlers. For this reason they own most of it."

B. Traven.

ROUTE 7

INTERSTATE 90 NEAR CARDWELL to HELENA to WOLF CREEK
95 miles/152 kilometers

General description: The southern half of this route is rich with mining history. Montana's capital city, Helena, offers travelers her historical district. The northern end of Route 7 provides access to a wildlife management area, Gates of the Mountains (Montana's most scenic canyon), and a wilderness area.
Unique features: Helena Historic District, Montana Historical Society, Gates of the Mountains Wilderness Area.
Wildlife viewing opportunities: Beartooth Wildlife Management Area, Gates of the Mountains.
Activities: Golf, boating, snowmobiling, mountain biking, downhill and cross-country skiing.
Events: Vigilante Parade, Dixieland Jazz Festival, East Helena Rodeo, Last Chance Stampede and Rodeo.
Travel season: Year-round.
Services: Limited services are scattered along this route and found in Boulder. Helena is a major service center with an airport.
Road conditions and route description: From Interstate 90 near Cardwell, Highway 69 provides 32 mi/52 km of good, two-lane, and lightly traveled road that connects with Interstate 15. The route remains on Interstate 15 for 27 mi/44 km to Helena. The northern half of Route 7 follows Interstate 15 to the Wolf Creek exit, 36 mi/58 km beyond Helena.

The route: Highway 69 follows the Boulder River drainage, through agricultural land flanked by rolling mountains. Just south of the town of Boulder, a right turn on Elkhorn Road leads, via 18 mi/29 km of gravel road, to Elkhorn State Park (406-994-4042). This historic ghost town, that boomed during the late 1800s, is best viewed (and photographed) in morning or early-evening light. Two of the most interesting structures are the Gillan and Fraternity halls. The Fraternity Hall, listed on the National Register of Historic Places, is an architectural masterpiece and an excellent example of a Neoclassical Western facade; it's reputed to be the most photographed ghost town building in the United States. There is a campground in the area and good cross-country skiing come winter. Those interested in historical architecture should stop in Boulder and visit the century-old courthouse with its three-story entryway and grinning gargoyles.

Gold country

From Boulder, Interstate 15 snakes its way over subdued mountains, covered by open sagebrush, grassland, and forests of Ponderosa pine and Douglas-fir. Along Prickly Pear Creek, about 12 mi/20 km beyond Boulder, the spoil-heaps of a gold-dredging operation are still visible from the road. In the 1950s, a barge-like gold dredge chewed its way upstream for several miles until the Montana Department of Fish, Wildlife and Parks finally halted the destruction. Some of Montana's earliest mining districts are located off the Interstate between Jefferson City and Helena. A variety of structural relics still stand and can be seen from local roads that cross the area.

These short-lived towns owed their ephemeral existence to good geologic timing and the Boulder Batholith. This molten reservoir of igneous rock (which cooled into granite) heated water that circulated deep beneath the earth's surface. The water rose, hot enough to dissolve quartz and gold. When the water reached a certain level, it cooled and released its precious mineral load along veins of quartz. "As it happens," wrote David Alt in *Profiles in Montana Geology*, "we came along at just the right moment in geologic time to find the roof of the Boulder Batholith stripped by erosion down to the level where the quartz veins are rich in valuable minerals. In fact, the upper parts of some veins have already been eroded so the gold they contained is now in placer deposits."

Placer mining is what most people envision when they think of gold mining—the rugged individualist who sloshes water around in a pan beside a stream. Placer gold is gold that eroded loose from its original hiding place and collected in pockets along streambeds (which act like a giant sluice box). While placer mining proved far less romantic than many people imagine, it probably wasn't as dreary as hardrock mining at the dark end of a tunnel. Should you find an abandoned mine and feel compelled to explore it, be advised "to leave the keys in the car so your survivors won't have to jump the ignition when they come to claim it," wrote Alt. "Old mines offer abundant potential for unusual outdoor adventures...rotting timbers ready to crumble at a touch, ladders that suddenly get rotten at about the twenty-fifth rung, and deep shafts that descend hundreds of feet...Any of those can provide instant interment and save your estate the expense of a funeral."

Helena

The abandoned settlements south of Helena deliver a stark, though silent, testimony to how silly it is for a community to stake its financial well-being on a finite resource. The people of Helena realized that the gold in Last Chance Gulch would peter out; they fought for the State Capital to be located in their city. After five elections, they won, but only by a narrow margin, and only with the help of Copper King William Clark, and only because he hated Marcus Daly.

The battle over where to establish the State Capital started in 1867 with an election between Helena and Virginia City; Virginia City won. Two years later, the Legislature ordered another election with Virginia City and Helena as the contenders. An *accidental* fire destroyed the results. By 1874, Virginia City had slipped far into economic decline and the election was simply a for-or-against Helena vote. Corruption tainted the results; the United States Supreme Court refused to consider the case on appeal, so Montana's Supreme Court ruled in favor of Helena. But the state's constitution left the final outcome up to the citizenry. An 1892 election failed to produce a winner. And so, in an election to decide once-and-for-all, Helena and Anaconda stepped into the ring. Marcus Daly deeply desired Anaconda, the town he created, to be the Capital. William Clark sided with Helena, due to his interests there but mostly because he hated Daly. (For more about Daly and Clark see Route 4: Butte.) Anaconda was portrayed as a company-town with a feudal grip on its population; Helena was ridiculed for putting on social airs, and cultural pretensions. In *Montana: A History of Two Centuries*, Malone and Roeder wrote that,

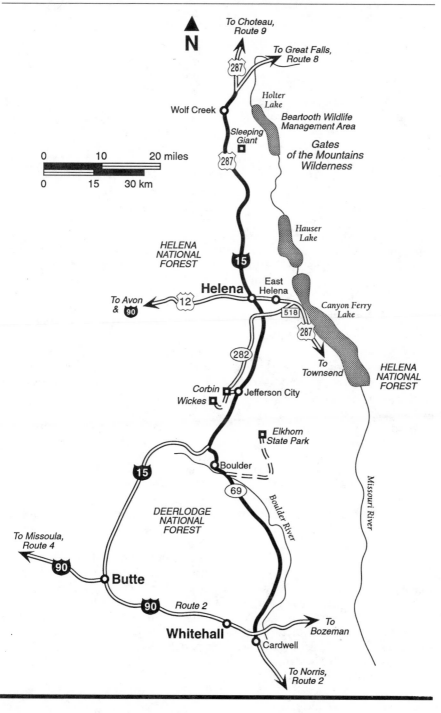

"There were gala parades with imported bands, barrels of free booze, even free money on occasion. Daly spent over $2,500,000 and Clark at least $400,000 on this campaign...that meant roughly $56 invested for each vote!" Helena won by a narrow three percent and, today, is the Montana State Capital with a population of 24,000.

The route: Helena, Montana's capital, offers a big dose of history as well as modern conveniences and contemporary entertainment, including a commercial airport, two golf courses, and a nearby downhill ski area. There are also myriad opportunities for outdoor recreation in the Gallatin Valley. Helena is surrounded by national forest and boasts a city park with a 5,468-foot mountain, Mt. Helena. Canyon Ferry Recreation Area, Hauser Lake, and Holter Lake Recreation Area all accommodate skiing, fishing, and boating. And the swimming is great at Spring Meadow Lake. All these areas provide outstanding wildlife viewing.

The Montana State Historical Society (406-444-2694), located near the Montana Capitol Building, includes the Mackay Gallery of C.M. Russell Art and F. Jay Haynes Gallery of historical photography, as well as changing historical displays. The St. Helena Cathedral (406-442-5825), completed in 1914, offers tours by appointment. The Cathedral is designed after the Votive Church in Vienna. The Holter Museum of Art (406-442-6400) displays traveling art shows and permanent collections ranging from contemporary to historical western. The Archie Bray Foundation (406-443-3502) hosts resident ceramics artists from around the world, and residents' work is shown and sold in the Archie Bray Gallery. The grounds also feature a unique walking tour sponsored by the local Audubon Society.

The Helena Historic District in the downtown area contains a number of historically and architecturally significant buildings from the 1870s and 1880s. Among the more significant areas are Last Chance Gulch, the original Governor's Mansion, and Reeder's Alley. The Helena Tour Train, sponsored by the Montana Historical Society, conducts tours through Helena's historical areas, June through Labor Day, twice a day.

Annual events in Helena include the Vigilante Parade in May, the Dixieland Jazz Festival in late June, the East Helena Rodeo the first weekend in July, and the Last Chance Stampede and Fair in late July.

From about 25 mi/40 km north of Helena almost to Wolf Creek, the route follows Prickly Pear Canyon. The red and green rock of the canyon is Precambrian mudstone which means it's ancient mud, probably one billion years old. A graphic geology lesson to remember when you reach Glacier National Park is visible at a roadcut 1 mi/1.5 km from Wolf Creek. What you see here are layers of volcanic ash with offset vertical columns of dark basalt (these are called dikes). At one time, the basalt dike formed a continuous column. Horizontal faulting caused rock layers to slide over each other in much the same fashion that a deck of playing cards can be slid across a table. Pressurized water, sandwiched between layers, made this unusual movement possible, as it greased-the-skids, so to speak, and allowed one layer to slip along the top of the lower layer. Remember this when you read about the Lewis Overthrust that formed the mountains of Glacier and Waterton national parks.

On July 19, 1805, Captain Meriwether Lewis wrote, "This evening we entered much the most remarkable clifts that we have yet seen. These clifts rise from the waters edge on either side perpendicularly to the hight of 1,200 ft. The

The ghost town of Elkhorn.

towering and projecting rocks in many places seem ready to tumble on us. The river appears to have forced it's way through this immense body of solid rock for the distance of 5 3/4 Mi. . .I called it the *gates of the rocky mountains."*

Lewis was wrong about the river forcing "it's way," because water doesn't work any more than it has to. For all the work that water performs, it's really a pretty lazy element. Water follows the easiest route available and busting through an "immense body of solid rock" isn't easy; plus, water doesn't flow uphill. The Gates of the Mountains actually started to form, three million years ago, prior to the appearance of the hills we see here today. At that time, the river, we now call the Missouri, slowly carved a channel through easily eroded material. Eventually the river hit the more resistant limestone, but by then it was too late for the river to turn back. So, the river didn't burst through, it lowered itself down through white limestone.

The best way to enjoy Gates of the Mountains is from a boat, either your own (there is a public boat launch) or the tour boat (406-458-5241). The two-hour tour costs $2.50 to $5.50 and follows the steep-walled, limestone canyon named by Lewis. Watch for bighorn sheep, mountain goats, mule deer, peregrine falcons, osprey, and bald eagles. Gates of the Mountains is wildly beautiful, one can't help but wonder how much more scenic the canyon appeared to Captain Lewis a century before.

To the east and beyond the canyon rim, the Gates of the Mountains Wilderness Area covers more than 60,000 acres/24,000 ha and abuts the Beartooth Wildlife Management Area. The terrain varies from rolling hills to deep canyons and rocky ridges frequented by mountain goats. Few people utilize this wilderness area. The best way to gain access to the wilderness area is to follow Highway 280, out of Helena and across the Missouri River, to County Road 4 where a left turn leads to a trailhead.

The 31,798 acre Beartooth Wildlife Management Area is comprised of gently rolling terrain, covered by grasses and sagebrush, with rocky outcrops jutting up through the forest at higher elevations. Numerous elk and bighorn sheep make the area their home. From the Interstate, take the Missouri River Road (near Wolf Creek) to the Holter Lake access road and follow it for 6 mi/10 km (there are four campgrounds along the way) to the Beartooth Wildlife Management Area. While wildlife is often visible from the road, some roads are closed to vehicles and provide pleasant mountain biking. A short ways after entering the area, an interpretive sign indicates the presence of an interesting prairie dog town. The Beartooth Wildlife Management Area is closed from December 1 to May 14. (For more information contact the Montana Department of Fish, Wildlife and Parks: 406-454-3441.)

On the other side of Holter Lake, 11,000 acres of open and grassy BLM land contains the 6,200 ft/1,890 m Beartooth Mountain. The skyline of this mountain forms a locally renowned landmark, the Sleeping Giant, who lies stretched out on his back.

The end of Route 7, at Wolf Creek, marks the beginning of two routes that merge in Choteau. Route 8 continues up Interstate 15 to Great Falls and then jogs over to Choteau while Route 9 remains closer to the Rocky Mountain Front.

For More Information About Route 7:

Events and Services

Gold West Country: 1155 Main Street, Deer Lodge, Montana 59722; 406-846-1943.

Helena Area Chamber of Commerce: 201 East Lyndale Avenue, Helena, Montana 59601; 406-442-4120.

Whitehall Chamber of Commerce: Box 667, Whitehall, Montana 59759; 406-287-3343.

Montana Historical Society: 12 E. Lawrence, Helena, Montana 59601; 406-444-2694.

Archie Bray Foundation: 2915 Country Club Avenue, Helena, Montana 59601; 406-443-3502.

Elkhorn (Ghost Town) State Park: Montana Fish, Wildlife and Parks, FWP-Region 8, 1404 8th Avenue, Helena, Montana 59620; 406-444-4720.

Gates of the Mountains Scenic Boat Cruises: 406-458-5241.

National Forest and Wilderness Areas

Gates of the Mountains Wilderness: District Ranger, Helena Ranger District, Helena National Forest, 2001 Poplar, Helena, Montana 59601; 406-449-5490.

Helena National Forest: Federal Building, Room 334, 301 South Park, Drawer 10014, Helena, Montana 59626; 406-449-5201.

Wildlife Viewing

Beartooth Wildlife Management Area: Montana Department of Fish, Wildlife and Parks; 406-454-3441.

Sailboats on Canyon Ferry. Darrin Schreder photo.

Out onto the Prairies

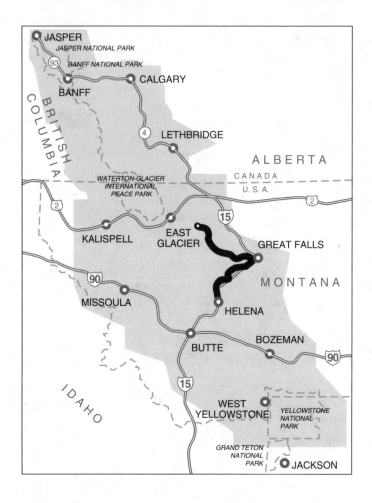

"...a smooth even sheet of water falling over a precipice...forms the grandest sight I ever beheld...the water after descending strikes against the abutment on which I stand and seems to reverberate and being met by the more impetuous courant they roll and swell into half formed billows of great height which rise and again disappear in an instant."

Captain Meriwether Lewis at the Great Falls of the Missouri River, 1805.

ROUTE 8

WOLF CREEK to GREAT FALLS to CHOTEAU
103 miles/166 kilometers

General description: Route 8 follows the Missouri River past some world-renowned geologic features as it makes its way out onto the prairies where grizzly bears once roamed. Two major attractions in Great Falls are the Charles M. Russell Museum Complex and Giant Springs. The route also provides access to two wildlife refuges where massive gatherings of waterfowl occur.
Unique features: Missouri River, Ulm Pishkun Buffalo Jump, C.M. Russell Museum, Paris Gibbon Center for Contemporary Arts.
Wildlife viewing opportunities: Freezeout Lake Wildlife Management Area, Giant Springs State Park, Benton Lake National Wildlife Refuge.
Activities: Boating, fishing, golf.
Events: State Fair, C.M. Russell Auction of Original Western Art, Western Heritage Artists Annual Art Show, Annual Native American Inter-Tribal Celebration of Sobriety, Montana Roundup Days, Lewis and Clark Festival.
Travel season: Year-round.
Services: Cascade and Vaughn can provide basic services. Great Falls is a major service center and has an international airport.
Road conditions and route description: From Wolf Creek, Route 8 remains on Interstate 15 to Great Falls (50 mi/81 km) and on to Vaughn (12 mi/19 km beyond Great Falls). From Vaughn, follow Highway 89, a high-quality-two-lane road, for 41 mi/66 km to Choteau.

The route: Beyond Cascade, the Mesa Buttes come into view on the left (north) side of the Interstate. This is the best array of *laccoliths* in the world. About fifty million years ago, molten igneous rock rose from within the depths of the earth. The layers of earth above the rising volcanic reservoir cracked and the cracks (some of them 20 mi/32 km long) filled with liquid igneous rock (or *magma*). The magma cooled, the surrounding material eroded away and exposed what we see today—the rugged *dikes* that look like the ruins of great walls. These dikes reveal the ancient subterranean duct-work that allowed magma to pool like massive blisters that remained sandwiched, between layers of sedimentary rock, until they cooled and subsequent erosion unveiled these laccoliths. One of the largest laccoliths, Square Butte, appears in many of Charlie Russell's paintings. The vegetation on top of Crown Butte, protected by the steep cliffs surrounding it, grows as it did before ranchers grazed cattle in the area and the plow blades of sodbusters erased the prairie where grass once grew belly-high to a horse.

From Wolf Creek, an alternative to the high-speed interstate follows the Missouri River through rocky canyons and over rolling prairie. Upstream from the settlement of Cascade, the Missouri River is considered a "blue-ribbon" trout stream. Downstream from Cascade, the vegetation is comprised of grasslands, riparian cottonwood forests, willow thickets, and wetlands. In addition to a more relaxed pace, this drive offers a number of wildlife viewing opportunities; golden eagles at Eagle Rock (6 mi/10 km south of the town of Craig), beaver dams along Little Prickly Pear Creek, and raptor watching in the spring near Ulm. The Ulm Pishkun Buffalo Jump State Park (406-454-3441) is located 4 mi/6 km north of Ulm. There is an interpretive trail in this 170-acre park and an interesting black tailed prairie dog town. (For more information about buffalo jumps, see Route 12.)

The section of the Missouri River between Wolf Creek and Great Falls provides good floating and "blue-ribbon" fishing opportunities. A majority of the land bordering the river is private with few official public access points. The Montana Department of Fish, Wildlife and Parks offers an excellent map of the Missouri River and access points between Holter Lake and Great Falls. (Write to Region 4 Headquarters, P.O. Box 6610, Great Falls, Montana 59406.)

Two views of the Great Falls of the Missouri

In Great Falls, five dams plug the Missouri, taming the waterfalls for which the city was named. On June 13, 1805, Captain Lewis described the falls and mentioned seeing "several skelletons of the buffaloe lying in the edge of the water... which I presume have been swept down by the current and precipitated over this tremendious fall." He continued, "of the sun on the sprey or mist which arises from these falls there is a beatifull rainbow produced which adds not a little to the beauty of this majestically grand scenery. I wished... I might be enabled to give to the enlightened world some just idea of this truly magnifficent and sublimely grand object, which has from the commencement of time been concealed from the view of civilized man...this moment fills me with such pleasure and astonishment."

Seventy-five years later, *civilized man* brought the *enlightened world* west and they built the first dam across the Missouri River at Great Falls. Here's what Paris Gibson, founder of Great Falls, wrote, "In magnitude, the falls are unsurpassed in the United States except by the falls of Niagara...it is safe to assume that the power of the Falls of the Missouri available for industrial progress is fully equal..."

Great Falls

Great Falls is Montana's second largest city with a metropolitan population of 80,000. According to the Guiness Book of World Records, the world's shortest river flows through Great Falls. The Roe River originates in Giant Springs State Park where the largest freshwater spring in the United States pours 400 million gallons of water into the Missouri each day. The spring offers great trout-watching but the adjacent hatchery is even better. The area also offers good bird-watching (more than 150 species have been seen here). The visitor center exhibits stuffed animals, wildlife photography, and wildlife videos; it's open during the summer from 8 a.m. to 7 p.m. on weekdays and 10 a.m. to 7 p.m. on weekends. The weekday hours during the off-season are 8 a.m. to 5 p.m. Giant Springs is located (east of and) beyond the municipal golf course off River Drive. (For more information call the Montana Department of Fish, Wildlife and Parks: 406-454-3441.)

Located in downtown Great Falls, the Paris Gibson Center for Contemporary Arts displays a variety of works in expressive styles that vary from traditional to experimental and offers classes, speakers, workshops, and special events throughout the year. From Memorial Day to Labor Day, the center is open on weekdays from 10 a.m. to 5 p.m. and on weekends from 12 p.m. to 5 p.m. During the off-season the center is closed on Mondays. (For more information,

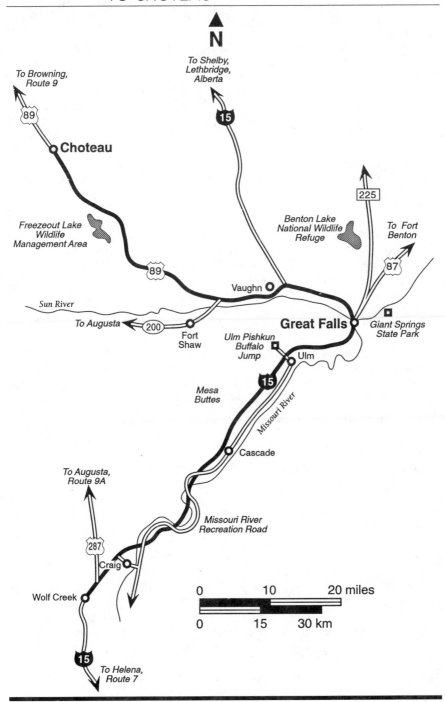

write Paris Gibson Center for Contemporary Arts, 1400 First Avenue North, Great Falls, Montana 59401 or call 406-727-8255.)

"To have talent is no credit to its owner; any man that can make a living doing what he likes is lucky, and I'm that. Any time I cash in now, I win," wrote Charlie Russell a short time before he died. The most complete collection, displaying the talent of America's Cowboy Artist, is offered to the public at the Charles M. Russell Museum Complex. The complex, that covers an entire city block, includes the Russell home, Charlie's log cabin studio (Nationally Designated Historical Sites), and seven galleries that exhibit 7,500 works of art which include masters such as O.C. Seltzer, Olaf Wieghorst, Edward Curtis, and Joseph Henry Sharp. The Gallery charges a modest admission. The complex is open in the summer (May 1 to September 30), Monday to Saturday from 9 a.m. to 6 p.m. and Sunday from 1 p.m. to 5 p.m. During the winter the complex is closed Mondays and open 10 a.m. to 5 p.m. from Tuesday thru Saturday and on Sunday from 1 p.m. to 5 p.m. (For more information, write C.M. Russell Museum Complex, 400 13th Street North, Great Falls, Montana 59401 or call 406-727-8787.)

Beginning the first Saturday of July and continuing through the first Saturday in August, Great Falls hosts the State Fair. Three big events take place over the third weekend of March. The works of international artists are exhibited all over town during the Western Heritage Artist Annual Art Show and Native American Art Show. For the past twenty-four years, artists and craftspeople have displayed and sold their work during the C.M. Russell Auction of Original Western Art. Artistic creations are displayed at the Heritage Inn prior to an auction; admission to the auction is $75 which includes a buffet meal. The event benefits the C.M. Russell Museum and has sold more than $5,000,000 worth of western art. (For more information contact the Great Falls Advertising Federation, Box 634, Great Falls, Montana 59403; 406-761-6453.) Montana Roundup Days, celebrated during the last weekend of June, includes historic exhibits, cowboy poets, music, a broomstick rodeo, a barn dance, and a real rodeo (for information call 800-443-3733; in Montana call 800-452-0700). The Lewis and Clark Festival is held the last weekend in June. Visitors can view a Lewis and Clark encampment, attend a buffalo barbeque, or take a Missouri River float. For more information contact the Great Falls Area Chamber of Commerce, 406-761-4434.

Native people share their customs, rituals, and dancing with the general public during the Annual Native American Inter-Tribal Celebration of Sobriety at the Great Falls College. For general information about Great Falls, contact the Chamber of Commerce at 617 10th Street South, Great Falls, Montana 59405; 406-761-4434.

Difficult as it may be to imagine today, grizzly bears freely roamed the prairies around Great Falls only a few generations ago. Contrary to popular belief, settlement on the prairies did not *push* grizzlies into the mountains; grizzlies already lived there. The plains grizzlies were simply killed due to conflicts with ranchers and farmers. The Lewis and Clark Expedition killed its share of bears. Read the Lewis and Clark journals and you're likely to believe that the plains grizzly acted more aggressively than bears today. But as historian Duane Hampton points out, "Those guys took pot-shots at every bear they saw. Usually, the first half-dozen shots just wounded the animal. And you know as well as me that a wounded bear isn't very amiable."

Benton Lake National Wildlife Refuge and Fort Shaw

Not far from Great Falls, the 12,383-acre Benton Lake National Wildlife Refuge is one of the most important waterfowl refuges in the United States. To reach the refuge, take Highway 87 and turn left (north) onto Secondary 225 (Bootlegger Trail) and follow it 12 mi/19 km to the refuge entrance on the left. During March to April and September to October, more than 100,000 waterfowl, such as ducks, Canada geese, snow geese, and tundra swans, stop at this shallow prairie marsh to take a break from their migration. The refuge is also one of two sites in Montana nominated to be part of the International Shorebird Reserve. A brochure, available at the main information sign (located 1.5 mi/2.5 km from the entrance), provides a self-guided interpretive tour along the 9 mi/15 km Prairie Marsh Drive. Check at the Refuge headquarters for area closures before canoeing or hiking. The Refuge is open from March 1 to November 30 though occasionally closed due to a wet road. (For more information contact the U.S. Fish and Wildlife Service: 406-727-7400.)

Beyond Great Falls, 12 mi/20 km, the route parts ways with Interstate 15 and follows Highway 89 which traverses agricultural and ranch lands. In 1913, Charlie Russell lamented the coming of the plow when he wrote to a friend, "Bob you wouldn't know the town [Great Falls] or the country either, it's all grass side down now. Where once you rode circle and I night wrangled, a gopher couldn't graze now. The boosters say it's a better country than it ever was but it looks like hell to me, I like it better when it belonged to God..."

Eight mi/13 km later, a left turn onto Highway 200 leads (6 mi/10 km) to what remains of Fort Shaw. While there is little more than a roadside sign to provide interpretation, the site is historically significant. Constructed in the heart of Blackfeet country (at least it was in 1867), the fort served as a base to protect the Mullan Road and mining camps from Indian attack. From 1866 to 1892, the army established a dozen forts in Montana. "To these wilderness outposts came the nondescript troopers," wrote historian Harry Fritz, "enlistees who, at $13 per month, were often either seeking adventure or shirking creditors." It was from Fort Shaw that Major Eugene Baker launched a punitive action against a small group of Peigans who had killed a retired fur company agent, Malcolm Clark (who, ironically had married a Peigan woman and was considered a friend to the Indians). Baker encountered the winter camp of Heavy Runner. The lodges were full of smallpox victims; the healthy men were out hunting. Without warning or provocation, Baker ordered an attack on what turned out to be the wrong band of Indians. A barrage of bullets cut down Heavy Runner as he walked forward with papers proclaiming his loyalty to the United States Government. The massacre claimed the lives of 173 Peigans, fifty-three of them women and children. Baker left the survivors to fend as best they could on the frozen plains. The army conducted an investigation; Baker was absolved of any wrong-doing. Fort Shaw later became the focal point of settlers in the Sun River Valley. The army closed the fort in 1891.

Freezeout Lake Wildlife Management Area

The Freezeout Lake Wildlife Management Area is 11,350 acres of wetland and marsh; more waterfowl congregate here than anywhere else in Montana. The lake occupies an ancient and shallow glacial basin. During the peak of migration (March to May and September to November), more than a million birds rest their weary wings here. The *Montana Wildlife Viewing Guide*

Grain silos in Fairfield. John Reddy photo.

recommends the road around Pond Five as a popular drive and the first week in November as a peak period for tundra swans (10,000) and the first week in April and November for snow geese (300,000). If all those snow geese lined up end-to-end, they'd form a line 142 mi/229 km long; that's longer than the route you're currently driving! The refuge is closed from October to December to give the birds a reprieve from the hunting season.

In their quest to bag a duck, responsible hunters switched from lead shot to steel shot, and for good reason. The lead pellets from a shotgun shell, that don't end up in a hunter's target, fall to the ground. According to *The Birder's Handbook* by Ehrlich, Dobkin, and Wheye, "1,400 pellets (about half a pound) are left behind for every bird carried out. A single pellet swallowed with food or taken as grit and ground in the gizzard can introduce enough lead into the bloodstream to kill a duck." Every year, 1.5 to three million waterfowl die from lead poisoning. Some hunters resist the change to steel shot because of inferior ballistics and increased barrel wear. Lead weights used for fishing also cause poisoning, but the impact is minor in comparison to lead shot. "Poisoned waterfowl show characteristic behaviors, including holding wings in a 'roofshaped' or drooped position, a walking with staggering gait, showing reluctance to fly, seeking isolation, or remaining behind after others migrate."

Highway 89 continues across rolling grass and agricultural lands to the community of Choteau. This is a beautiful drive at daybreak when the morning sun illuminates the Rocky Mountain Front.

For More Information About Route 8:

Events and Services

Charlie Russell Country: P.O. Box 3166, Great Falls, Montana 59403; 1-800-527-5348 or 406-761-5036.

Great Falls Chamber of Commerce: P.O. Box 2127, Great Falls, Montana 59403; 406-761-4434.

Choteau Chamber of Commerce: Route 2, Box 256, Choteau, Montana 59422; 406-466-5897

Paris Gibson Center for Contemporary Arts: 1400 First Avenue North, Great Falls, Montana 59401; 406-727-8255.

Charles M. Russell Museum Complex: 400 13th Street North, Great Falls, Montana 59401; 406-727-8787.

Ulm Pishkun Buffalo Jump: Montana Department of Fish, Wildlife and Parks; 406-454-3441.

Missouri River access points between Holter Lake and Great Falls: Write for map to Montana Department of Fish, Wildlife and Parks, Region 4 Headquarters, P.O. Box 6610, Great Falls, Montana 59406.

Wildlife Viewing

Giant Springs State Park: Montana Department of Fish, Wildlife and Parks; 406-454-3441.

Benton Lake National Wildlife Refuge: U.S. Fish and Wildlife Service; 406-727-7400.

Freezeout Lake Wildlife Management Area: Montana Fish, Wildlife and Parks; 406-467-2646.

Blackfeet Country

"We did not think of the great open plains, the beautiful rolling hills and the winding streams with tangled growth as 'wild.' Only to the white man was nature a 'wilderness' and only to him was the land 'infested' with 'wild' animals and 'savage' people. To us it was tame. Earth was bountiful and we were surrounded with the blessings of the great mystery."

Chief Standing Bear (Lakota).

"When the colonists arrived in America, the whole continent was one continued dismal wilderness, the haunt of wolves and bears and more savage men. Now the forests are removed, the land covered with fields of corn, orchards bending with fruit and the magnificent habitations of rational and civilized people."

John Adams, 1756.

ROUTE 9

134 miles/216 kilometers

General description: Beginning in a volcanic landscape of grassland, rimrock, scattered conifers, and rocky ridges, this low elevation route offers scenic panoramas of the Rocky Mountain Front and access to the Sun River Game Reserve, Pine Butte Swamp Preserve, and Bob Marshall Wilderness Complex. The road rolls along as it passes between the eastern edge of foothill grasslands and the agricultural empire that stretches across the Great Plains. The route descends into several river valleys and crosses the Dearborn, Sun, Teton, and Two Medicine rivers and Dupuyer, Birch, and Badger creeks. Croplands extend through much of the route's middle section; at the northern end, it enters the Blackfeet Indian Reservation with access to the Badger/Two Medicine area.

Unique features: Bob Marshall Wilderness Complex, Blackfeet Indian Reservation, Museum of the Plains Indian, Badger/Two Medicine area.

Wildlife viewing opportunities: Sun River Game Reserve, Pine Butte Swamp Preserve, Blackleaf Wildlife Management Area.

Activities: Backpacking, cross-country skiing, mountain biking, downhill skiing.

Events: North American Indian Days Celebration.

Travel season: Year-round.

Services: Basic services available in Augusta, Choteau, and Browning.

Road conditions and route description: Turn off Interstate 15 at Wolf Creek and proceed north on Highway 287 for 65 mi/105 km to Choteau; turn left (north) on Highway 89 and continue for 73 mi/118 km to Browning. Highways 287 and 89 are good-quality, two-lane roads and are maintained for travel on a year-round basis. Signs that warn drivers to reduce speed for curves should be heeded.

The route: At Wolf Creek, Highway 287 rolls up and down over the remains of a massive lava flow that dates back fifty million years and covered sedimentary rock formed on the ancient shores of a shallow sea (some sixty to eighty million years ago).The volcanic rock is dark in color and the sedimentary is a lighter shade of pale brown and yellow. There is a mystical quality to this rugged landscape with its rimrock, rolling grasslands, scattered limber pine, ponderosa pine, Douglas-fir, and skunkbrush, dissected by rocky ridges (which are really *dikes*, see Route 8) that look like the ruined walls built by giant stone masons.

Beyond the junction with Highway 200, the Clark Range (on the left) forms the Rocky Mountain Front and also the Continental Divide. From the agricultural community of Augusta, the Sawtooth Range takes over the role of forming the Front. This dramatic escarpment formed when horizontal sections of sedimentary rock slid (or were pushed; the distinction inspires heated arguments between geologists) eastward over the plains and stacked in a slanted fashion, like so many dominoes, one on top of the other. The Front and the country behind it comprises the Bob Marshall Wilderness Complex which covers more than 1.5 million acres. This extensive wilderness area provides important habitat for grizzlies, mountain goats, bighorn sheep, elk, moose, and deer. The *Lewis* and Clark National Forest Visitor Map (Rocky Mountain Division) graphically details various roads, along Route 9 that provide access to trailheads that lead into the "Bob" (as the Bob Marshall Wilderness Complex is called by locals). The map is available from the Augusta Forest Service Information Station, Box 365, Augusta, Montana 59410; 406-562-3247, or Rocky Mountain Ranger District, Box 340, Choteau, Montana 59422; 406-466-5341, or Forest Supervisor's office, Lewis and Clark National Forest, Box 871, Great Falls, Montana 59403; 406-791-7700.

If you're going to visit the Sun River Canyon and Wildlife Management Area, the turnoff is in Augusta (see Route 9A). From Augusta, the main route continues over the plains where grizzlies and wolves lived surrounded by massive herds of bison, elk, and antelope; this once was truly the Serengeti of North America.

Clouds and Choteau

A short distance from Choteau, the road reaches a high point that provides a good vista of the Front Country. This is a good place for a little ART (Attitude Readjustment Time). Sure, private lands border the highway, but you can still pull over and walk about. Watch the wind move the grass like waves upon the sea. Crush some juniper needles between your fingers and smell the fragrant scent. If intermittent clouds blow through the sky, watch the play of sunlight across the land. This is also one of those areas along the Trail of the Great Bear where cactus grow.

Should you spend time cloud-gazing, it's nice to know what you're looking at. Clouds are divided into three basic groups which are sub-divided again (because scientists love lots of categories) to bring the total to twenty-seven types. We'll stick to the three basic clouds. **Stratus** clouds occur closest to the ground, spreading across the sky in a uniform and featureless manner. When stratus clouds occur at ground level, we call it fog. Higher up, **cumulus** are the archetypal cloud—those fluffy, white, cotton balls in the sky that most people envision when they hear the word cloud. Way up high and composed of ice crystals, float the **cirrus** clouds that look like wispy mare's tails, feather plumes, or streaks in the sky. Often times, they denote an approaching storm or at least a change in the weather (this is a pretty safe statement to make in the Rockies, where the weather changes rapidly to begin with).

Clouds form because all air contains some moisture or invisible water vapor. Warm air can hold more moisture than cold air. As air rises it cools and loses its ability to hold moisture. When the cooled air becomes saturated, the water vapor expands into visible (though tiny) droplets and a cloud forms. To envision this, think about what happens when you open a teapot. Inside the pot, hot air contains invisible water vapor. As air from inside the pot rises, it cools, becomes saturated, loses its ability to hold invisible moisture, and visible steam forms.

A cloud sub-type of particular interest while traveling the Front Country is the **lenticular** cloud. These clouds look like flying saucers or curved pancakes and denote strong, mid-level air movement. Mountains deflect the fast moving air up where it develops a wavecrest and forms lenticular clouds. Under the right conditions, a fantastic congregation of lenticular action creates a standing wave that extends along the Front for miles; this

ROUTE 9 *WOLF CREEK TO BROWNING*

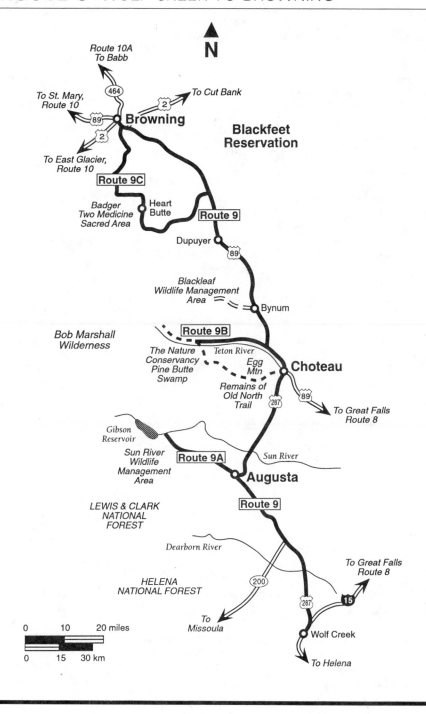

N

Route 10A
To Babb

To St. Mary,
Route 10

464

89   **Browning**

2

2

To Cut Bank

**Blackfeet
Reservation**

To East Glacier,
Route 10

Route 9C

Badger
Two Medicine
Sacred Area

Heart
Butte

Route 9

Dupuyer

89

Blackleaf
Wildlife Management
Area

Bynum

Bob Marshall
Wilderness

Route 9B

The Nature
Conservancy
Pine Butte
Swamp

Teton River

Egg
Mtn

Choteau

Remains of
Old North
Trail

287

89

To Great Falls
Route 8

Gibson
Reservoir

Sun River
Wildlife
Management
Area

Route 9A

Sun River

Augusta

LEWIS & CLARK
NATIONAL
FOREST

Route 9

Dearborn River

HELENA
NATIONAL FOREST

200

287

To Great Falls
Route 8

15

To
Missoula

Wolf Creek

To Helena

0   10   20 miles

0   15   30 km

formation is the most spectacular and photographic in the evening or morning and often foretells the coming of a chinook (see Route 11).

A gravel county road, 1 mi/2.5 km south of Choteau, leads to The Nature Conservancy's Pine Butte Swamp Preserve. Choteau's origins are associated with the establishment of the second Blackfeet Agency, which was abandoned as the Native People lost more land and their reservation shrank. The town was surveyed in 1883; it became a regional center for ranching and later farming. Today Choteau, with a population of 1,800, is a good example of an agricultural community that has begun to expand its economic base by taking advantage of the natural resource-based tourism possibilities that surround it. The Teton County Court House is listed on the National Register of Historic Places; the town, like Fort Macleod on Section 12 is a good example of western small town architecture. The Teton Trail Museum displays some standard exhibits in addition to dinosaur bones and fossilized dinosaur eggs like those found on Egg Mountain. The best exhibit is the skeleton of a Canadian trapper with arrowheads embedded in his spine and two bullet holes and a tomahawk gash in his skull. (Choteau Chamber of Commerce, Route 2, Box 256, Choteau, Montana 59422; 406-466-5897.)

In Choteau, Highway 287 connects with Highway 89. A short ways up Highway 89, a left turn (west) on the Teton River Road leads to the Rocky Mountain Hi (downhill) Ski Area (406-466-2422). North of Choteau, the 19,430-acre Blackleaf Wildlife Management Area can be reached by turning left (west) at the settlement of Bynum and following the Blackleaf Road for 16 mi/26 km. The area is home to grizzly and black bears for part of the year (portions are closed from spring to July 1 due to grizzly use). The area also offers an impressive array of wildflowers in bloom (summer and spring) and a variety of raptors. The *Montana Wildlife Viewing Guide* points out that, "A herd of about seventy-five mountain goats can be seen year-round where the road deadends in stunningly beautiful Blackleaf Canyon." (For more information contact the Montana Department of Fish, Wildlife and Parks: 406-278-7754.)

Highway 89 continues north through agricultural land, occasionally crossing a stream flanked by riparian vegetation. Concerning the population density of the area, one traveler said, "I just passed through Dupuyer and saw a little road sign that indicated the mileage to someone's ranch. You know there's not many people living in an area when you can do that."

The only shootout on the Lewis and Clark Expedition

Just south of the Blackfeet Reservation, a road sign mentions the only violent cultural conflict that occurred during the Lewis and Clark Expedition. On July 3, 1806, Lewis and Clark split up during the homeward journey in order to increase their area of exploration. Lewis and nine men passed through Hellgate Canyon (near Missoula), ascended the Blackfoot River, crossed the Continental Divide, and entered the plains where they observed 10,000 bison within a 2 mi/3 km area. On July 12, Natives pilfered seven horses. Ten days later the party met a group of Piegans (one of three Blackfoot tribes), that Lewis mistook for Gros Ventre. His journal entries indicate that Lewis felt suspicious of the group, which seems justifiable; the size of his party and theft of their horses probably rendered him a bit paranoid. Nevertheless, as he wrote, "I thought it best to please them and gave to one a medal to a second a flag and to the third a handkerchief." The two groups camped together that night. "I . . . did not wake until the noise of the men and indians awoke me a little after light in the morning." Three of the Piegans ran off with four of the Lewis party's guns. One of the whites pursued and "as he seized his gun stabed the indian to the heart with his knife the fellow ran about 15 steps and fell dead . . ." Lewis threatened a Piegan with his pistol and the man laid down the gun. Two of the whites wanted to shoot the Piegan but Lewis forbid it "as the indian did not appear to wish to kill us." Lewis chased another Piegan, shouting at him to return the horse or he would shoot. "I shot him through the belly, he fell . . . and fired at me.., being bearheaded I felt the wind of his bullet very distinctly." Having killed two Piegans, Lewis and company high-tailed it, covering 100 miles in twenty hours! In a timely rendezvous worthy of a Hollywood adventure film, they joined the expedition below Great Falls, abandoned their horses, jumped in the boats, and continued downriver before any Blackfeet arrived.

Curly Bear Wagner, cultural director for the Blackfeet tribe, presents a slightly different view of the same story. Lewis encountered Blackfeet on their land. The Blackfeet expected tribute in return for passage, like a toll-keeper collecting from those who drive across a bridge. Lewis gave some rather worthless stuff and the Blackfeet decided the whites were cheapskates who could part with more. Whatever the case, the unfortunate incident resulted in the first deaths of Native Americans by New Americans out West and set the stage for future hostilities.

Blackfeet country

Route 9 enters the Blackfeet Indian Reservation at Birch Creek. Between 1856 and 1895, the reservation underwent considerable reduction. The first agency was at Fort Benton located east of Great Falls, the second agency near Choteau. In 1874, the southern boundary was moved more than 40 mi/65 km from the Teton River (which flows next to Choteau), to Birch Creek. Today, the 1.5 million-acre Blackfeet Reservation comprises the United States' portion of the Blackfeet Nation which consists of three other tribes, all in Alberta, Canada: The Bloods, Piegan, and Northern Blackfoot. Not so long ago, these people, known to other Native people as "The Lords of the Great Plains," claimed a vast portion of the prairies. Folklore attributes the name *Siksika*, meaning "Blackfooted People," to moccasins blackened by the soot of prairie fires.

Where Highway 89 crosses Badger Creek, look to the left and back (southwest) to see Ghost Ridge. By the winter of 1883-84, the bison had been exterminated. Hunters returned to camp empty handed; the Blackfeet relied entirely on the Agency which lacked the means to sustain them due to drastic funding cuts by Congress. That winter, more than 600 Blackfeet starved (an estimated twenty percent of the tribe) and were buried on Ghost Ridge.

"So, like the mighty grizzly bear who, when Fall approaches, goes into a winter sleep, we went into our sleep," wrote Curly Bear Wagner. "Now, the winter of our suffering is over and we arise, refreshed with due strength, declaring to all men that we shall form a new government, a new way of life, recapturing our pride and dignity and fostering our culture and our heritage." A number of interesting and historic sites exist on the reservation but there is little in the way of interpretive signs. Curly Bear leads half- and full-day historic tours that provide insights to tribal life from pre-historic times to the present. For more information write Blackfeet Historical Tours, Box 238, Heart Butte, Montana 59448, or call 406-338-2058.

A turn right (east) on the road just past Two Medicine River leads to a buffalo jump site. As no interpretive signs indicate the jump's location, spotting it will be a good test provided you've seen the Madison (Route 3), Ulm Pishkun (Route 8), or Head-Smashed-In buffalo jump (Route 12a). If you've never seen a buffalo jump then turn on the imagination; what portion of the cliff would you drive a bison over? Bear in mind that bison, being heavy and therefore greatly influenced by gravity, wouldn't need to fall far to be crippled or killed.

The Reservation's headquarters and largest town is Browning where the prairie wind blows so hard that it knocks down street signs. The Museum of the Plains Indian exhibits a permanent display of the rich and diverse historic arts from tribal people who lived on the Plains. The museum also devotes two galleries to changing exhibits of contemporary Native artists and craftspeople. A highlight at the museum is the five-screen, multi-media presentation of the *Winds of Change* that documents the evolution of Native culture on the Northern Plains. Admission is free; the museum is open year-round: June to September, daily from 9 a.m to 5 p.m. and October to May, Monday through Friday from 10 a.m. to 4:30 p.m. (For more information: Museum of the Plains, Box 400, Browning, Montana 59417; 406-338-2230.) Adjacent to the museum, the Blackfeet Tribal Fairgrounds is the site of North American Indian Days during the second week in July. This is one of the largest gatherings of United States' and Canadian tribes and includes four days of dancing, games, sport events, and socializing. (For information: North American Indian Days Committee, Box 850, Browning, Montana 59417; 406-338-7276.)

ROUTE 9A: SUN RIVER GAME RESERVE: 19 Mi/30 Km:

Road conditions and route description: From Augusta, turn left (west) on the Sun River Road. Follow it for 4 mi/6.5 km to a fork in the road; go right and continue for 15 mi/24 km to the Sun River Canyon. This good gravel road passes the Sun River Wildlife Management area.

The route: On the way to Sun River Canyon, the Sun River Road provides access to the 20,000-acre Sun River Wildlife Management Area (406-466-5341). The area's primarily functions as critical winter range to Montana's largest elk population. Though the area is closed in the winter when this gathering occurs, the Sun River Road offers good vantage points for watching elk. Mountain biking on the wildlife management area's dirt roads is fun; watch for Canada geese, herons, and tundra swans.

Where the prairies meet the Rocky Mountain Front, the road enters the steep-walled Sun River Canyon. One of North America's largest herd of bighorn sheep commonly roams in the area between Hannan Gulch and Wagner Basin. The Home Gulch Campground is a good place to watch for sheep; also keep your eyes opened for elk, deer, and raptors.

The Nature Conservancy's Pine Butte Swamp Reserve.

ROUTE 9B: PINE BUTTE SWAMP PRESERVE 24 Mi/39 Km

Road conditions and route description: The entire loop is approximately 24 mi/39 km long, half of which is a paved secondary road and the other half is gravel. One mi/2.5 km south of Choteau, turn left (towards the mountains) and follow a gravel county road. At Forest Service Road 109, turn left (towards the mountains) and proceed 9 mi/15 km to the (west) end of the road. On the return trip, at the (east) end of Forest Service Road 109, turn left (north). This road crosses the Teton River and makes a turn to the right and becomes the Teton River Road which proceeds for 15 mi/24 km to Highway 89. Choteau is 5 mi/8 km to the right (south).

The route: The dirt road that departs from Highway 89 (1mi/2.5 km south of Choteau) heads toward the Front over rolling agricultural and grasslands. The road passes Egg Mountain; this is where paleontologist Jack Horner discovered the fossilized remains of dinosaur nesting colonies. The discovery pointed out that dinosaurs exhibited maternal behavior and ushered in a significant change in the way we view dinosaurs. Today, the Museum of the Rockies (through a cooperative arrangement with the Nature Conservancy) runs the Paleo Field School where amateurs can actively work in the field with professional paleontologists.

Introductory to advanced paleontology courses offer field work, lectures, and meals. For more information write Paleo Field School, Museum of the Rockies, Montana State University, Bozeman, Montana 597171-004. The

119

school requests that people leave the dig sites at Egg Mountain undisturbed.

The Old Trail Museum in Choteau offers sessions in Paleo instruction. Two-day sessions run from June 1 through September 15. For more information, phone 406-464-2314.

About 7 mi/11 km beyond Egg Mountain, the road passes a kiosk (an informational sign with a roof on it). The sign provides information about the Nature Conservancy's Pine Butte Swamp Preserve which is the result of a unique cooperative effort between the Nature Conservancy, the Forest Service, BLM, and local ranchers. In addition to being the largest wetlands habitat along Montana's Rocky Mountain Front, the preserve is the only place where grizzly still freely roam on the prairie, their native home. Only a hundred years ago, grizzlies' habitat extended from the Pacific Coast east to Minnesota, and from Alaska south to Mexico. Of an original population estimated at 100,000, something like 800 remain. The 18,000-acre Pine Butte Swamp Preserve provides extremely important habitat to grizzlies, though your chances of seeing one here are slim. The only hike you can take on the preserve without permission starts at the kiosk and heads south, across the road, and up to the ridge top.

Atop the ridge, limber pine (often called jack pine) grow with an average age of 350 years. The stunted size of these trees should help you realize that organisms don't lead a lavish life of opulence here, what with high winds, cold temperatures, and spartan moisture. To the east, Pine Butte rises up from the wetlands that provide habitat to forty-three mammals and 150 birds. Native people on a vision quest trekked to Ear Mountain (8,580 ft/2,615 m), the prominent mountain due west of the ridge. While on top of the ridge, look down at the kiosk and follow the fence (on the left) for 150 yd/450 m to the north and you might spot a circle of stones. This is a tipi ring left by Native people hundreds, maybe thousands of years ago.

Should you walk out to the tipi ring, don't do something silly like take a rock for a souvenir—just leave things the way they've been for years and years. (So often, people who remove artifacts get their souvenirs home and think, 'This is only a rock in my house, it has no meaning here. The true value of this rock existed out on the prairie where it formed part of a tipi ring. I feel like a mindless moron for taking it.") This campsite was used time and again by nomadic bands of Native people.

Sit in the center of the ring, close your eyes, and let the quiet take hold of your imagination. Picture the land before fences, buildings, and roads. Off in the distance, the snort of a grizzly rises above the morning breeze. The only people for miles are you and your band, camped here during a yearly journey south along the Old North Trail. Your one objective today is to procure food before night.

Remnants of the Old North Trail still exist from Calgary, Alberta, to Denver, Colorado. Just 1 mi/2.5 km farther up the road, a section of the 10,000-year-old travel route can been seen. Where the fence comes down to the road, you'll see a depression (which may have water in it depending on the season) to the right (east). From this point, walk about 100 yd/30 m to the right (to the northeast) and you'll see a rut. At first, you may think this is a jeep road, but look close; it's too narrow. This is the Old North Trail, which really isn't an awesome sight until you start thinking about what you're seeing. During the most recent ice age, a land bridge formed at the Bering Strait and allowed people to migrate from Asia to North America. These travelers and their dogs,

THE SPIRIT OF THE
Great Bear

GOING-TO-THE-SUN HIGHWAY, GLACIER NATIONAL PARK. TOM & PAT LEESON PHOTO.

The Spirit Bear prevails on the Trail of the Great Bear. From its southernmost habitat in Yellowstone National Park to its Canadian Rockies' range, the majestic grizzly is interwoven in history and legends as a symbol of nature's power and fragility.

Pilgrims on the Trail of the Great Bear may be fortunate to catch a glimpse of the magnificent animal, but all will sense its presence in the roar of a wilderness waterfall and the melody of a mountain bluebird.

COLUMBIA ICEFIELDS. TOM & PAT LEESON PHOTO.

Fire and Ice

An adventure of epic proportions, travelers on the Trail of the Great Bear traverse millions of years in time, from the molten geothermals of Yellowstone National Park to the glacial ice fields of Banff and Jasper national parks.

In Celebration

The Trail of the Great Bear celebrates North America's visionary dream, the national park. It links the world's first national park, Yellowstone, through the world's first international peace park, Waterton-Glacier, to Canada's first national parks, Banff and Jasper as an international scenic corridor.

OLD FAITHFUL GEYSER. TRAVEL MONTANA PHOTO.

Prince of Wales Hotel and Waterton Townsite, Waterton Lakes National Park, Alberta, and the Goat Haunt region of Glacier National Park, Montana. Alberta Tourism photo.

Spanning Two Nations

The Trail of the Great Bear is an international tour linking Canada and the United States, Alberta and Montana.

Waterton-Glacier is the bridge between the two nations.
Designated as the world's first international peace
park, Waterton-Glacier commemorates
friendship amongst nations and recognizes
that Nature knows no political boundaries.

MOUNTAIN GOAT. BRUCE WEIDE PHOTO.

Watchable Wildlife

The Trail of the Great Bear region is often referred to as the Serengetti of North America reflecting the impressive number of wildlife species found within the corridor. Watchable Wildlife programs offered in Montana and Alberta will alert the traveler to rich viewing opportunities particularly spectacular in the spring, fall, and winter.

SILVER-TIPPED GRIZZLY BEAR. TIM CHRISTIE PHOTO.

Essential Habitat

The Trail of the Great Bear encompasses eco-regions on both the east and west sides of the Continental Divide. These natural ecosystems provide the essential habitat that allows the diverse variety of plants and animals to flourish within the corridor. National, state, and provincial agencies, together with private landowners and resource managers are the stewards of this fragile environment. The Grizzly is endangered. These wildlands are his last vestige. As increased pressure is placed on the land, both steward and user must strive to insure the protection and consideration of wildlife habitat. The Trail of the Great Bear is committed to this objective.

WHEN THE LAND BELONGED TO GOD, A PAINTING BY CHARLES M. RUSSELL.

When the Land Belonged to God

The Trail of the Great Bear traverses the land where the Rocky Mountains run head-on with the Great Plains. At one time this region was home to millions of free-roaming buffalo. Today, only remnants of those huge herds remain at

sites like the National Bison Range, and Yellowstone, Waterton, and Banff national parks.

Images of the era of great herds were preserved in the paintings of famed western artists like Charles M. Russell, (1864-1926). Exceptional western art exhibits are found along the Trail of the Great Bear in Montana at the CM Russell Museum in Great Falls, the Montana Historical Society in Helena, the Buffalo Bill Historical Center in Cody, Wyoming, and the Glenbow Museum in Calgary, Alberta.

CHIEF MOUNTAIN, NINASTAKIS, THE SACRED MOUNTAIN OF THE BLACKFOOT AND NEIGHBORING TRIBES. AL CLUCK PHOTO.

Kunaitupii

The Blackfoot word Kunaitupii means "All the people." The Trail of the Great Bear is a window to the history and culture of the diverse population living along the corridor.

For time immemorial native people have inhabited the region. The First Nations found along the corridor include the Blackfoot in Alberta, and the Blackfeet and Ktunaxa in Montana.

THE ORIGINAL DESIGN IS THE WORK OF PEIGAN ARTIST WILLIAM BIG BULL. RED AND BLACK ARE THE TRADITIONAL PEIGAN COLORS. THE DESIGN INCORPORATES A NUMBER OF TRADITIONAL PEIGAN SYMBOLS. THE BEAR IS THE MEDICINE GRIZZLY. ON THE LARGE BEAR PAW TO THE LEFT IS THE PICTOGRAPH OF WHITE MAN. ON THE PAW ON THE RIGHT IS THE PEIGAN PICTOGRAPH FOR PEIGAN. ACROSS THE BOTTOM ARE TRADITIONAL PEIGAN SYMBOLS FOR MOUNTAINS, EARTH, AND WATER.

FOR MANY, THE SPIRIT OF THE LAND IS BEST COMMUNICATED THROUGH THE PHILOSOPHY AND CUSTOMS OF THE NATIVE PEOPLE. TRAVELERS CAN GAIN INSIGHT INTO THIS UNIQUE PERSPECTIVE AT LOCATIONS LIKE HEAD-SMASHED-IN BUFFALO JUMP IN FORT MACLEOD, ALBERTA, THE MUSEUM OF THE PLAINS INDIAN, BROWNING, MONTANA, AND EVENTS LIKE THE FLATHEAD NATIONS ANNUAL POW-WOW.

ALICE LITTLE MOUSTACHE AND CHAD FRITZ BRIDGE THE GAP AT NAPI FRIENDSHIP CENTER, PINCHER CREEK, ALBERTA.
DAVE OKAMURA PHOTO.

THE HEAD-SMASHED-IN BUFFALO JUMP. ALBERTA TOURISM PHOTO.

THE CAPITOL DOME, HELENA, MONTANA.
DARRIN SCHREDER PHOTO.

GHOST TOWN, ELKHORN, MONTANA.
DARRIN SCHREDER PHOTO.

The Old West

The European settlement of the West was one of the most dramatic periods in North American history. That migration occurred in remarkably different ways in Canada and in the United States which is reflected in the industry, architecture, and even the lifestyles of today. Great Bear travelers are invited to experience that past.

THE NORTHWEST MOUNTED POLICE MUSEUM, FORT MACLEOD ALBERTA.
ALBERTA TOURISM PHOTO.

TRANSPORTATION PLAYED A VITAL ROLE IN THE
SETTLEMENT OF THE WEST. FROM THE DOG DRAWN
TRAVOIS TO THE HORSE AND WAGON, THE RIVER
BOATS ON THE WIDE MISSOURI, TRANSCONTINENTAL
TRAINS, AND THE MODEL T. INVENTION IS
EXPLORED AT THE TOWE FORD MUSEUM IN DEER
LODGE, MONTANA, AND THE REMINGTON CARRIAGE
COLLECTION IN CARDSTON, ALBERTA.
JOHN REDDY PHOTO.

ANACONDA
AND
PHILIPSBURG
ARE BUT TWO
MONTANA
COMMUNITIES
WITH A RICH
LIVING MINING
HISTORY. THE FRANK SLIDE
INTERPRETIVE CENTRE AND ECOMUSEUM
IN CROWSNEST PASS, ALBERTA,
PRESENTS THE COAL MINING HISTORY OF
THE REGION. LARRY MAYER PHOTO.

THE TRAIL OF THE GREAT BEAR IS CRISS-
CROSSED WITH THE ROUTES OF HISTORIC
EXPEDITIONS TO THE WEST. JOHN REDDY
PHOTO.

THE COWBOY IS ALIVE AND WELL ALONG THE
TRAIL. THIS IS THE LAND OF GREAT RANCHES,
FROM CHOTEAU TO DEER LODGE AND LONGVIEW
TO PINCHER CREEK. PRACTICALLY EVERY TOWN
ALONG THE TRAIL HOSTS AN ANNUAL RODEO; THE
MOST FAMOUS IS THE CALGARY STAMPEDE.
WILLIAM R. SALLAZ PHOTO.

THE TRAIL OF THE GREAT BEAR ENCOMPASSES MANY OF THE MAJOR TOWNS AND CITIES OF ALBERTA AND MONTANA. THE COSMOPOLITAN CITY OF CALGARY AND THE COMMUNITIES OF LETHBRIDGE, KALISPELL/WHITEFISH, GREAT FALLS, BOZEMAN, BUTTE, AND MISSOULA ARE BUT A FEW LOCATIONS OFFERING URBAN ENTERTAINMENT, FINE DINING, AND SHOPPING. SCOTT ROWED PHOTO.

Live the Adventure

Y ou can live the spirit of the Trail of the Great Bear. There are outdoor activities for every interest from downhill skiing to biking, golfing, auto touring, hiking, and floating.

WILLIAM R. SALLAZ PHOTO.

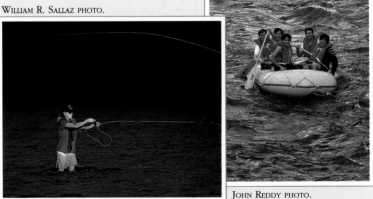

JOHN REDDY PHOTO.

BLUE-RIBBON TROUT STREAMS FROM THE BOW TO THE MADISON FLOW THROUGH THE GREAT BEAR CORRIDOR. WHETHER YOUR PASSION IS TO HIKE BACKCOUNTRY TRAILS OR FISH IN A CATCH-AND-RELEASE RIVER, ACCESSIBLE WILDLANDS ARE AT YOUR REACH ALONG THE TRAIL OF THE GREAT BEAR.

TAKE AN INTERNATIONAL SCENIC BOAT
CRUISE ON WATERTON LAKE.
VIEWING THE SCENERY FROM ABOARD
A BOAT IS AN EXCELLENT WAY TO
ENJOY THE SIGHTS. THE GATES OF
THE MOUNTAINS NEAR HELENA, ST.
MARY LAKE IN GLACIER PARK, LAKE
MINNEWANKA IN BANFF, AND
JASPER'S MALIGNE LAKE OFFER SCENIC
BOAT TOURS.

MANY OF THE ROADS ALONG THE TRAIL OF THE
GREAT BEAR ARE GREAT FOR BICYCLE TOURING.
SCOTT ROWED PHOTO.

TOM & PAT LEESON PHOTO.

SCOTT ROWED PHOTO.

MANY OF THE GREAT SKI HILLS OF THE NORTHERN ROCKIES ARE FOUND ALONG THE TRAIL OF THE
GREAT BEAR. YELLOWSTONE'S BIG SKY, BRIDGER BOWL, SHOWDOWN, BIG MOUNTAIN, BANFF,
LAKE LOUISE, JASPER, AND KANANASKIS COUNTRY OFFER SKIER'S A VARIETY OF TERRAIN AND SOME
OF THE BEST POWDER SNOW TO BE FOUND ANYWHERE. NUMEROUS SNOWMOBILING AND CROSS-
COUNTRY SKIING OPPORTUNITIES CAN ALSO BE FOUND ALONG THE TRAIL. FOR A TRULY UNIQUE
EXPERIENCE TRAVELERS CAN EXPLORE THE COLUMBIA ICEFIELDS IN A SNOW COACH.

Trail *of the* Great Bear

**Trail of the Great Bear
LEGEND:**

Route
Route Number   00
National Parks
TGB Corridor

N

pulling travoises, eroded this trail into the prairie.

For permission to explore the wetlands or Pine Butte, contact the preserve managers at 406-466-5526. The Nature Conservancy operates a guest ranch at the preserve where workshops concentrate on natural history. For information or reservations write to Pine Butte Guest Ranch, HC58 Box 34C, Choteau, Montana 59422 or call 406-466-2158.

The road continues, winding on past The Nature Conservancy's guest ranch and the preserve manager's residence. A left turn (west) on Forest Service Road 109 provides a scenic 9 mi/15 km drive along the South Fork of the Teton River, over prairie hills, through montane and subalpine vegetation, up a steep-walled canyon, past the Mills Falls Campground, and on a short ways farther to the Our Lake trailhead. The 3.5-mi/5.5-km hike to Our Lake makes a good overnight backpack trip.

Mountain goats live in the area around the lake and often walk right through camp; there are also possibilities for some breathtaking ridge walks from Our Lake. The Mill Falls Campground is a nice place to car-camp. Consider yourself fortunate should one of the Front Country's infamous electrical storms pass over with the brief but torrential rains, thunder-boomers that shake tent poles, and flashes of lightning that illuminate the night. A right turn (east), on the other side of the bridge over the Teton River, leads back to the main route via the Teton River Road. A left turn (west) leads to the Rocky Mountain Hi Ski Area on Teton Pass via Forest Service Road 144.

ROUTE 9C: HEART BUTTE LOOP   50 Mi/81 Km

Road conditions and route description: A couple miles north of the Highway 89 and Highway 44 junction, on the other side of Birch Creek, turn left (west) on a secondary road. This 50-mi /81-km route passes through the settlement of Heart Butte and joins the main route just south of Browning.

The route: The Badger-Two Medicine area is the site of a potential wilderness area and a great deal of controversy because the Blackfeet claim it as a religious site of great spiritual importance that traditional Blackfeet feel should be not be desecrated. Oil and gas interests (in conjunction with the Forest Service) feel that roads should be built in the area to enable exploration for and development of oil and gas. Environmentalists, siding with traditional Blackfeet, want the area left alone due to its natural beauty and the role it plays as a critical wildlife corridor between Glacier National Park and the Bob Marshall Wilderness Complex.

This route provides access to the Badger-Two Medicine via a turn left (west) on the secondary road on the other side of Birch Creek which forms the southern boundary of the Blackfeet Reservation. Consult the Forest Service offices listed in Route 9 for more information and maps. This route passes through the Native settlement of Heart Butte and offers excellent foothills scenery in addition to good examples of glacial geology. Should you want to gather more information about the Badger-Two Medicine area, write to Dale Gorman, Supervisor's Office, Lewis and Clark National Forest, Box 871, Great Falls, Montana 59403; 406-791-7700.

For More Information About Route 9:
Events and Services
Glacier Country: 945 4th Avenue East, Suite B, Kalispell, Montana 59901; 1-800-338-5072, or 406-756-7128.

Charlie Russell Country: P.O. Box 3166, Great Falls, Montana 59403; 1-800-527-5348 or 406-761-5036.

Choteau Chamber of Commerce: Route 2, Box 256, Choteau, Montana 59422; 406-466-5897.

Paleo Field School: Museum of the Rockies, Montana State University, Bozeman, Montana 597171-004.

Blackfeet Historical Tours: Box 238, Heart Butte, Montana 59448; 406-338-2058.

Museum of the Plains Indian: Box 400, Browning, Montana 59417; 406- 338-2230.

National Forests and Wilderness Areas
Bob Marshall Wilderness Complex: Augusta Forest Service Information Station, Box 365, Augusta, Montana 59410; 406-562-3247, or Rocky Mountain Ranger District, Box 340, Choteau, Montana 59422; 406-466-5341, or Forest Supervisor's Office, Lewis and Clark National Forest, Box 871, Great Falls, Montana 59403; 406-791-7700.

Badger-Two Medicine potential wilderness area: Lewis and Clark National Forest, Box 871, Great Falls, Montana 59403; 406-791-7700.

Wildlife Viewing
Blackleaf Wildlife Management Area: Montana Department of Fish, Wildlife and Parks, 406-278-7754.

Sun River Wildlife Management Area: Montana Department of Fish, Wildlife and Parks, 406-466-5341.

The Nature Conservancy's Pine Butte Swamp Preserve: 406-466-5526. Pine Butte Guest Ranch, HC58 Box 34C, Choteau, Montana 59422; 406-466-2158.

Cross-country skiing possibilities abound along the East Front.

Across the Great Divide

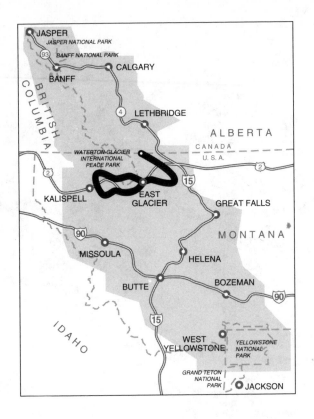

"There's a lot of pressure to... aspire to bigger and better things. People ask me why I never got out into the real world." Jerry gestured to the snow-covered mountains. "I told them, 'This is the real world'."

From an interview with
retired Glacier Park ranger, Jerry DeSanto (in *Montana Magazine*).

ROUTE 10

WEST GLACIER to ST. MARY   *87 miles/140 kilometers*

General description: This route offers a variety of landscapes and vegetation types that range from moist timberland around West Glacier to subalpine forest on the Marias Pass on the Continental Divide to low-lying foothills on the East Front. From West Glacier, Highway 2 follows the southern boundary of Glacier National Park offering access to the Middle Fork of the Flathead River and an overlook from which mountain goats are often observed. The route continues over the Continental Divide down to the intermittent open and forested lands so characteristic to the East Front country. From East Glacier, the route winds through aspen parklands to St. Mary.

Unique features: Glacier National Park, Great Bear Wilderness, Going-To-The-Sun Road, Museum of the Plains Indians.

Wildlife viewing opportunities: Walton Goat Lick Overlook, Going-To-The-Sun Road, Highline Trail, Logan Pass.

Activities: Backpacking, mountain biking, river floating, cross-country skiing, golf, fishing, hiking.

Travel season: Year-round.

Services: Basic services can be found in West Glacier, Essex, East Glacier Browning, and St. Mary.

Road conditions and route description: Highway 2 from West Glacier to East Glacier is a good, two-lane road that makes a low crossing of the Continental Divide over Marias Pass. At East Glacier, turn left (north) on Highway 49. This narrow road winds its way to Kiowa and the junction with Highway 89; turn left here and continue to St. Mary. Some roads are maintained on a year-round basis. This road is open only on a seasonal basis. In the winter continue on to Browning then turn north at Highway 89.

The route: From West Glacier, Highway 2 skirts the southern boundary of Glacier National Park as it ascends from lush forests of Douglas-fir, lodgepole pine, and larch to the subalpine fir and Engelmann spruce found atop Marias Pass. For 30 mi/48 km, from West Glacier to Essex, the road follows the Middle Fork of the Flathead River. River rats with a taste for whitewater adventure can quench their thirst on the Middle Fork; watch for the Moccasin Creek (before Nyack), the Paola (beyond Pinnacle), and Bear Creek (beyond Essex) river access signs. However, from the Paola or Bear Creek put-ins, it's "plainly not a stream for the faint-hearted," as Hank Fischer wrote in *The Floater's Guide to Montana.* "Those who have floated the Middle Fork know why it's called Montana's wildest river."

The Great Bear Wilderness is accessible along Highway 2 at Essex, Nimrod, and the Devil's Creek Campground. The Great Bear forms the northern portion of the 1.5-million-acre Bob Marshall Wilderness Complex, which in conjunction with Glacier and Waterton national parks comprise over 2.5 million acres of habitat for grizzly bears, elk, deer, wolves, bighorn sheep, mountain goats, and lots of other wildlife.

The historic Izaak Walton Inn, originally built (in 1939) to house winter train crews, displays photographs of the Great Northern's glory days and the railroad activity to which the little town of Essex owes its existence. Westbound freights used to stop in Essex where additional locomotives hooked on for the steep pull over the Continental Divide. Today, the Izaak Walton Inn still provides pleasant lodging to visitors who travel by car and AMTRAC train passengers. During the winter, the Inn becomes one of the premier cross-country ski resorts in the United States with 19 m/30 km of groomed trails for track and skate skiing (406-888-5700).

Two mi/3 km beyond Essex, turn off the highway, walk to the end of a short paved trail, peer out over the railing, and watch for mountain goats (especially from April through mid-July). A naturally occurring salt lick on the north side of the river attracts wild goats that come down for a dose of minerals. The record number of goats seen here at one time is eighty-nine. In 1981, reconstruction of Highway 2 through this area was completed. As a result, the average speed of travel increased from twenty-five mph to forty-five mph. The Park Service anticipated an increase in the number of goats killed by automobiles, so a tunnel was built. During one observation interval, biologists counted over 1,200 goats that came down to the salt lick and 99.6 percent used the underpass. Deer and other wildlife also utilize the tunnel for safe passage beneath Highway 2.

Marias Pass

A few miles beyond the salt lick, on the right hand (south) side of Highway 2, Devil's Creek National Forest Service Campground offers overnight camping. The road crosses Marias Pass at 5,280 ft/1,610 m, Montana's lowest pass over the Continental Divide. The pass derives its name from the Marias River which is over 50 mi/80 km to the east and was named after Maria Wood, cousin of Captain Meriwether Lewis. The historic and real name for this gap in the Rockies, "the Backbone Pass," came from the Blackfeet. The Kootenai, Flathead, and Salish traveled east over Backbone Pass for access to the plains where they hunted bison. Blackfeet raiding parties crossed west to steal horses from the Salish, Kootenai, and Flathead. In 1810, an early trapper, Finian MacDonald, crossed the divide over Marias Pass with 150 Indian allies. On the plains, they encountered Blackfeet and a battle ensued. MacDonald decided to follow safer routes to the north or south after that.

The Theodore Roosevelt Obelisk commemorates the opening of the pass to far more travelers whose passage is far less dramatic than MacDonald's. This is a good place to see evidence of the Lewis Overthrust Fault, the geologic player responsible for providing the raw mountain material that glaciers later refined. Around sixty million years ago, a massive slab of ancient earth began sliding east. Over the course of a million years, the sedimentary slab traveled as far as 50 mi/80 km. Usually, according the geologic law of superposition, the youngest sedimentary layer sits on top of the stack with the layers below becoming progressively older. The Lewis Overthrust Fault set up a unique situation wherein rocks more than a billion years old came to rest on top of youngsters (only sixty to eighty-million-year-old rocks). "The best way to obtain a grand view of the Lewis Overthrust Fault," wrote geologist David Alt in *Glacier Country*, "is to look north from Marias Pass. You can see the tan Altyn limestone just above the fault as a straight band of tan rock that slopes like a railway grade descending gently down to the west." During the most recent ice age, a sea of ice enveloped this area on such a mammoth scale that only the tops of the highest peaks protruded above the glacier. Ice bulldozed its

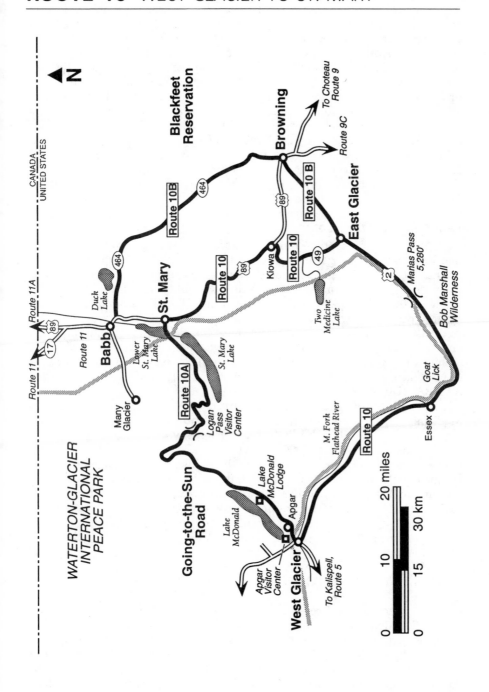

way down drainages carving U-shaped valleys and gouging out basins like those now filled by McDonald and St. Mary Lakes (seen along Route 10A). Were you standing at this exact spot 12,000 years ago, you'd quite literally feel very depressed (beneath a few thousand feet of ice). The glaciers of today are pygmies compared to the titans of the past; in fact, they've even shrunk since they were first mapped in the early 1900s. Geologists believe that today's glaciers formed after, and thus are not remnants of, the last ice age.

The Forest Service Summit Pass Campground sits atop the divide. The road down the east side passes through forests of Engelmann spruce and subalpine fir and then aspen parkland pocketed with prairie potholes, beaver ponds, and interspersed with lush meadows where impressive fields of wildflowers bloom in the spring and early summer. The *Montana Wildlife Viewing Guide* recommends the area around the Firebrand Pass Trail Trailhead (6 mi/10 km prior to East Glacier) as a "great birding spot, especially in the spring and fall." This is also a good place to watch for bears. A few miles before East Glacier, the road crosses onto the Blackfeet Reservation. (For more about the Blackfeet, read Routes 9 and 10B.)

Down to the Front country

Along the East Front, the Trail of the Great Bear passes many aspen groves that look as if a giant gardener pruned the tree-tops to maintain a uniform height. The wind is the gardener here. Trees survive the powerful prairie winds by growing on the wind-sheltered side of a hill, just below the summit. Branches that stick up above the shelter of the hill and surrounding trees are sheared off by the wind.

At East Glacier, where the mountains meet the plains, the route turns (north) onto Highway 49. The Glacier Park Lodge, noted for its remarkable log architecture, was built by the Great Northern Railway prior to World War I. East Glacier is also an entry or exit point to the Trail of the Great Bear for AMTRACK travelers.

A few miles up Highway 49, a left turn takes you to Glacier Park's Two Medicine Lake, where there's a campground and trails that lead into rugged alpine backcountry. Beyond the turnoff, Highway 49 continues past aspen parkland as it ascends for 1,000 ft/300 m to a saddle forested with lodgepole pine. The road drops to the junction with Highway 89 where you turn left. For the next 19 mi/31 km, the road winds through gentle foothills as it descends into the St. Mary Valley. While this section is quite scenic any time of the day, it's especially impressive at sunrise when the morning mists drift between the mountains. South of St. Mary (5 mi/8 km) the road crosses the Hudson Divide; on one side the water flows into the Gulf of Mexico and on the other side, Hudson's Bay.

ROUTE 10A: GOING-TO-THE-SUN ROAD   53 Mi/85 Km

General description: Crossing the width of Glacier National Park, Going-To-The-Sun Road is one of if not the most scenic roads in the world. This route also attains the highest driveable point on the Trail of the Great Bear north of Route 1B. The alpine passage begins in West Glacier, crosses the Continental Divide at Logan Pass (6,646 ft/2,026 m), and continues down to the end of St. Mary Lake. Hikes accessible from Logan pass offer excellent opportunities to see grizzlies and other wildlife.

Travel Season: Closed by snow.

Road conditions and route description: From Highway 2, turn left (north) into West Glacier and enter Glacier National Park. Within a short distance from the park entrance, the road T's; turn right (east) and continue for 51 mi/82 km over Logan Pass and down to St. Mary. This two-lane road is well maintained, however it is narrow and heavily used during the peak tourist season. Be prepared to drive slowly. Going-To-The-Sun closes after the first major snowfall, which usually occurs sometime in October, and opens in the late spring around mid-June. Vehicular length restrictions are in place. Contact the park office for details.

The route: For the first couple decades of Glacier National Park's existence travelers followed routes established by the Great Northern Railroad. After the train delivered them to East Glacier, they traveled on horseback to Two Medicine Chalet, then to the St. Mary Chalet, on to Going-To-The-Sun Chalet, over Logan Pass to Lake McDonald Lodge, and finally back to the train station at West Glacier. Such a tour required at least a week and many people spent an entire month; but that all changed with the construction of one road.

The Going-To-The-Sun Road, completed in 1933 after a decade of construction and an expenditure of $3 million, spanned the breadth of the park. The road, first called the "Transmountain Highway," was an engineering marvel as well as a logistical challenge. The final survey team of thirty-three men worked, for three months, on terrain that only mountain goats and mountaineers dared traverse; the crew succeeded despite a 300 percent turnover rate. The National Park Service insisted that contractors construct bridges, retaining walls, and guardrails from native rock and that explosive blasts be as small as possible to reduce collateral destruction. In one blast area, workers wore wool socks over their boots to prevent the possibility of sparking off a charge. The 405 ft/123 m East Side Tunnel proved one of the most difficult tasks; construction progressed at a bit less than 5.5 ft/1.5 m per day and as power equipment couldn't reach the tunnel, workers removed the debris by hand. The elegant Triple Arches was spontaneously designed on the spot to replace the original plan for a massive retaining wall. Though the park officially opened the road in 1933, it wasn't entirely paved until 1952. Today, ninety-five percent of Glacier is still wilderness but only five percent of the park visitors venture beyond the road. A study in 1990 showed that sixty percent of Glacier's visitors stayed one full day or more. For the adventurous few, backcountry permits are required for backpackers and horsepackers. Permits are free and issued on a first-come-first-served basis and must be obtained within twenty-four hours of the backcountry trip.

A trip up Going-To-The-Sun begins in West Glacier, location of the park headquarters and the Glacier Natural History Association, which sells books and maps at park visitor centers; profits remain in the park and support interpretive and educational programs. Membership includes a fifteen percent discount on most publications; write Glacier Natural History Association, Box 327, West Glacier, Montana 59936, or call 406-888-5756. Also located in West Glacier is the Glacier Institute, which offers field courses in the park, taught by experts, that examine cultural and natural resources, management policies and research efforts, and creative arts. (For information: Glacier Institute, Box 1457, Kalispell, Montana 59903; 406-888-5215.) AMTRAK still stops at the West Glacier train station.

East Front south of St. Mary.

A journey up Going-To-The-Sun commences a short ways beyond West Glacier, with a right turn at the junction. A left turn, however, leads to the Apgar Visitor Center and campground. There are four other campgrounds along this route at Sprague Creek and Avalanche Creek on the west side of the pass, and Rising Sun and St. Mary on the other side. A bike trip over Logan Pass is the best way to experience the Going-To-The-Sun Road, however much of the road is closed to bicycles from 11 a.m. to 4 p.m., June 15 to Labor Day due to heavy vehicle traffic. Due to the narrow and winding road, vehicle length restrictions are in effect from July 1 to August 31—no vehicle or vehicle-and-towed-unit more than 28 feet in 1992, 24 feet in 1993, and 20 feet in 1994. During May, June, September, and October, the length limit will be relaxed. Consult Glacier National Park. Be aware that extended rear-view mirrors present a hazard. Plan to spend at least two to three hours (you really ought to spend the day) traveling this route. People in a hurry are better off sticking to the main route on Highway 2.

Built primarily of native materials in 1913, the Lake McDonald Lodge furnished posh accommodations in a rustic setting. The lodge, now on the National Register of Historic Places, overlooks the lake that was named in memory of Duncan McDonald who distinguished himself by carving his name on a tree trunk in 1878, an act for which he'd be fined today. The Kootenai people conducted religious ceremonies at this lake; they called it *Yakilahkwilnamki,* "The Sacred Dancing Place." In the fall, the lake's beauty is enhanced when the soft light of evening sets the golden larch aglow (for more about larch, see Route 6). The winter-closure gate is located at the head

The fine craftsmanship that went into the Going-to-the-Sun Road is displayed in the "Triple Arch."

of Lake McDonald; this is a great place to begin a cross-country ski trip. (The park does not permit snowmobile travel.)

Trail of the cedars

A little farther up the road, McDonald Creek flows over the Sacred Dancing Cascades which are especially beautiful in the winter when ice adds to their magic. The Trail of the Cedars is an excellent place for ART (Attitude Readjustment Time); if a walk around this boardwalk loop doesn't calm the road-weary beast within, you'd better consult a therapist. Common to the Northwest coast, but rare in this neck of the woods, a cedar-hemlock plant community grows here, due to the unique conditions of abundant moisture, relatively high humidity, and cool air funneled down between Snyder and Howe Ridge. Some of the red cedars, also known by the name *Tsuga plicata* (the tree of life), grow up to 220 ft/67 m high with a diameter of 7 ft/2 m. Cedar boughs produce a pleasant fragrance and Natives fashioned the stringy, fibrous bark into clothing and baskets.

As you start the ascent to Logan Pass, watch the avalanche chutes for bear and the rocky outcrops for mountain goats. There are numerous places to pull over, so be wise and courteous and don't stop in the middle of the road. Going-To-The-Sun Road is flanked on the north by the rocky ramparts of the Garden Wall. Be sure to notice the careful crafting that went into the bridges, guardrails, and retaining walls; the Triple Arches Bridge is an excellent example of how elegance, harmony, and function can be blended.

Logan Pass

Logan Pass (6,646 ft/2,025 m) presents a number of reasons to get out of the car: the visitor center, the Logan Pass Boardwalk, mid-summer skiing on the alpine snowpack, and the Highline Trail to name only four. The 1.5 mi/2.5 km Logan Pass Boardwalk gains 460 ft/140 m of elevation as it traverses a spectacular alpine landscape on its way to the Hidden Lake Overlook where mountain goats are commonly seen. Bring binoculars as grizzly bears often forage about the basin that contains Hidden Lake. In the summer, wildflowers bloom in profusion. Stay on the boardwalk; it can handle the thousands of tromping feet far better than the delicate alpine vegetation.

The Highline Trail remains fairly level for most of the 7.5 mi/12 km journey beneath the Garden Wall to the Granite Park Chalet. As the trail nears the chalet, it overlooks Bear Valley (closed to humans), where grizzlies are regularly observed. People equipped with a spotting scope or binoculars have the rare opportunity to watch bears for an extended time without disturbing them. The Granite Park Chalet offers overnight accommodations and meals; up here no phones ring and the only light after sundown comes from candles. The concessioner that operates Granite Park (6,690 ft/2,040 m) also runs Sperry Chalet (6,500 ft/1,982 m), both are listed on the National Register of Historic Places. The chalets usually open, when snow allows, in July and close Labor Day, and begin accepting reservations (by mail only) in January. (For more information: Belton Chalets, Inc., Box 188, West Glacier, Montana 59936; phone April through September: 406-888-5511.)

The road descends from Logan Pass above the north shore of St. Mary Lake. No one knows what missionary deemed it necessary to rename this long, and often windswept lake that the Blackfeet called "The Lakes Inside" (referring also to Lower St. Mary Lake just over the park boundary and on the Blackfeet Reservation). For a century, with the aid of guns and superb horsemanship, the Blackfeet ruled the Northern Plains. They drove the Kootenai, Pend d' Oreille, and Flathead over the divide and into western Montana.

ROUTE 10B: EAST GLACIER—DUCK LAKE   55 mi/89 km

General description: Route 10B traverses the Blackfeet Reservation, passing through Browning, the tribal headquarters for the reservation and home of the Museum of the Plains Indians. It continues north over rolling foothills, pastureland, and past Duck Lake.
Travel season: Year-round.
Road conditions and route description: From East Glacier, continue (east) to Browning on Highway 2, a very good, two-lane, all-season highway. At Browning, turn left onto Highway 464, a two-lane, well maintained road that's open year-round; continue 55 mi/89 km to the junction with Highway 89 at Babb.

The route: From East Glacier, Highway 2 proceeds in straight line, for 13 mi/21 km, to the town of Browning. With a population of 8,851, Browning is the largest town on the Blackfeet Indian Reservation. The terrain of the 1.5 million acre/500,000 ha reservation ranges from the level eastern plains to the rolling western foothills. Originally, the Lame Bull's Treaty of 1855 set aside two-thirds of eastern Montana for the Blackfeet and their allies the

Sacred Dancing Cascades.

Gros Ventre. Treaties written in the mid-1860s redefined the southern boundary as the Missouri River, a sizeable reduction. In 1874, by order of President Grant, a southwestern section larger than today's reservation was taken away. Following the 1883-84 winter of starvation, when more than 600 Blackfeet died, the tribe agreed to sell part of the reservation for survival needs. The Sweetgrass Treaty of 1888 reduced the reservation by more than eighty percent.

The final reduction to the reservation came in 1896, when the federal government desired Blackfeet lands for mining exploration. The tribe agreed to sell, for $1.5 million (they asked $3 million) and certain conditions, a strip of their land that extended from the Canadian border south to Birch Creek and from the Continental Divide to the present-day reservation boundary. The United States Congress consented to the Blackfeet conditions to "cut and remove... wood and timber for agency and school purposes and for their personal uses for houses, fences, and all other domestic purposes... to hunt upon said lands, and to fish in the streams, so long as the same shall remain public lands of the United States." In 1910, after the search for precious metals proved fruitless, that land became part of the new Glacier National Park.

The Blackfeet people and their reservation

Grasslands comprise most of the area's vegetation, in addition to aspen parkland, pine forest, wetland, and riparian habitat found in river valleys. Agriculture accounts for thirty percent of the employment on the reservation. Two manufacturing plants, Blackfeet Writing Company (pencils, pens, and markers) and Heart Butte Industries (gloves, cap, and coats), employ a hundred people. The Blackfeet tribal enrollment is about 13,000 with half of the members living on the reservation; unemployment here is more than fifty percent. For more information about Browning, see Route 9.

From Browning, the route follows Highway 464 north. The road traverses rolling grasslands that, despite agricultural alterations, still retain some of the pastoral characteristics of the days when Blackfeet led their nomadic existence. Beyond the incredible panoramic views of the Rocky Mountain Front, this stretch of road offers little in the way of obvious attractions; so stop and take time for the subtle beauty that surrounds you. Get out of the car, stand beside a fence, and feel the cool morning breeze, listen to the cry of a hawk, and watch clouds change shape over the mountains. If your mind is destination-oriented, think about something else for a few minutes; what would life be like in an isolated area surrounded by such stark beauty, where wildflowers carpet the rolling prairie in spring, and winter winds blow down street signs?

Located at the north end of Highway 464, Duck Lake offers you a chance to play a land-locked Captain Ahab in quest of Moby Trout. Before you fish for these monster fish, be sure to purchase a non-member fishing permit, which costs: $7.50—daily, $20—three days, or $30—seasonal. (For more information contact: Blackfeet Fish and Game Department, P.O. Box 850, Browning, Montana, 59417; 406-338-7207.) From Duck Lake, Highway 464 drops down to the junction with Highway 89 where a right turn (north) takes you into Babb and the beginning of Route 11.

Crown of the Continent Ecosystem Project
By Gil Lusk, Superintendant, Glacier National Park

Both Canada and the United States are involved in community-wide programs which might one day lead to an international Crown of the Continent Ecosystem centered around Waterton-Glacier International Peace Park. While the concepts differ slightly in approach, they are both process-oriented, dealing with ways to integrate long-term natural resource management issues at the community level.

The philosophy of the concept can be summarized as follows:

1. Management of natural resources within political boundaries fails to recognize that existing natural systems cross such borders. This often results in uneven or checkerboard management of large systems.

2. Our future, and how successful it is, will depend on our ability to plan and implement systems predicated on necessary economic growth and environmental qualities being in harmony and not as either/or discussions.

3. Existing processes, or paradigms, are based on systems which have evolved out of the Industrial Age and the initial emergence of complex governmental systems. As a result, they too often serve specific interests rather than community or system needs. Processes need to be developed which allow for broader input and non-territorial discussions.

4. Science and our understanding of complex natural systems will be ever more important in making the complex decisions of our future. Ways to mainstream science at the community level are needed.

Embodied within the Crown of the Continent concepts are processes to achieve the above and more. If successful, they could one day lead to an international natural system from Jasper National Park in Canada to Grand Teton National Park in Wyoming, encompassing several ecosystems and all providing for the necessary planned economic growth of the region along with the protection of underlying natural values and qualities. As such, it could well represent a world model for our future.

For More Information About Route 10:

Roads and Trails of Waterton-Glacier International Peace Park. 1986. George C. Ruhle. Glacier Natural History Association.
Hikers Guide to Glacier National Park. Dick and Sharon Nelson.
Motorists Guide to Glacier National Park. Roberta Seibel and Barbara Blair. 1979. Glacier Natural History Association.
Going-to-the-Sun: The Story of the Highway across Glacier National Park. Rose Houk, Pat O'Hara and Danny On. 1984. Woodlands Press.
The Grizzlies of Glacier. 1978. Warren L. Hanna. Mountain Press.

Events and Services

Charlie Russell Country: P.O. Box 3166, Great Falls, Montana 59403; 1-800-527-5348 or 406-761-5036.
Glacier Institute: Box 1457, Kalispell, Montana 59903; 406-888-5215.
For fishing on the Blackfeet Reservation: Blackfeet Fish and Game Department, P.O. Box 850, Browning, Montana 59417; 406-338-7207.
Blackfeet Reservation: Browning, 406-338-7181.

National Parks

Glacier National Park Information: Superintendent's Office, Glacier National Park, West Glacier, Montana 59936; 406-888-5441. People with a telecommunication device for the deaf (TDD) can call 406-888-5790.
Glacier Natural History Association: Box 327, West Glacier, Montana 59936; 406-888-5756.

National Forests and Wilderness Areas

Bob Marshall Wilderness Complex: Augusta Forest Service Information Station, Box 365, Augusta, Montana 59410; 406-562-3247, or Rocky Mountain Ranger District, Box 340, Choteau, Montana 59422; 406-466-5341, or Forest Supervisor's Office, Lewis and Clark National Forest, Box 871, Great Falls, Montana 59403; 406-791-7700.

Wildflowers in Glacier National Park.

Crown of the Continent

"I remember my first sight of Buffalo on the plains of Western Canada. It was Blackfeet territory then... There were no Indian Reserves in those days. There were only two white men nearer than Hudson Bay Fort at what is now Edmonton. Calgary at that time had not been thought of and no one had drilled for gas at Medicine Hat. The prairie as far as we could see East, North, and West was one living moving mass of buffalo..."

Kootenai Brown, first Superintendent
of the park that would become Waterton Lakes National Park.

"Today, the 15 to 20 bison [in the paddock]... occupy this portion of their native range..."

Waterton Lakes National Park pamphlet.

ROUTE 11

ST. MARY to PINCHER CREEK　　　　*119 kilometers/74 miles*

General description: With impressive views of the abrupt transition from plains to mountains, this route provides access to Glacier Park's Many Glacier area and then climbs out of the St. Mary Valley, over a forested saddle, and drops into the Waterton Basin. Waterton Lakes National Park offers good wildlife viewing. A variety of views of Chief Mountain lend interest to the southern end of this section. The northern portion of the route travels over rolling grass and pastureland.

Unique features: Many Glacier, Chief Mountain, Waterton Lakes National Park, Remington-Alberta Carriage Collection, Alternate Energy Farm.

Wildlife viewing opportunities: Many Glacier in Glacier National Park, Waterton Lakes National Park, Police Outpost Provincial Park Wetlands.

Activities: Biking, backpacking, mountaineering, fishing, golf, cross-country skiing, downhill skiing, sailboarding, ice climbing, scenic boat cruises.

Travel season: The Chief Mountain border station is closed from mid-September to early-May. The Carway Crossing is year-round.

Services: Services are seasonally available at St. Mary and Waterton Townsite. Full service available in Cardston and Pincher Creek. Limited services in Waterton year-round.

Road conditions and route description: From St. Mary, follow Highway 89 for 21 km/13 mi to the junction with Highway 17; turn left (west) and continue 23 km/14 mi to the Port of Chief Mountain Customs. The border station is closed from mid-September to early May. Also, be aware of highway signs that post the border crossing hours. The year-round border crossing is at Carway. On the Canadian side of the border, the road becomes Highway 6. North of the border, 24 km/15 mi, a left turn on Highway 5 leads to Waterton Lakes National Park. Beyond this junction, 51 km/32 mi, Highway 6 enters Pincher Creek.

The route: Two major factors contributed to the designation of Glacier National Park. First and foremost, mining in the area didn't pan out and oil development proved commercially unfeasible. Second, George Bird Grinnell, an outdoors enthusiast and editor of *Forest and Stream* magazine, loved the mountainous region. In essays, he wrote about the hunting, fishing, and "unexcelled" scenery, and people in the eastern United States learned about the mountains of Glacier for the first time. In 1901, Grinnell wrote an article entitled, "The Crown of the Continent." He insisted that the recreational and aesthetic values of Glacier deserved formal protection. While exerting influence through his writing, Grinnell also played politics; he garnered the support of Great Northern Railway officials who realized there was money to made from Glacier tourism. Glacier became a national park in 1910.

Meanwhile, across the border in Canada, a colorful character known as Kootenai Brown expressed concern that uncontrolled development would destroy Waterton Lakes. Due to the efforts of Brown and local ranchers, in 1895, the Department of Interior established Kootenay Lakes Forest Park. In 1911, Canada followed the United States' lead and bestowed national park status on the Waterton Lakes area. Upper Waterton Lake straddles the international border which was established by Britain and the United States in 1818. With a desire to define their fur trapping territories the two countries drew an arbitrary line along the forty-ninth parallel.

In a brilliant move (and one quite ahead of its time in 1932), Canada, the United States, and Rotary International created the Waterton-Glacier International Peace Park. Since then, the two parks have worked in cooperation to protect, interpret, and manage the Waterton-Glacier International Peace Park. The concept behind the Crown of the Continent Ecosystem goes one step further by recognizing that the needs of the plant and animal communities extend beyond the Peace Park boundaries and include the surrounding wildlands, national forests, native reservations, and privately held lands. Further recognition for this unique ecosystem came in 1979 when the United Nations designated the Crown of the Continent Ecosystem as two international Biosphere Reserves.

Many Glacier

West of Babb, the paved road (closed in the winter) skirts the shore of Sherburne Reservoir (that flooded Montana's first oil field developed in 1904) and leads to Many Glacier (inside the park). During the drive along the reservoir watch for eagles. The treeless slopes overlooking Many Glacier harbor grizzly bears. On the eastern shore of windswept Swiftcurrent Lake stands the Many Glacier Hotel with its Swiss motif. This grand hotel, one of the first buildings in Glacier, was built in 1914-15 during the heyday of Great Northern Railway service to the park. The beautiful hike to Grinnell Glacier traverses alpine

The Many-Glacier Hotel.

country and provides a good chance of seeing mountain goats. Outstanding trailheads are located here. A scenic boat cruise takes visitors farther into the valley backcountry.

Chief Mountain

Seven km/4 mi beyond Babb, the turnoff onto Chief Mountain International Highway (Highway 17) ascends out of the St. Mary Valley from montane to subalpine forests. The road passes Chief Mountain, one of 50-60 vision quest sites still actively used along the Trail of the Great Bear. Whether you're a geologist or on a spiritual quest, there's no denying that there's something unusually special about this mountain. To a geologist, Chief Mountain is a *klippe*, a remanent of the thick slab that over-rode the region sixty million years ago (see Route 10). Erosion around the mountain rendered it a graphic example of the transition between the ancient slab smitten by wanderlust and the younger surface on which it finally settled. Native people didn't need a scientist to tell them that the mountain possessed exceptional qualities. For thousands of years Chief Mountain has been the focus of spiritual activities. Today, offering, fasting, and vision quest sites can be seen along the base and on top of the mountain. Should you venture up Chief Mountain respect these sites and leave things where they lay; you wouldn't want people walking into your church plucking religious icons from the alter to add to their souvenir collection.

Just below the International Border, there's a parking area for the Belly River trailhead. While passing from the United States to the Canadian Customs station, notice the treeless swath in-between; this is the International Border. (See Sidebar.) The Port of Chief Mountain border crossing is opened from early-May to mid-September. Port of Peigan crossing is open year-round. (For more about the border, see Route 11A.) A short ways past the border, a road on the left leads down to the Belly River Campground (in Waterton Lakes National Park).

Crown of the continent

On the way to Waterton Lakes, the road passes extensive riparian habitat dotted with little lakes and beaver ponds. After crossing a saddle covered by a subalpine forest, the route drops rapidly with excellent views of Waterton Valley and the dramatic transition between prairie and mountains. Stop at the Waterton Valley Overlook to enjoy this view better and get a visual idea of the Crown of the Continent Ecosystem. Within this ecosystem, you can distinguish four vegetational or eco-zones; the obvious and treeless alpine zone, the subalpine with Engelmann spruce, larch, subalpine fir, and lodgepole, the montane with lodgepole, aspen, and poplar, and the obvious prairie grassland banded with riparian habitat and patchy aspen groves. The foothill parkland and prairie that extends east of Waterton Lakes are known as the Waterton Fringe. This area provides critical habitat to elk, moose, deer, nesting trumpeter swans, and sustains an incredible variety of birds. Due to unique climatic conditions that foster chinook winds (see Chinook Winds at conclusion of this route), the Waterton area supports remarkable vegetational diversity. More than half of the plants found in Alberta can be seen at Waterton which means the area is wildflower heaven come springtime.

Most of the valley bottom below would be under water now had plans formulated in the early 1920s come to fruition. Farmers pressured the govern-

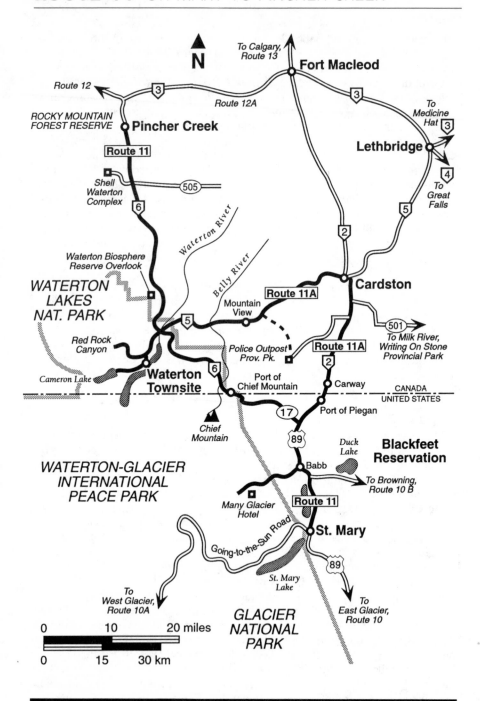

Ninaiistako
By Brian Reeves

Ninaiistako (Chief Mountain) is the sacred mountain of the Blackfoot and many Native tribes in the region. Ninaiistako is a focus of sacred power and traditional Blackfoot spiritual activities. The home of Thunderbird, the most powerful of the Up Above People, it was here, thousands of years ago, that the first medicine pipe, The Long-Time-Pipe, was given by Thunderbird to the People. The Blackfoot elders speak of Ninaiistako as a place of great power where particularly powerful and significant visions could be obtained through fasting and prayer. According to Percy Creighton, a Kaina (Blood) Elder, the People "knew there was a person up on Chief Mountain. They call it Chief Mountain because it is an outstanding mountain and because Dream Person lives up there. That is where the big man of their tribe prayed and fasted."

Ninaiistako (2,768 meters) lies half within the Blackfeet Reserve and half within Glacier National Park. The mountain is one of the world's sacred places, and like other holy mountains—Mt. Sinai, Mt. Fuji—it is being inappropriately used by non-traditional Native and white people. It is also being logged by Blackfeet business interests. Traditional Blackfoot religious activities are being disrupted and offerings taken as souvenirs. The Blackfeet Tribal Business Council recently passed a tribal resolution restricting trespass by motor vehicles and prohibiting individuals from intruding upon spiritual activities or removing sacred items.

If you wish to climb Ninaiistako, inquire first with the Blackfeet Tribal Office (406-338-7207) and the St. Mary's Visitor Center (406-732-5571).

Respect this sacred place. Visit Ninaiistako as you would your church. Take nothing with you but your memories. Leave nothing behind but your footsteps.

ment for more irrigation water and proposed a dam on Waterton Lake. (Believe it or not, people flocked to the arid plains east of the Rockies fully believing that "rain followed the plow." When they woke up to the fact that they had moved to an area where only a few more inches/centimeters of precipitation fell than in a desert, they looked to government assistance.) Due to fortuitous rains in 1923, the pressure eased. However, the plans weren't abandoned until the United States realized that the reservoir would flood part of Glacier National Park and refused to allow members of the Canadian Irrigation Survey entry into the park.

A picturesque farm in the foothills of the Rockies just north of Waterton Lakes National Park.

Waterton Lakes National Park

Admission to Waterton Lakes National Park is $4.25 daily (valid until noon the following day); $9.50 four-day pass; $26.75 annual pass; Canadian Senior Citizen pass is free. (For general park information call 403-859-2224.) Park entrance permits are not interchangeable between Glacier and Waterton but are for all other Canadian National Parks. Watch for osprey nests near the registration office. As you drive into the Waterton Townsite, be aware that mountain sheep and deer commonly roam the streets and yards; drive slow and with care, help preserve this unique situation where humans and wildlife mingle. The Heritage Centre, run by the Waterton Natural History Association and located on Waterton Avenue, offers the public interpretive exhibits, an art gallery, and a sales area with numerous books that relate to natural history. Profits from sales are applied to cover the cost of operating the centre and the Heritage Education Program that conducts natural history and photography field course. (For more information: Box 145, Waterton, Alberta, TOK 2MO; 403-859-2624.) The International Peace Park Pavilion, located in the Marina, provides information about the establishment of the Peace Park. The Prince of Wales Hotel, built by the Great Northern Railroad in 1925, stands singularly atop the hill overlooking Middle and Upper Waterton Lakes and the townsite. A book by the Waterton Natural History Association tells the tale of the history of the building.

Waterton oil

There are two short and scenic roads in Waterton. Just past the Park Information Centre, a right turn onto the Akamina Highway leads to Cameron Lake. On the way up, the road passes Oil City where a plaque commemorates the first oil well drilled in Western Canada during 1901. The Kootenai people pointed the oil seep out to Kootenai Brown; they used the oil to heal wounds. Brown *pumped* oil from the seep ponds by soaking gunny sacks and wringing them out into cans; he used it to lubricate wagons. In 1901, The Rocky Mountain Development Company drilled the first well to a depth of 310 m/1,017 ft and struck oil; five years later operations shut down. Others tried, drilling to 612 m/2,007 ft, but to no avail; the entire enterprise was abandoned in the early 1930s. Apparently, oil from far deeper in the earth seeped up via faults. Today, wells bordering the park and drilled to a depth of 5 km/3 mi produce oil and gas. Fortunately, for the formation of Waterton Lakes National Park, the drillers of yesteryear didn't possess the technology of today.

While Waterton Park provides important habitat and a much-needed sanctuary for grizzlies, that doesn't mean they're easy to see. At Cameron Lake however, people with binoculars regularly spot grizzlies in the avalanche chutes above the opposite shore.

The Red Rock Canyon Road follows the Blakiston Valley, an old travel route from British Columbia used by Native people and later traversed by Lieutenant Thomas Blakiston of the 1857-60 Palliser Expedition. At the end of the road, a short interpretive trail loops around Red Rock Canyon where some of the oldest rock in the Canadian Rockies is exposed. The red, greenish, and white layers are all mudstone and all contain iron that, when it was exposed to air, oxidized and turned red. The greenish and white layers didn't oxidize because they remained beneath the surface of a primeval sea that advanced and retreated numerous times. In some places you'll see ripple marks etched in the rock by ancient waves, elsewhere mud cracks tell of blazing heat beneath a prehistoric sun.

The fishing is supposed to be good in Waterton Park; a National Park Fishing Permit is required and valid in all Canadian national parks. An annual permit is $10.75 and seven-day permit, $5.25. The wind, that so often blows through Waterton, attracts sailboarders. Waterton Inter-Nation Shoreline Cruises offers scenic boat trips on Upper Waterton Lake; the cruise from the townsite to Goat Haunt (U.S.A.) takes about two hours with a half-hour layover. (Weather permitting, the cruises operate from May 4 to September 29; contact 403-859-2362.) The popularity of ice climbing has also increased here. There are two campgrounds in this portion of Waterton Lakes National Park. A left turn (indicated by a sign) 1.5 km/1 mi after regaining Highway 6 headed north, leads to the paddock that contains fifteen to twenty bison.

Sour gas beneath the foothills

Proceeding up Highway 6, you can see the Rockies extending far to the north. The farms appear neat and well maintained, like the idyllic vision of a farm complete with a red barn. South of Pincher Creek, 21 km/13 mi and just before Secondary Road 505, a left (west) turn leads to the Shell Waterton Complex, a sour gas processing and sulphur recovery plant. Situated out on the foothills and backed by the rugged Rocky Mountain Front, this installation with its gleaming network of ducting, pipe, and minarets of steel, appears like an apparition from science fiction placed on a western movie set. The plant converts sour natural gas into marketable products such as methane, butane, propane, and sulphur. In order to accomplish this, the plant safely removes hazardous hydrogen sulfide (which is what makes the gas sour). This byproduct is converted into sulphur which is used in fertilizer, paper products, sugar, drugs, and matches. Pipelines pump ninety percent of the methane to California. In operation since 1961 and employing 300 people, the plant produces 200 million cubic feet of gas daily, enough to heat one million homes for a day. The Shell Waterton Complex conducts public tours of the facility on an appointment basis and appreciates at least an hour advance notice (403-627-7200).

The snow eater

Before concluding this route description, a brief word about the dramatic chinook winds that influence life in this area so much. Chinook is a Native word meaning "snow-eater." These winds bring a rapid increase in temperature; one weather observer watched the mercury rise 80 degrees f/48 degrees C in a few hours and 30 inches/ 75 cm of snow melt in half a day. This weather phenomenon begins over the Pacific Ocean and moves east as a warm, moist air mass. As the air moves up and over the mountains, it cools and causes the moisture to condense. Now here's the weird part. While cooling causes condensation, condensation generates heat—thus the air that slides down the east side of the mountains is warmer than it was at a similar elevation on the west side, plus the rush downhill further warms the air. In the *Handbook of the Canadian Rockies*, Ben Gadd writes that a "way of predicting a chinook is to note how you are feeling, for many people become irritable or restless a few hours before the wind hits. A jump in the number of auto accidents, crimes, and suicides is associated with chinook weather."

The town of Pincher Creek stands at the end of Route 11. The town's name came from a miner who lost a set of horseshoe pinchers in the creek. The area, first settled by the Northwest Mounted Police who grazed horses on the rich prairie, is now one of southern Alberta's major stock-raising centers. An alternate energy farm here explores ways to utilize the power of the Chinook. Just west of Pincher is the West Castle Recreation Area offering year-round opportunities including downhill skiing.

ROUTE 11A: CARDSTON LOOP   219 Km/136 Mi

Travel season: Year-round.
Road conditions and route description: From the junction with Highway 17, Highway 89 continues for 10 km/6 mi to the Port of Peigan Customs. This border crossing is open year-round and operates for longer hours in the summer than the Chief Mountain border station. (May 16 to October 31: 7 a.m. to 11 p.m., and November 1 to May 15: 9 a.m. to 6 p.m.) In Canada, the road becomes Highway 2 which extends 24 km/15 mi to the town of Cardston; turn left onto Highway 5 and continue 45 km/28 mi to the junction with Highway 6 adjacent to Waterton Lakes National Park.

The route: Route 11A provides a year-round travel corridor to Waterton Lakes National Park and the rest of the Trail of the Great Bear. The route continues up Highway 89 to the Port of Peigan border stations.

Borders

Humans seem to be the only animal fixated on pencil-thin boundary lines; for the rest of the life on earth, boundaries definitely exist but they're pretty fuzzy. So there you are, approaching the international border; what do you need to know? Though Canada and the United States share a lot of similarities, real changes occur as you cross the border line. For one thing, Canadians tack "eh" to the end of every sentence and people from the United States speak with a funny accent. The money is different; Canadian money is colorful and a U.S. dollar is worth more. Canadians use the metric system based on units of ten and the United States hangs on to an odd system of measurement based on who-knows-what. Canada doesn't shoot fireworks into the night sky on the Fourth of July (they do celebrate Canada Day on July 1) and the United States doesn't pay attention to Queen Victoria Day (though they seem mesmerized by the Prince and Princess of Wales).

If you require narcotic medicine, carry a quantity appropriate to personal use and be ready to produce a prescription or note from your doctor. You are allowed one carton of cigarettes and one liter of alcoholic beverages duty free. In the event that you have to prove citizenship, a passport, birth certificate, or naturalization certificate will accomplish this. If you have a dog or cat on board, be sure to carry a certificate signed by a licensed Canadian or United States veterinarian certifying that the animal has been vaccinated for rabies in the past three years. Firearms may not be transported across the border.

For travelers who live outside Canada and are entering, you'll note that there's a GST (Goods and Services Tax). Visitors can claim a rebate on GST goods. Write to Revenue Canada, Customs and Excise, Visitor's Rebate Program, Ottawa, Canada, K1A 1J5. Trans-border traveler's enjoy duty-free shops at the Alberta/Montana border which offer substantial savings on liquor, cigarettes, fragrances, cosmetics and luxury gift items such as watches, jewelry and fashion accessories.

You've passed into another country now! If you're a Canadian traveling south convert mileage and speed limit signs like this: distance (in miles) or miles-per-hour divided by .62 equals the speed or distance you're used to dealing with. If you're from the United States: distance (in kilometres) or kilometres-per-hour times .62 equals the speed or distance you're used to dealing with.

Border Crossing Hours:
    Coutts: 24 hours all year.
    Carway/Peigan: May 16 to Oct. 31: open 7 a.m. to 11 p.m.
                   Nov. 1 to May 15: open 9 a.m. to 6 p.m.
    Del Bonita: June 1 to Sept. 15: open 9 a.m. to 9 p.m.
                Sept. 16 to May 31: open 9 a.m. to 6 p.m.
    Chief Mountain: Open June to mid-Sept.: 7 a.m. to 10 p.m.

Prairies and the East Front of the Rockies.

Police Outpost Provincial Park

About 18 km/11 mi beyond the border, a sign indicates that a left (west) turn leads to Police Outpost Provincial Park. This park is located in ungrazed foothills covered by grass and aspen parkland and adjacent to the marshy Outpost Wetlands Natural Area. The area is especially colorful in the spring and early summer with blooming wildflowers and in the fall from golden aspen. Twenty-two of Alberta's twenty-six wild orchids thrive here, in addition to a tremendous variety of birds including sandhill cranes. (For more information: call 403-653-2522.)

In Cardston, the Remington-Alberta Carriage Centre (a major Alberta Culture interpretive facility, scheduled for opening in 1993) will display 215 historic carriages. The facility will also house a theater, exhibit galleries, and offer special events, tours, and classes. For information call 403-653-3981 or 403-653-4686. Cardston is also the site of the first Mormon Temple to be built outside the United States; this impressive structure is an architectural landmark. From Cardston the route crosses rolling ranchland, with breathtaking views of the Rocky Mountain Front via Highway 5 until it joins the Highway 6.

For More Information About Route 11:

A Guide to Waterton Lakes National Park, Heather Pringle. 1986. Douglas & McIntyre.

Short Hikes and Strolls in Waterton Lakes National Park, Elizabeth Russell and Valerie Haig-Brown. 1987. Waterton Natural History Association.

Waterton and Northern Glacier Trails for Hikers and Riders. Charles Russell, Elizabeth Russell, John Russell, and Valerie Haig-Brown. 1984. Waterton Natural History Association.

The Flora of Waterton Lakes National Park. Job Kuijt. 1982. University of Alberta Press.

Rocks, Ice and Water: The Geology of Waterton-Glacier Park. David D. Alt and Donald Hyndman. 1973. Mountain Press Publishing Company.

Kootenai Brown: His Life and Times. William Rodney. 1969. Grays Publishing, Ltd.

Plants of Waterton-Glacier National Parks. Richard J. Shaw and Danny On. 1979. Mountain Press Publishing Company.

Events and Services

Waterton Park Chamber of Commerce: Box 55, Waterton Park, Alberta T0K 2M0; 403-859-2303.

Chinook Country Tourist Association: 2805 Scenic Drive, Lethbridge, Alberta T1K5B7; 1-800-661-1222 or 403-329-6777.

Cardston Chamber of Commerce: Box 280, 67 3rd Ave. West, Cardston, Alberta T0K OKO; 403-653-2798.

Pincher Creek Chamber of Commerce: 659 Main Street, Pincher Creek, Alberta T0K 1WO; 403-627-3333.

Heritage Education Program: Box 145, Waterton, Alberta, T0K 2MO; 403-859-2624.

Remington-Alberta Carriage Centre: 403-653-3981 or 403-653-4686.

Shell Waterton Complex: 403-627-7200.

Waterton Inter-Nation Shoreline Cruises: 403-859-2362.

National and Provincial Parks

Glacier National Park Information: Superintendent's Office, Glacier National Park, West Glacier, Montana 59936; 406-888-5441. People with a telecommunication device for the deaf (TDD) can call 406-888-5790.

Waterton Lakes National Park: Waterton Park, Alberta T0K 2M0; 403-859-2224.

Police Outpost Provincial Park: 403-653-2522

The International Boundary
by Jerry DeSanto

National Geographic *characterized Jerry DeSanto as "the last of [Glacier] Park's old-time" and tough-as-tacks rangers. Now retired from the Park Service, DeSanto pursues his original calling as a historian with a keen interest in the International Boundary and a botanist specializing in alpine vegetation.*

The boundary line, a forty-foot-wide swathe through the forest between the two customs stations, marks the International Boundary between Canada and the United States. The boundary from Lake of the Woods in Minnesota and Ontario to the Continental Divide on the Rocky Mountains was established by the Convention of London in 1818. The line at this point was first surveyed in 1874 by a joint British and American party and stone monuments were built at widely separated locations. The boundary was resurveyed in the early 1900s and in 1908 aluminum-bronze monuments were placed at conspicuous spots at intervals not to exceed four miles. Concrete markers were added later at major crossings.

The boundary between the two countries in this area is the forty-ninth parallel of north latitude. In the nineteenth century, however, technology did not exist to determine a parallel of latitude on the curved surface of the earth. The astronomers and surveyors of the boundary survey did as good a job as possible but their calculations rarely placed the boundary exactly on the forty-ninth parallel. So, instead of actually curving with true latitude, it is actually a series of straight lines connecting monuments; as a result, the boundary is on one side or the other of the forty-ninth parallel. At Chief Mountain Customs, the boundary is over 800 feet south of the forty-ninth parallel and the entire Alberta boundary is south of the parallel.

The International Boundary Commission, as it exists today, was established in 1925 and a joint staff carries out the work of maintaining the line. By treaty, the commission is responsible for inspecting the line, repairing or replacing monuments as needed and clearing the boundary vista. The entire line needs to be cleared about once every ten years. At the time of this printing, the boundary was last inspected and cleared in 1987.

Hiker crosses the Belly River.

Leaping Buffalo, Marching Mounties, and Exploding Mines

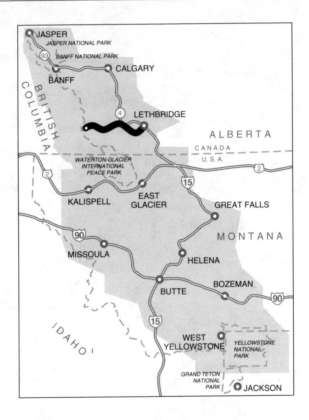

"The arid district [the Palliser Triangle of southern Alberta] . . . can never be of much advantage to us as a possession."

Dr. James Hector of the Palliser Expedition, 1859.

"Desolate? Forbidding? There was never a country that in its good moments was more beautiful. Even in drouth or dust storm or blizzard it is the reverse of monotonous, once you have submitted to it with all the senses. You don't get out of the wind, but learn to lean and squint against it. You don't escape sky and sun, but wear them in your eyeballs and on your back. You become acutely aware of yourself. The world is very large, the sky even larger, and you are very small. But also the world is flat, empty, nearly abstract, and in its flatness you are a challenging upright thing, as sudden as an exclamation mark, as enigmatic as a question mark."

Wallace Stegner, *Wolf Willow*.

ROUTE 12

PINCHER CREEK to CROWSNEST PASS   64 kilometers/40 miles

General description: From the prairies surrounding the town of Pincher Creek, Route 12 ascends to the top of Crowsnest Pass, the lowest pass in the Canadian Rockies, which straddles the boundary between Alberta and British Columbia. The Municipality of Crowsnest Pass is coal country with a rich mining history and the site of the Frank Slide, one of the most spectacular landslides in North America. Two of the best interpretive centres found along the Trail of the Great Bear are on Routes 12 and 12A, the Frank Slide and Leitch Collieries, Head-Smashed-In Interpretive Centres.
Unique features: Frank Slide and the Frank Slide Interpretive Centre, Head-Smashed-In Buffalo Jump Interpretive Centre, Fort Museum.
Wildlife viewing opportunities: Crowsnest Lake and River.
Activities: Fishing, mountain biking, caving, cross-country and downhill skiing, snowmobiling, golf, hiking, backpacking.
Events: Empress Summer Theatre, Rum Runner Days, Midnight Days, Santa Claus Parade, Peigan Indian Days.
Travel season: Year-round.
Services: All services found at Pincher Creek including a small airport, Fort Macleod, and along the road through the Municipality of Crowsnest Pass.
Road conditions and route description: Just north of Pincher Creek, Highway 6 intersects Highway 3 at Pincher. Turn left (west) and follow this well-maintained, two-lane highway to the summit of Crowsnest Pass at 1,396 m/4,579 ft; return via the same route.

The route: The first 20 km/12 mi of Route 12 traverse intensively utilized ranch land; this is, after all, the beef-raising centre of southern Alberta. Ready for a little ART (Attitude Readjustment Time), or maybe it's time to put the fly rod to use? Lundbreck Falls, accessed by a turn left (south) where the sign on Highway 3 indicates, is a nice place to stop for a picnic. The area beneath the falls provides a cool and misty retreat from the heat of the day and the Crowsnest River is a "blue-ribbon" trout stream. There is a Provincial Parks campground here.

The Crowsnest Municipality contains a string of five communities (incorporated into one municipality) bordering Highway 3 and situated in a valley that ascends from the foot of the mountains to the border between Alberta and British Columbia atop Crowsnest Pass. This historic district is rich with the memories of the coal mining days. The site of one of the largest mines in the area, the Leitch Collieries, provides a self-guided tour with interpretive signs that explain the workings of this operation above and below ground. The sandstone walls of the power house and manager's residence still stand as well as the long row of 101 coke ovens. Due to financial setbacks and a strained relationship with the Canadian Pacific Railroad, the coal facility, established in 1907, ceased production in 1915. This is also the site of Police Flats where the Northwest Mounted Police established an outpost to round up rustlers that herded pilfered beef over the International Border.

Though much of the history recounted along the Crowsnest Pass drainage

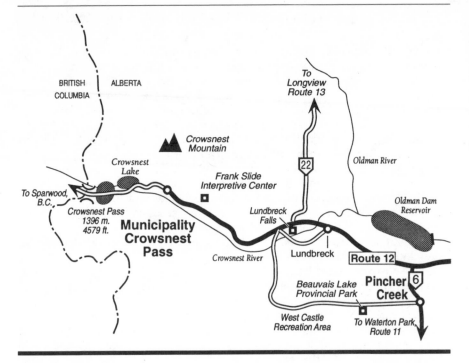

revolves around coal mining, use of the area extends back at least 10,000 years. Ancestors of the Kootenai, who for the most part resided on the west side, crossed the pass on foot in the late spring and in September for month-long bison hunts. An archaeological survey conducted in 1973 located extensive evidence of prehistoric camps around the top of the pass. Europeans didn't cross the pass until 1873 when Michael Phillipps (of the Hudson Bay Company) and John Collins (a trapper) interrupted their prospecting to follow ancient native trails. Despite the presence of trails, their journal states, "This is the first trip ever made by what is now known as the Crow's Nest Pass."

The track layin', coal minin' blues

The Crowsnest area remained relatively quiet until 1897 when the Canadian Pacific Railway company received from the Canadian government $11,000 and 20,000 acres/18,000 ha of land for every mile of track laid, so they ended up with $3.6 million in federal subsidies, thousands of acres of land, plus an additional 6 square mi/1.6 square km of choice coal fields in the Crowsnest Pass area. In return, the Canadian Pacific Railway promised reduced freight rates for western grain and settler's goods. Laborers worked on the railroad for twelve to fourteen hours a day, earning eleven cents an hour ($1.50 a day) with $4.00 deducted each week for food.

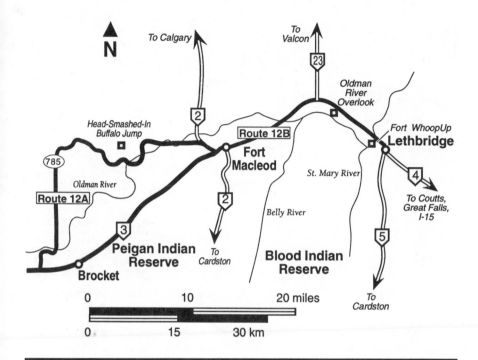

While coal mining had been going on in the area for some time, the appearance of a railroad increased mining activity dramatically. Emigrants flocked to the area following illusive dreams of prosperity in a new land. On December 9, 1910, forty-two men entered the Bellevue mine to work their shift. That night, rocks fell somewhere inside the mine. The sparks set off a methane gas explosion that consumed oxygen in the mine leaving behind a deadly concentration of carbon monoxide and carbon dioxide. Thirty men died. (The Crowsnest Pass Ecomuseum has reopened the Bellevue mine for visitation: 403-562-8831.)

Four years later, at the Hillcrest Mine, the 7:00 a.m. shift commenced as 235 men turned their backs to the morning sun and filed into the darkness. Two-and-a-half hours later, a powerful explosion roared through the tunnels killing men and consuming oxygen. Deadly gases killed most of the 189 men; many were found face down, their rigid fingers holding wet rags against pale lips in a futile struggle to filter the air. Rescuers pulled one man to the surface where he learned that two of his sons were still below; the man walked back into the mine and died from the gases. Three mass graves contain most of the bodies from Canada's worst mine disaster. The Hillcrest Cemetery is on the south side of the river across from Bellevue.

Long ago, the Crowsnest drainage provided a passage way to ancestors of the Kootenai. According to local folklore, these Native people started avoiding this route due to legends about Turtle Mountain, "the mountain that moved."

The Leitch Collieries along the Crowsnest Pass Highway, a remnant of the coal mining days.

By 1903 the Crowsnest valley was "civilized" by people who scoffed at such legends. On April 29 at 4:10 a.m., as 600 people slept in the town of Frank, Turtle Mountain moved. A slab of limestone 150-m/500-ft thick parted company with the mountain and during the next ninety seconds, an eighty-two-million-ton avalanche of stone covered the valley below killing at least seventy people. Only twelve bodies were recovered, the others rest beneath the slide.

Frank Slide Interpretive Centre

One of the three best interpretive centres found along the Trail of the Great Bear, the Frank Slide Interpretive Centre, is located the on the right (north) side of the road above the debris from one of North America's most awesome landslides. There's an entertaining interactive video game that provides information about what triggered the Frank Slide. Displays in the centre depict what life was like during the coal mining days and offer geologic insights about the Frank Slide. Be certain to watch the award-winning presentation, *In the Mountain's Shadow*. This stunning nine-projector, multi-media documentary does an excellent job of describing the hopes, dreams, and day-to-day life of miners and their families. The centre with its extremely hospitable staff, is opened year-round; summer hours are 9 a.m. to 8 p.m. and the rest of the year, 10 a.m. to 4 p.m. (For more information: Frank Slide Interpretive Centre, Box 299, Blairmore, Alberta, T0K 0E0; 403-562-7388.)

According to archaeologist Brian Reeves, the pass is named after the mountain which was named "Raven's Nest" by a band of Kootenai. The name became Crowsnest because, to early whites, ravens and crows were both black birds that all looked the same.

Crowsnest Peak.

In terms of geology, Crowsnest Mountain is similar to Chief Mountain back on Route 11; it's an isolated piece of the Lewis Overthrust. From 1987-88 the Blairmore Coal Pile Reclamation Project removed 660,000 tons of coal slack thereby improving the water quality of Crowsnest River (now a "blue-ribbon" trout stream) and rehabilitated 57 acres of land.

The Crowsnest Municipality celebrates Rum Runner Days during the first weekend in July. The celebration commemorates Emilio Picariello, a former Blairmore merchant, town councilor, and bootlegger. Festivities include a polyathlon that traces the rum runner route, a raft race down the Crowsnest River, golf tournament, the Great Quacker (duck) Race, a parade, and dancing. (For more information call 403-562-2000.)

The Crowsnest Museum in Coleman, a community museum (403-563-5434) inside the old Coleman High School, displays lots of relics from the coal mining days including equipment used inside the mines. The museum offers an interpretive pamphlet for a self-guided driving tour of the area. Summer hours, Victoria Day to Labor Day, 10 a.m. to 4 p.m. daily; museum closed in the winter on Saturday and Sunday. Also visit the Crowsnest Pass Eco-museum and take the Bellevue Mine tour, the only underground mine tour along the trail (403-562-8831). A number of high-country snowmobile access points are found along the valley—the Atlas Road Snowmobile Area in particular—make Crowsnest popular with snowmobilers. A winter snowmobile fest is held

157

annually. The Allison Creek area is a popular destination for cross-country skiers.

Beyond Crowsnest Lake, Highway 3 crosses the Island Lake Natural Area. Watch for long-toed salamanders in wetlands and loons on the lakes. At 1,396 m/4,579 ft, Crowsnest Pass is the lowest pass crossing the Rockies. Due to its low elevation, the pass supports a montane forest of lodgepole pine, Douglas-fir, and aspen that provides habitat to species of birds usually found farther west.

ROUTE 12A HEAD-SMASHED-IN LOOP   140 km/87 mi

General description: Route 12A crosses the Oldman River and traverses the prairies, beneath a bluff that provided Native people with sites for buffalo jumps, to the Head-Smashed-In Buffalo Jump Interpretive Centre and UNESCO World Heritage Site. From Head-Smashed-In, the route continues to Fort Macleod, where the legendary Northwest Mounted Police built their first fort and based their operations in Western Canada. The route loops back crossing prairie land as it traverses the Peigan Indian Reserve.

Road conditions and route description: At the intersection of Highways 6 and 3, turn right (east). Within 10 km/6 mi turn left (north) onto Secondary 785 (if you enter Brocket, that's too far—turn around); follow the gravel road and signs that lead to Head-Smashed-In. Beyond Head-Smashed-In, Secondary 785 becomes a mediocre paved road that meets Highway 2. Turn right (south) and follow this well-maintained road a very short distance to the intersection with Highway 3 and turn left (east) to reach Fort Macleod. For the return trip, follow Highway 3 west; this road is a high-quality, well-maintained, two-lane highway.

The route: This route travels east from the Rocky Mountain Front over rolling prairie dominated by ranches and farms. Just before the town of Brocket, a left turn (north) onto Secondary road 785 leads to the Head-Smashed-In Buffalo Jump, designated a United Nations World Heritage Site by UNESCO.

The road crosses the Oldman River; the portion of the river that flows through this route contains some of Canada's most extensive riparian woodland and bordering wetlands. It provides productive habitat for deer, a variety of songbirds, and great blue herons. However, the river is bounded by private lands and is therefore unprotected. Explorer Peter Fidler translated the river's original name into English in 1792 (a rather novel idea considering all the natural features named after government officials); Oldman refers to the Blackfoot creator deity, Napi.

Blackfoot Origins
By Brian Reeves

The Oldman river region of southwestern Alberta is very important in traditional Blackfoot Culture, for it is here that the Blackfoot elders say the People originated. Ethnologists, missionaries, and early travelers first inquired as to the origins of the Blackfoot (who traditionally refer to themselves as the Nitsitapii (the people who speak the same language). Elders of the three Blackfoot tribes, the Kainai (Many Chiefs also known as the Blood), Piikani(Peigan), and Siksika (Blackfoot), told these white people two stories relating to their origins.

These stories are at odds with theories developed by white ethnographers and historians who chose to ignore or dismiss the elders' accounts as myth or fairy stories with no historical validity. But the archaeology, linguistics, and population genetics of the Blackfoot tends to support the stories of the elders. Science tells us that the Blackfoot have been here for a very long time, supporting the elders' insistence that the People originated here rather than migrating some three centuries ago. Archaeology shows, from sites such as Head-Smashed-In, that the People have been here for thousands of years. Archaeology also tells us that the general historical events, described in the origin story of the three tribes, is not a myth, but actually happened some 5,000 years ago, when a new archaeological culture which originated south and west of the mountains in the Northeastern Great Basin suddenly appeared on this side of the mountains.

The first and oldest of these stories, also told by the Arapaho, tells of a time when the People were traveling south crossing a frozen lake or river. A part of the tribe had crossed the river and were on the other side. A child saw a buffalo horn frozen in the ice. Someone pulled it loose, and the ice parted, drowning many of the Indians and separating the tribe. The Blackfoot were on the north side. It was long thought that the people on the south side had perished, but it is now thought that somewhere off to the south they still remain as a tribe. The Arapaho version speaks of traveling north, with the Arapaho remaining on the south side, and an unknown tribe living to the north. The river is said to be the Missouri River. There was a now extinct tribe of the Arapaho whose language was closer to Blackfoot than any of the others. The events described in this myth account for the original division of these distant linguistically and genetically related people which occurred very far back in the past, possibly at the end of the last ice age 10,000 years ago.

The other story the Blackfoot elders related to their inquisitive white visitors is the only story they have which accounts for the origin of the three Blackfoot tribes. In the very long ago time the People lived far to the south on the other side of the mountains. Game became very scarce and the People began to starve. An old man of the tribe who had three

married sons, was very sad to see them and their little children starving. One morning, he called them together and told them of a vision
he had in which his dream person had told him to go across the
mountains with his children, beyond which was a very big land with
plenty of food. They followed the dream person's advice, traveling east
with great difficulty and much hunger until they reached the great
prairie stretching to the end of the world. It was full of game.

In the morning the young men started to hunt but had bad luck.
They could not get close enough to the game to kill it. The old man
made a powerful black medicine which he applied to his eldest son's
feet, enabling him to run so fast that he ran right up to a fat cow and
killed it. They feasted and gave thanks to the Sun; the old man gave
his eldest son a new name "Siksika" (Blackfoot) which was to be the
names of his children too. The younger sons were envious of their
elder brother's good fortune. The old man promised them they too
would have new names for themselves and children, once they had
gone to war. The old man said: "Here we will found three tribes, and
this shall be their country."

Treaty No. 7

Although the Blackfoot and other tribes had signed a treaty with the United
States government in 1858 no comparable treaty was signed with the government of Canada until some twenty years later in 1877. After Canada became
a country in 1867, traditional Blackfoot lands became part of Canada's Northwest Territory—a vast expanse of lands east of British Columbia and west
of Ontario. As white settlement expanded, a series of treaties were
"negotiated" between the Native tribes and the new government of Canada.
The seventh of these known as Treaty No.7—signed at Blackfoot Crossing
on the Bow River below Calgary—covered the southern area of today's Alberta.
It included three Blackfoot tribes, and their allies, the Sarci and the Stony.

Census figures determined the number of acres allotted to each tribe. Unfortunately for the Piikani who then were the largest of the three Blackfoot tribes,
most of the North Piikani who generally wintered in southern Alberta were
in Montana, and were not counted in the census. They were allotted a much
smaller reservation (116,000 acres) than they should have been granted in their
traditional wintering area on the Oldman River south of the Porcupine Hills.
The Stony took up a reservation in their traditional wintering area on the Bow
River above Fort Calgary, while the Siksika, Kainai, and Sarci resided on a
common reserve centered on the Bow River downstream of Fort Calgary. The
common reservation proved to be an unsatisfactory arrangement for these
three tribes and in 1883, the Sarci moved to their present reservation west
of Calgary and the Kainai to their's between Fort Macleod and Cardston.
Theirs, the Blood Reserve, at 350,400 acres, is the largest Indian reserve in
Canada.

In the United States, with the passage of the Dawes Act in 1887 individual
Indians took title to their allotments and could dispose them as they wished.
Hence over forty percent of the Blackfeet Reservation in Montana is in fact

Head-Smashed-In Buffalo Jump Interpretive Center.

held by whites. This was not the case in Canada, where sale of Indian lands was prohibited. Although the Canadian Blackfoot Reserve has always remained "Indian land," reserve lands were "surrendered" by the tribes. The Piikani and Siksika were persuaded by the government of Canada to sell off portions of their reserves in 1909 and 1910 to white ranchers and land development companies. The Siksika surrendered 115,000 acres, nearly half of their lands (300,800 acres). The Piikani surrendered 23,000 acres.

Although Indian policy and its application in Canada was different than the United States, it still resulted in the loss of lands, forced acculturation in Indian Residential Schools, and suppression of traditional culture and religion.—*Brian Reeves*

Head-Smashed-In and the wind

The dirt road bears east along the base of the Porcupine Hills; from here and on past Head-smashed-In comes because it is one of the largest, best preserved, least vandalized, and most continuously used bison jumps in the world. Wind played a major role here. This is one of the windiest areas in Canada, with an average wind speed of 28-km/18-mi-per-hour. A local from Fort Macleod stated that, "Last winter, there was a period when the wind blew over thirty km-per-hour for more than sixty days in a row." Such winds, an average of thirty-five each year, helped erode the cliffs.

The meteorological explanation for chinook winds (see Route 11) is a bit different from the mythological account. After winter settled in, the Old Man

Native People of the Trail of the Great Bear
By Brian Reeves

For thousands of years the Trail of the Great Bear has been the traditional homeland for Native First Nations, some of whose descendants reside today, many in abject poverty, on Indian reservations along the Trail. On the east are the three Blackfoot tribes, once the largest and most powerful of the First Nations: The Kaina, who reside on the Blood Reserve in southern Alberta; the Piikani, comprised of the South Peigan, who reside on the Blackfeet Reserve in Northern Montana and refer to themselves as the Blackfeet; the North Peigan, who reside on the Peigan Reserve in southwestern Alberta; and the Siksika (Blackfoot) who reside on the Blackfoot Reserve southeast of Calgary.

Blackfoot territory for the last 1,000 or more years extended from North Saskatchewan River south along the eastern slopes, foothills, and western plains to the Missouri River. Eastward, their traditional lands encompassed the Sweet Pine (Sweet Grass) and the Cypress Hills, lands they shared with their allies, the Atsina (Gros Ventre), a northern nation of the Arapaho.

Traditionally the Atsina's and other Arapaho tribes' lands included the Upper Missouri and Yellowstone rivers. Some 500 years ago, the Crow, whose original homelands were on the Middle Missouri River, occupied the Upper Yellowstone River, while the Upper Missouri River was occupied by Shoshone from the northern Great Basin. By 1800 the Blackfoot and Atsina had displaced the Shoshone intruders from these lands. A group of Shoshone, known as the Sheep Eaters, lived in the mountainous region of Greater Yellowstone. The last survivor died in the late 1800s.

In the northern foothills and mountains of today's Alberta lived bands of northern forest hunters, including the Sarci, who shifted their territory to the southeast, becoming allied with the Blackfoot in the 1700s. Today they reside on the Sarci Reserve at Calgary. Tunaxa (Kootenai) territory lay to the south, extending from the Northern Saskatchewan River to today's Glacier National Park, and on west from the headwaters of the Columbia, along the Kootenai River, to the northern end of Flathead Lake. Today, the Tunaxa reside on reserves in Idaho, Montana, and southeastern British Columbia. Around 300 years ago the Nakota (Assiniboine) moved westward up the Saskatchewan River. Today, three Nakota bands reside on the Stoney Reserve west and north of Calgary.

Salish people have been residents in the Flathead and tributary valleys in western Montana for the past 1,000 years, where they continue to live on their reservation today. For a brief time, after they acquired horses in the late 1600s, they traveled east over the passes to hunt buffalo. Like the Shoshone, they too were driven back across the mountains by the Blackfoot and Atsina.

from the West ran over the mountains followed by warm winds. This upset the Old Man from the North. He chased the Old Man from the West and shot arrows at him bringing back the cold northern winds. Back and forth the two Old Men raced until the Old Man from the West won, but only for awhile and during that time it was summer.

Use of the Head-Smashed-In Buffalo Jump dates back more than 8,000 years. Little is know about these early hunters. The first Blackfoot people, who used the jump until the early nineteenth century, were quite different from the Plains Indians portrayed in movies. Prior to the appearance of horses, during a time the Blackfoot called the "Dog Days," they walked and used dogs as pack animals. The basic social unit of the Blackfoot was a *band* and it consisted of ten to thirty lodges or about eighty to 240 people. People could move freely from one band to another (making disputes easy to settle). A leader possessed the qualities of a good warrior, but most important of all, he was generous. Bands located winter camps in wooded river valleys about a day's walk apart. In the spring, the bison moved out onto the prairie and the bands soon followed on what they called the "seasonal round." The Blackfoot bands traveled along traditional routes dictated by bison movement, weather, and seasonal changes. Large tribal gatherings centered around the Sun Dance in the mid-summer. Afterwards, the tribe split up and bands headed for wintering areas where a number of bands might join forces for a communal hunt at places like Head-Smashed-In.

Meanwhile, the bison had traveled their own seasonal round. In the spring the bison moved from sheltered valley bottoms onto the plains. Their movement, like those of the Blackfoot, were not haphazard; as more efficient grazers than cattle, they timed their movements according to the ripening forage along the course of their travel. (An interesting relationship existed between the bison and the prairie grasses they ate. Not only did bison provide fertilizer, their hooves, backed by the pressure of their mass, pushed native grass seeds to just the right depth to sprout. The hooves of cattle are incapable of accomplishing this.) In the summer, the bison gathered during the annual rut; this was a bad time to attempt a large communal hunt due to the agitated nature of the vast herds. After the rut the herd split up; males took off on their own and small herds of cows and calves headed towards wintering grounds led by one or two matriarch cows.

How the jump worked

Perhaps as a child, you heard of bison jumps and envisioned cliffs taller than the Empire State Building. Now you look at Head-Smashed-In and feel a little disappointed; the cliff is only 10 m/33 ft high, but bear in mind that it wouldn't take much vertical displacement to put a bison out of commission. But here's what you probably didn't think about as a child: all the work, cooperation, skill, and luck involved in a successful hunt. If a band of Blackfoot spotted a herd of bison gathered on the plateau above the jump site and if the wind blew favorably, then they began the operation. The proper ceremonies had to be performed to prepare the people and the buffalo or the entire hunt could prove fruitless. Afterwards, two men who dedicated their lives to being *runners*, joined the bison herd; one wore a coyote of wolf pelt and the other a bison calf skin.

Bison possess a great sense of smell but their eyes aren't too good. The man in the calf skin bellowed like a frightened calf luring the matriarch towards the cliff; the herd followed. The man in the coyote skin flanked the herd from behind making them nervous. Sometimes days passed but eventually, if the runners were successful, they moved the herd between the drive lanes—two rows of cairns that extended 8 km/5 mi back from the cliff. While runners lured the herd closer to the precipice, down below at the kill site, the band of Blackfoot readied themselves. Camp was set up, drying racks erected, drive lanes repaired, and each person instructed as to his or her duties. Finally, when the herd was in position, people ran in from behind shouting and waving skins. The herd rushed forward and more people jumped up from behind brush piled along the drive lane. The runner in the calf skin ran for a crevice at the brink of the cliff and the bison followed. Bison, when stampeding, can reach and maintain a speed of 50 km-/30 mi-per-hour. Sometimes the runner was trampled beneath the hooves of his intended victims. When the lead matriarch spotted the precipice and tried to turn around, it was too late; the momentum of the herd pushed the forerunners to their doom. Many bison were only wounded or stunned by the fall, so hunters dashed up and killed them; they believed that if an animal escaped, it would warn others of the fatal trick.

Head-Smashed-In Interpretive Centre

You probably think that the way Head-Smashed-In got its name is self-explanatory. Bison fell, smashed their heads, and there you have it. Wrong. "About 150 years ago, according to legend, a young brave wanted to witness the plunge of countless buffalo as his people drove them to their deaths. Standing under the shelter of a ledge, like a man behind a waterfall, he watched the great beasts cascade past him. But the hunt was unusually good that day, and as the bodies mounted, he became trapped between the animals and the cliff. When his people came to do the butchering, they found him with his skull crushed by the weight of the buffalo. Thus they named the place 'Head-Smashed-In.' " (from the Head-Smashed-In Buffalo Jump brochure.) The interpretive centre offers a world-class facility with a theatre and thematic displays on five different levels that explain Native mythology of the area, the lifestyle of the Plains people, use of the buffalo jump, the consequences of contact with whites, and the science of archaeology at the jump site. Native guides provide a tour quite unique compared to tours usually offered by museums or interpretive centres. The guides include wonderful stories, legends, and myths. The centre, with a cafeteria and a gift shop with an excellent selection of books, also hosts special events and is open daily with winter hours of 9 a.m. to 5 p.m. and summer hours of 9 a.m. to 8 p.m. Admission is adults $5, children $2, and families $12. For more information: Head-Smashed-In Interpretive Centre, Box 1977, Fort Macleod, Alberta TOL OZO; 403-553-2731.

Whiskey traders

From Head-Smashed-In, a secondary paved road leads to Highway 2 and Fort Macleod, the original outpost of the legendary Northwest Mounted Police. Two major factors launched the 1874 march of the Mounted Police across a thousand miles of Canada. One was whiskey traders and the other was fear of Manifest Destiny. While the Hudson Bay Company, to the north of the Blackfoot people, and the American Fur Company to the south, traded liberal quantities of whiskey for furs, at a certain point, both companies corked the bottle for fear of destroying the golden goose. In 1864, the American Fur Company went belly up and whiskey traders from Fort Benton in the United

States moved into the vacuum. The Civil War (in the United States) ended and a wave of embittered and cynical war veterans traveled west; some took up the whiskey trade. These men lived for the day and conducted business in a similar fashion. At whiskey forts such as Whoop-Up, Slide-out, and Standoff, Blackfoot passed a bundle of furs through a slot in the stockade and received a mug full of whiskey. "And such whiskey," wrote James MacGregor in *A History of Alberta*. "Tobacco, old tea leaves and molasses brought to a full rolling boil, then cooled, seasoned to taste with Perry's painkiller and alcohol and dolled up to a dubious pink with red ink." Under the influence of this delirium, invoking elixir, Natives traded away everything—furs, rifle, horses, and more.

Ill treatment of the Native people disturbed some eastern Canadian politicians, as did traders from the United States openly conducting business in southern Alberta and not paying customs taxes for goods transported over the border. Canadians feared that the United States would send troops to protect the unsavory entrepreneurs as it had done so often in the past. It was time to send in the Mounties.

The Great March

In June 1874, a two-mile-long column comprised of 275 men (totally inexperienced in frontier skills), 339 horses, 235 oxen and cattle, cannons, mowing machines, forges, and kitchen equipment set out to put a stop to the whiskey trade and United State expansionism. Ironically, they dropped below the medicine line (as the Natives referred to the border) to procure supplies at Fort Benton, the very source of their problems. The Mounties turned north and found that word of their coming had proceeded them. Fort Whoop-Up was deserted. Five months after beginning the Great March, the Mounties (now seasoned troops with a proud sense of *esprit de corps*) established Fort Macleod on an island in the Oldman River. That trek is commemorated in the Red Coat Trail designation. Law and order became synonymous with their red tunics, that were red for a very good reason. The Natives associated red with the anti-American British troops; they equated the blue uniforms of the United States Calvary with deceit and treachery. While the Mounties maintained a show of dominance, they strove to deal honestly with the Native people and thereby earned their respect.

Today, the Fort Museum offers a replica of the first Fort Macleod (the corner bastions and catwalks are fun but fanciful additions) and displays of artifacts and paraphernalia concerned with Native people and the Northwest Mounted Police. The museum also conducts interpretive programs about the Northwest Mounted Police. During the summer, the Mounted Patrol Musical Ride is a special highlight. This is a rendition of the original musical ride performed in authentic uniforms. (For more information: Fort Macleod Historical Association, Box 776, Fort Macleod, Alberta, T0L 0Z0; 403-553-4703.)

Historical downtown Fort Macleod

Fort Macleod's classic, early twentieth-century Main Street, constructed in brick and sandstone, is Alberta's finest example of a restored downtown; it has earned designation under the Alberta Historical Act and as a Provincial Historic Area. A self-guided walking tour of the town is available at the Chamber of Commerce on Main Street (403-553-4955). Also in Fort Macleod, the Empress Theatre is Alberta's oldest operating theatre. The building was completely restored with special care taken to retain its original ambience and character;

live Summer Theatre in July and August is the real attraction here though first-run, foreign and classic movies are also screened. (For information: Empress Theatre, Box 99, Fort Macleod, Alberta, T0L 0Z0; 403-553-4151.) Fort Macleod also celebrates two fun events in a big way: Midnight Days, on the last weekend of May, includes baseball in the pool, mud volleyball, cabaret, a parade, and midnight shopping. Alberta's oldest Santa Claus Day Parade also takes place here (during the weekend closest to the beginning of December) with ethnic foods offered by vendors, crafts, skating, concerts, the parade, and of course, midnight shopping. The return portion of this route follows Highway 3 and traverses the Peigan Indian Reserve where the Peigan Indian Days is celebrated at Brochet during the third weekend of July with dances, games, and socializing.

ROUTE 12B: FORT MACLEOD-LETHBRIDGE   31km/50mi

General description: Route 12B follows Highway 3 across the prairie east to Lethbridge following the general course of the Oldman River. The lands are primarily dry and irrigated flat farmlands developed on rich glacial lake sediments left by the retreating glaciers 20,000 years ago. Lethbridge, a major city of 60,600 people, Southern Alberta's main service centre, has many attractions and services. From Lethbridge, you have the option of returning back west to Fort Macleod via Highway 3, or looping southwest via Highway 5, to rejoin Route 11A at Cardston.
Travel season: Year-round
Road conditions and route description: Highway 3 is an all-weather, two-lane highway, becoming a four-lane divided highway 26 km east of Fort Macleod. The route is known as the Crowsnest Trail. In Lethbridge, the Crowsnest Trail is a limited access through city expressway.

The route: The route travels east over rolling and flat farmland east of Fort Macleod, following in part the old wagon trail which connected Fort Macleod to the Whoop-Up Trail. The Whoop-Up Trail ran from Fort Benton, the head of steamboat navigation on the Missouri, to Fort Whoop-Up, located at the junction of the St. Mary and Oldman rivers, just south of Lethbridge. Until the construction of the Canadian Pacific Railway in 1882, all goods were shipped into today's southern Alberta by bull trains traveling up the Whoop-Up Trail to Fort Macleod and Fort Calgary.

In 1885 a narrow-gauge railroad was constructed from the CPR at Medicine Hat to Lethbridge, replaced by a standard gauge in 1893. Grade work began on the Crowsnest Pass Branch in 1897. The crossings of the Oldman River was the most formidable obstacle faced by the railroad engineers. The first line avoided the issue by crossing the St. Mary near Fort Whoop-Up, staying on the south side of the Oldman west to Fort Macleod. Frequent floods would wash the trestles on this line out. The problem was solved with the construction of the Canadian Pacific High Level Bridge across the Oldman River at Lethbridge along with a new line to Fort Macleod.The bridge, completed in 1908, located just south of Highway 3 was an engineering feat. It is the longest (1.6km/1.2 mi) and highest (94m/280 ft) bridge of its kind in North America. You can best view the High Level Bridge by taking the first signed exit off the Crowsnest Trail on the east side of the Oldman River in Lethbridge.

Vistas of the Oldman River Valley and its extensive cottonwood forests appear as you drive east from Fort Macleod. Ten km/6 mi east of the intersection of Highway 23, the point where Highway 3 becomes a divided four-lane highway, is a view point looking out over the valleys of the Oldman and Belly rivers. This was the location of one of the small whiskey posts, Fort Kipp, constructed in 1872, and later taken over by the NWMP. In all some twenty small whiskey posts were constructed along the Oldman above Lethbridge as part of the network of posts operating out of Fort Whoop-Up. Interpretive signage tells you of the history of the valley.

An authentic reconstruction of Fort Whoop-Up is located in Indian Battle Park located in the Oldman River valley in the City of Lethbridge. The Fort Whoop-Up Interpretive Centre features historical displays, special events, and an excellent video on Whoop-Up and the whiskey trade. The fort has a small gift shop. The Fort is open from the May long weekend to Labour Day weekend. (For more information write Fort Whoop Up Interpretive Society, Indian Battle Park, P.O.Box 1074, Lethbridge, Alberta T1J 4A2 or call 403-329-0444).

Indian Battle Park

In 1870 the Blackfoot Confederacy fought the Cree and Assiniboine. It was the last major inter-tribal battle in the Canadian West. Today Indian Battle Park commemorates the conflict. The battle began three miles upstream of Fort Whoop-Up in the late fall when the Cree and Assiniboine attacked a Peigan camp. A running battle ensued, as the Peigan joined by nearby Blackfoot camps pursued the Cree downriver. It ended here with the routing of the Cree and Assiniboine by the Blackfoot. In the following year warfare between these two groups ended. You can learn more about the battle through interpretive exhibits at Indian Battle Park and at the Sir Alexander Galt museum located on the edge of the valley above. The museum has a fine viewing gallery overlooking the river valley.

Lethbridge

Lethbridge began as a coal town supplying coal to the CPR and to settlers in the late 1800s. During the 1930s there were eight major collieries operating. The last mines closed in the late 1950s. The earliest mines were located in the river bottom in and adjacent to Indian Battle Park. Interpretive exhibits in the museum there tell you about the early history of "Coalbanks" as it was known. The museum incorporates a historic structure, the city's first major hospital, named after Sir Alexander Galt. Galt, one of the fathers of Canadian Confederation (Galt, Ontario is named after him), was also High Commissioner of Canada to Great Britain, and responsible for arranging the financing for the first coal mines in Lethbridge and the construction of the railway branch lines. Early Lethbridge (named after the president of Galt's company) was very much a company town. It was planned by Galt's agent and manager Charles A. Magrath. He became the city's first mayor. The museum is open Monday to Friday 10:00 a.m. to 4 p.m., Saturday and Sunday 1:00 p.m. to 4:00 p.m., and Wednesday evenings until 8:00 p.m. (For more information: write Galt Museum, c/o City of Lethbridge Community Services, 817 4 Ave. S, Lethbridge, Alberta, or call 403-3320-3898.

Nikka Yuko Centennial Gardens

Among the many immigrant groups who came to the Lethbridge district were Japanese, who were brought in the early decades of the twentith century to work on the irrigation farms. They, and later Japanese-Canadians, relocated here from the Pacific Coast during World War II, played a very important role in developing the diversified agricultural economy in the region. The Nikka Yuko Centennial Gardens commemorates their role. It is an authentic 4 acre/1.6 ha Japanese Garden with paths, streams, and waterfalls and is a symbol of Japanese-Canadian friendship. Interpretation is provided by hostesses in full Japanese costume. The gardens are open from May to September. For more information call 403-328-3511.—*Brian Reeves*

For More Information About Route 12:

Exploring Southern Alberta's Chinook Country. Ken Liddel. 1981. Heritage House.
Canoeing Chinook Country Rivers. Hans Bhurmann and David Young. 1982.
Lethbridge: A Centennial History. Alex Johnston and Andy A. den Otter. 1985. The Whoop-Up Country Chapter Historical Society of Alberta.
The Landscapes of Southern Alberta: A Regional Geomorphology. Chester B. Beaty. 1975. University of Lethbridge.
Hiking Alberta's Southwest. Joey Ambrosi. 1984. Douglas & McIntyre.

Events and Services

Chinook Country Tourist Association: 2805 Scenic Drive, Lethbridge, Alberta T1K5B7; 1-800-661-1222, or 403-329-6777.
Crowsnest Municipality Chamber of Commerce: 1127 21st Avenue, Blairmore, Alberta TOK OMO; 403-562-8766.
Fort Macleod Chamber of Commerce: Box 940, Fort Macleod, Alberta TOL OZO; 403-553-4414.
Crowsnest Pass Ecomuseum: Box 1440, Blairmore, Alberta TOK OEO; 403-562-8831.
Frank Slide Interpretive Centre: Box 299, Blairmore, Alberta TOK OEO; 403-562-7388.
Crowsnest Museum (in Coleman): 403-563-5434.
Head-Smashed-In Buffalo Jump Interpretive Centre: Box 1977, Fort Macleod, Alberta TOL OZO; 403-553-2731.
Fort Museum: Fort Macleod Historical Association, Box 776, Fort Macleod, Alberta TOL OZO; 403-553-4703.
Lethbridge Chamber of Commerce: 529 6th Street, Lethbridge, Alberta T1J OMB; 403-327-1586
City of Lethbridge: 910 4th Avenue S., Lethbridge, Alberta T1JOM; 403-320-3000.

How Fort Whoop-Up Got Its Name

From *Fort Whoop-Up: Alberta's First and Most Notorious Whiskey Fort* by Georgia Fouks. 1983 Whoop-Up Country Chapter Historical Society of Alberta

Fort Whoop-Up was originally called Fort Hamilton after Alfred Hamilton one of the fort's two original builders. How the fort was renamed has over the years been a subject of considerable debate. One account says that a Pennsylvania Dutch trader, Joe Wye, returning to Fort Benton for supplies, when questioned by John Power, one of the suppliers, about the trade up in Canada, replied "Oh, we're just a whoopen-on-em-up." The phrase pleased the locals, who shortened it first to "whooping-it-up" and then "Whoop-up."

One of the old-time traders J.W. "Diamond R." Brown, however, said the name came from the habit of the whiskey traders secretly crossing the border. They were not allowed to carry whiskey on the Blackfeet Reserve and were always trying to avoid the U.S. army patrols and the Montana police. The traders "whooped it up" for the border at night, traveling up to fifty miles without a stop. Another account has it that the name came from the Indians who "whooped it up" after getting drunk on the whiskey they traded for at the fort. A French freighter on the trail, Charles Choquette, is also credited with the origin of the name, according to a Lethbridge Herald account. Choquette was not proficient in English and when he learned a new word tended to repeat it over and over again.

One night when Choquette's outfit was nearing the fort, after an eighty-mile stretch of particularly tiresome trail, someone said "Let's whoop it up and get to the fort." Charlie thought it was a great word and repeated it so often it became a byword. Another account says that name comes from an urgent letter sent by one of the traders who was doing a great trade but had run out of whiskey and sent an urgent letter to Fort Benton, asking Powers to send more whiskey as he was "whooping her up in good shape."

According to Paul F. Sharp in his award winning book, Whoop-Up-Country, "whoop you up" was a common Missouri River expression. It meant to be rounded up. Supposedly Hamilton and his partner Joe Healey were leaving Fort Benton to build the fort on behalf of I.G. Baker, when Baker shouted, "Don't let the Indians whoop you up."

Between the Prairie and Foothills

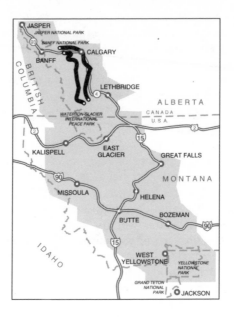

"I will lift up mine eyes unto the hills, from whence cometh my help."

The Bible, Psalms.

"These mountains are our temples, our sanctuaries, and our resting places. They are a place of hope, a place of vision, a place of refuge, a very special and holy place where the Great Spirit speaks with us. Therefore, these mountains are our sacred places."

Chief John Snow in *These Mountains Are Our Sacred Places.*

ROUTE 13

LUNDBRECK to BOW VALLEY PROVINCIAL PARK
251 kilometers/156 miles

General description: From the turnoff of Highway 3 to Longview, Highway 22 passes through wetlands and willow parklands flanked with occasional farms and grassy foothills with aspen, Douglas-fir, and lodgepole pine forests. While some travelers may feel this landscape isn't quite as spectacular as that found on other portions of the Trail of the Great Bear, it is important wildlife habitat. At Longview, the option exists to continue north on Highway 22 or turn onto Route 14 (closed in the winter) which traverses the Kananaskis Country and Peter Lougheed Provincial Park. The northern portion of this route, in addition to providing a winter route that connects with Route 15, offers access to the East Kananaskis Country and Calgary before entering the Bow Valley that leads to Banff National Park.

Unique features: Big Rock, Calgary, Fort Calgary, Glenbow Museum, Calgary Zoo, Cochrane Ranch Historic Site, and Western Heritage Center.

Wildlife viewing opportunities: Sheep River Wildlife Sanctuary, Fish Creek Provincial Park, Inglewood Bird Sanctuary, Bow Valley Provincial Park.

Activities: Golf, fishing, snowmobiling, hiking, cross-country skiing, horseback riding, big city entertainment in Calgary.

Events: Calgary Exhibition and Stampede, Cochrane Rodeo, Heritage Days.

Travel season: Year-round.

Services: No services exist for the first 165 km/102 mi of this route between Lundbreck and Longview after which services are readily available. Calgary is a major service center with an international airport.

Road conditions and route description: Remain on Highway 22 for 201 km/125 mi to Trans-Canada Highway 1; take the westbound on-ramp. Route 13 ends 50 km/31 mi later adjacent to the Bow Valley Provincial Park. Highway 22 is an all-weather, two-lane highway that varies in quality, but overall is in good condition. Some sections are unpaved.

The route: As you begin Route 13, be aware that no services exist until Longview, 165 km/102 mi away. Highway 22 traverses over agricultural and grazing lands, flanked to the east by the Porcupine Hills and to the west by the Chapel Butte foothills. The Chapel Butte area provides key habitat to moose and deer amid riparian and grassland habitats. However, the area is primarily on private land and therefore not open to the public. The route crosses the North Fork of the Oldman River which is a "blue-ribbon" fishery and also situated on private land; there is a campground just off the road at this crossing. Farther north and to the left (west) of the highway, the Whaleback is one of the more spectacular areas of foothill ridges in Canada. A variety of habitats ranging from wetlands to riparian to montane forest provides winter range to 1,300 elk; this area is also on private land.

Chain Lakes Provincial Park is located 72 km/45 mi up Highway 22 on the left (west) side. The area provides critical habitat to elk, moose, and deer that includes rolling willow parkland, foothills covered with grass, and rugged montane ridges to the west of Chain Lakes Reservoir. A Provincial Park (403-646-5887 in summer and 403-627-2021 in winter) is located next to the reservoir, which is a popular ice fishing destination. Twenty km/12.5 mi north of Chain Lakes you will pass the historic Bar-U Ranch being developed by the Canadian Park Service as a national historic park. The Bar-U is one of the oldest and most famous of the foothill ranches. Its history dates back to 1882, when the first ranch was established by the Northwest Cattle Company. George Lane, one of the "Big Four" founders of the Calgary Stampede was ranch foreman. He left in 1892 to purchase his first ranch, the Flying E. In 1902 Lane purchased the Bar-U, becoming the largest single ranch owner in Alberta. Together the Bar-U, Flying E, and Lane's other ranch, the Little Bow, ran 40,000 head and had an annual calf crop of 8,000. The Bar-U remained in Lane's hands until his death in 1925. It was then purchased by Pat Burns, another one of the "Big Four," a pioneering rancher and meat packer.

Two miles beyond the Bar-U is the old Prince of Wales E.P. Ranch. Its claim to fame being its second owner, Edward Prince of Wales (The Duke of Windsor). He purchased the ranch in 1919, and over the course of the next forty years visited it at various times. His first visit was in 1923 when he traveled incognito as Lord Renfrew (this is the title Prince Charles used when dating Princess Diana). King George V died in January 1936, and Prince Edward succeeded to the throne, abdicating it on December 10th to marry Wallace Simpson. They were given the titles the Duke and Duchess of Windsor. They visited the ranch once in 1941. The Duke sold the ranch in 1962.

For more information on the Bar-U National Historic Park development write The Canadian Parks Service, Box 2989, Station "M," Calgary, Alberta 72P 3H8, or call 403-292-4401.

Hell's Half Acre, situated in Turner Valley, is where Alberta's first major oil reserves were discovered in 1914. The most significant site remaining here is the Turner Valley Sour Gas Plant (the first sour gas processing plant in Canada) that performed the same function as the Waterton Shell Complex on Route 11.

Hells Half Acre

Legends fill the air as you approach the Turner Valley oilfield. As Western Canada's first oilfield, it boomed in 1914, again in 1924, and a third time from 1936 to 1945. It has produced more than 100 million barrels of oil and will continue sending its valuable products to markets for years to come. Turner Valley came by the name of Hells Half Acre through flaring off the natural gas when there was not a market for all the gas being produced. The gas was flared off so that the oil could be produced. At night the glow of "Hells Half Acre" could be seen from Calgary. Unfortunately removal of all this gas severely depressurized the resevoir, and despite the use of enhanced recovery techniques most of Turner Valley's oil will never be recovered. As a result of this profligate waste of resources the Alberta government in the late 1930s established the Oil and Gas Conservation Board, the first such regulatory authority in the world, to ensure this would never happen again.

Today, this area is getting ready for yet another boom as it prepares the world's largest permanent exhibit about the oil and gas industry. This exhibit will focus on the old Turner Valley Gas Plant, which you pass just east of the town of Turner Valley. This gas plant, a Provincial Historic Site, operated from just after the First World War to the 1980s when it was replaced by a modern facility elsewhere within the field. The old plant contains many of the only

N

To Route 16

To Edmonton

Banff

Canmore

Route 13B

Stoney Indian Reserve

1A

Bow River

Cochrane

2

Route 15

Bow Valley Prov Pk

1

Calgary

Sarcee Indian Reserve

Fish Creek Provincial Park

1

Bragg Creek

22X

To Medicine Hat

Kananaskis Village

Kananaskis Country

22

Peter Lougheed Prov Pk

Turner Valley

7

Sheep River Wildlife Sanctuary

546

Black Diamond

2A

Okotoks

40

541

Longview

High River

23

To Vulcan

Route 14

Bar U National Historic Park

Nanton

22

Route 13A

Chain Lakes Prov Pk

2

ROCKY MOUNTAIN FOREST RESERVE

Route 13

Claresholm

Oldman River

To Lethbridge, Route 12 B

3

Head-Smashed-In

Crowsnest Pass

3

22

Route 12A

Fort Macleod

Crowsnest River

Lundbreck

3

2

Route 12

6

To Cardston

To Pincher Creek, Route 11

0   10   20 miles

0   15   30 km

surviving examples of pioneering gas processing technologies; including gasoline, propane and sulphur recovery. When developed and open to the public it will provide a fascinating in-depth experience into the oil and gas industry, and the foundations of Alberta's economic growth and development.

Brochures and maps to Turner Valleys historic sites can be obtained at the tourist booth under the wooden drilling rig replica in Turner Valley. For more information about Hells Half Acre, the proposed oilfield petroleum exposition, write Hell Raising Centre, #506, 609 14 Street, N.W., Calgary, AB T2N 2A1 or phone 403-283-FIRE(3473).

Sheep River Wildlife Sanctuary and Northern Lights

The extensive grassland, montane forest, and steep canyon walls provide excellent habitat for bighorn sheep at the Sheep River Wildlife Sanctuary. Bring binoculars as sheep may be feeding off in the distance. According to the *Alberta Wildlife Viewing Guide*, "During the fall, mature rams can often be closely observed from the comfort of your vehicle." In the spring and fall, golden eagles and other birds of prey utilize updrafts created by the foothill ridges to aid them on their migration. To reach the sanctuary, from the settlement of Turner Valley on Highway 22, follow Secondary 546 for 25 km/16 mi into the East Kananaskis Country. In order to protect the bighorn sheep's winter range, the sanctuary is closed to vehicles from December 1 to May 15. The Bluerock Campground is situated at the western edge of the sanctuary. For more information call Fish and Wildlife Division, Calgary; 403-297-6423.

When camping out on the plains, there's a good chance of seeing the Northern Lights. This light show, the aurora borealis, usually hovers at least 161 km/100 mi above the earth's surface and extends 242 km/150 mi high. The display seen at latitudes along the Trail of the Great Bear is often a pale greenish glow that moves with ghostly slowness (consider yourself lucky to see crimson light). Much like the minute hand on a watch, you don't actually see it move but if you watch closely you know that it's moving. "Virtually everyone who wrote down his thoughts about the aurora described, first, the inadequacy of his language and second, a pervasive and stilling spiritual presence," wrote Barry Lopez in *Arctic Dreams*. The phenomenon originates on the sun where solar winds of ionized particles stream outward like the sunbeams in a child's drawing. As it passes the earth, the solar wind generates an electric current that's drawn down via magnetic force to an area, known as the aurora oval centered over the Magnetic North Pole. On the way down, due to a molecular process, energy is emitted in the form of infrared and ultraviolet light, radio waves, X-rays, and visible light that forms glowing curtains that float with almost imperceptible slowness across the night sky.

Highway 22 skirts Calgary along the base of the foothills. From Bragg Creek, Highway 6 leads up the Elbow Valley with access to campgrounds, snowmobiling, fishing, hiking, and cross-country skiing in the East Kananaskis Country. Highway 22 continues north over forested foothills and past scattered farms until it intersects Trans-Canadian Highway 1.

Calgary

For those who wish to visit Calgary, one of the three international oil capitols of the world (population 675,000), there are various access points: a right turn (east) off Highway 22 and onto Highway 773, 31 km/19 mi north of Black Diamond; a right turn (east) off Highway 22 and onto Highway 8, 14 km/9 mi

Whitetail deer can be spotted in Fish Creek Provincial Park.

beyond Bragg Creek; or follow the Trans-Canadian Highway eastbound into Calgary.

In *A History of Alberta*, James MacGregor wrote, "Calgary was conceived in confusion. The building of the fort was delayed, the Mounties sent north from Fort Macleod to man it crossed the [Bow] river from the north side to reach it, and it had difficulty in deciding what to call itself." For hundreds of years, Native people considered the area around the fork of the Bow and Elbow rivers as a choice campsite. In September 1875, Captain C. E. Denny wrote his impression of future-Calgary as viewed from atop North Hill. "Below us lay a lovely valley, flanked on the south by rolling hills. Thick woods bordered the banks of both streams; to the west towered mountains with their snowy peaks; beyond the Elbow stretched another wide valley, and heavy timber further west along the Bow. Buffalo in large bands grazed in the valley..."

The Fort received its name after Colonel Macleod learned that Inspector Brisbois (who led Troop F to present-day Calgary) wanted to name the fort after himself. Macleod suggested Calgary, believing that the Gaelic word meant "clear running water." (According to James MacGregor in his *History of Alberta*, it meant something else.) Today, surrounded by buildings instead of bison, Fort Calgary displays historical material pertaining to the Northwest Mounted Police with limited interpretation about Native people. The 40 acre-/16 ha-park is located on 9th Avenue SE and is open daily in the summer from 9 a.m. to 5 p.m. with the same hours in the winter from Wednesday to Sunday (403-269-7747).

The Glenbow Museum (403-264-8300 or 403-237-8988) is of international importance in terms of its scope, collections, exhibits, and programs. The Glenbow contains the most comprehensive collection of Blackfoot ethnographic material in the world, staged historical exhibits, and a western art gallery that features a number of artists including Russell and Remington. The Stephen Avenue Mall contains a number of historic buildings that provide insights to the architecture of early-day Calgary and offers a contrast with the historic districts in towns such as Helena, Fort Macleod, and Butte. Visitor Information Centres are located at the south end of Calgary off Highway 2, the east and west sides of Calgary off Trans-Canadian Highway 1, the International Airport, and in the heart of Calgary in the Burns Building.

During the second week of July, the city hosts the Calgary Exhibition and Stampede. Billed as the "Greatest Outdoor Show on Earth," the Stampede celebrates a fanciful Old West with rodeo, hot air balloon races, chuckwagon races, stage shows and performances, Native dances, and agricultural and craft exhibits. Calgary also hosts the Calgary Folk Festival and the Bow River Raft Race in August, and the Spruce Meadows International Horse Show in September. The cosmopolitan city of over 600,000 is an international community with all the big city amenities. For more information contact the Calgary Visitor and Convention Bureau, 237 8th Avenue SE, Calgary, Alberta T2G 0K8; 403-262-2766 or 800-661-1778.

Wildlife viewing in Calgary

Fish Creek Provincial Park is an urban wildland that stretches along the southern edge of Calgary. Whitetail and mule deer, beaver, badgers, coyotes, and more than 180 species of birds, including great blue herons, live along Fish Creek. The visitor centre host events all year long and provides interpretive exhibits. Some interpretive material includes information about the small buffalo jumps utilized in the winter by Peigan people. The jumps and winter campsites date back more than 3,000 years. There are various access points to the park.

The visitor centre is located at the end of the Bow Bottom Trail; from Highway 22, turn right (east) onto Highway 22X and left (north) on Highway 2. Turn right at the intersection of Highway 2 and Anderson Road (where there's a visitor information centre on the right) and continue to the Bow Bottom Trail. For more information, call the Provincial Parks Service: 403-297-5293.

Right on the edge of Calgary's busy city centre, the Inglewood Bird Sanctuary offers refuge to 216 species of birds, fox, deer, coyotes, and city-weary humans. Three km/2 mi of trails weave grassland and riparian habitat. The park is located at the end of 9th Avenue SE. For more information call Calgary Parks and Recreation: 403-269-6688.

Stony Indians

The obvious symptoms of suburban-blight become apparent as you travel west from Calgary and pass numerous country estates. Trans-Canada Highway 1 follows the Bow Valley and traverses the southern edge of the Stony Indian Reserve. Prior to Morley, the route passes through a unique highland western boreal forest not found anywhere along the Trail of the Great Bear south of this point.

Morley marks the extent to which Glacial Lake Calgary, created by an ice dam (like Glacial Lake Missoula on Route 5), flooded westward up the Bow Valley. The ancient shorelines are visible on the north side of the valley as you drop down to Morley.

Morley is the site of Alberta's first cattle ranch founded, in 1873, by Methodist missionaries. The fundamental Christian tenets of community—sharing, and respect for others—sounded like the common-sense approach to life that Stonys had practiced for centuries. "Our community was a sharing community," writes Chief John Snow in *These Mountains are Our Sacred Places*, "that is one of the reasons why we survived for so many centuries." Whereas the missionaries felt compelled to convert Native peoples, the Stonys "did not have disputes regarding religion. We had been taught not to question various forms or ways of worshipping the Creator. Who were we to question? We were not there when the religious experience happened to the individual or group. Therefore, we felt we were not qualified to question or dispute." (See sidebar.)

Today, the Stonys, like other tribes that preserved their language, customs, stories, and religion, are experiencing a slow revival of interest in traditional values among their young tribal members— self respect and confidence and dignity are returning. "Many bearers of Christianity teach that only man has a soul, but we Indian people believe that forms of life other than men have souls and spirits also," wrote Chief John Snow. "If an area is destroyed, marred, or polluted, my people say, the spirits will leave the area."

Overlooking Morley Flats, Mount Yamnuska stands as a bold natural monument to the beginning of the Front Ranges. Just off Highway 1 and across the Bow River, the Bow Valley Provincial Park offers a visitor centre (403-673-3663), picnic and campsites, and interpretive trails. The park, which caps the Kananaskis Country, is popular for Calgarians with easy access from Calgary which is only 80 km/50 mi away.

ROUTE 13A: HWY 2 FORT MACLEOD-CALGARY   150 km/94 mi

General description: Route 13A follows Hwy 2 north to Calgary passing from a flat and intensively farmed landscape to rolling ranchlands and country residential development south of Calgary. The highway passes through the towns of Claresholm and Nanton. The communities of High River and Okotoks lie just west of Hwy 2 on Hwy 2A.
Unique features: Museum of the Highwood, Big Rock.
Wildlife viewing opportunities: Willow Creek Provincial Park.
Activities: Golf, horseback riding, hiking, mountain biking opportunities in the Porcupine Hills.
Events: Claresholm Fair and Rodeo (August) 403-625-3381; High River; Little Britches Rodeo (June) 403-652-2110; Pro Rodeo (June) 403-652-2110; Nanton Round Up Days 403-646-2020; Okotoks Antique Days.
Travel season: Year-round.
Services: Full services are available in the towns of Claresholm, Nanton, High River, and Okotoks. Limited services are available in the communities of Granum and Stavely.
Road conditions and route description: Highway 2 north from Granum is a four-lane, divided highway to High River and a four-lane highway from High River to Calgary. Twinning of the 20-km/12.5-mi section from Granum to Fort Macleod will be completed by 1993.

The route: This route provides an alternative to Route 13 for travelers who are planning to return south along the Trail of the Great Bear. From Ft. Macleod, the route travels north along the eastern flanks of the Porcupine Hills following the general route of a branch line of the Canadian Pacific Railway constructed in 1892. The railway established the communities and small towns along the southern part of the route—Granum, Claresholm, Stavely, and Nanton to serve the settlers they had brought in to take up the agricultural lands they had been granted by the government of Canada for constructing the railroad. The railroad company also sold to those who could afford them "prepackaged" homes, barns, and outbuildings. Grain elevators and sidings were established every 16 km/10 miles, the distance a farmer could haul a horse-drawn wagonload of grain in a day. The communities were laid out on a standard T-shaped town plan with the railroad forming the bar of the T. Nanton is the best example along this route.

Highway 2 grew out of the Ft. Macleod-Ft. Calgary Trail, which had been used for hauling passengers and freight before the coming of the railway in 1892. Highway 2 has undergone considerable transformation in the years since. Originally it passed through all the communities. In the early 1960s the first four-lane sections were completed south of Calgary. A new route was selected passing well to the east of the towns of High River and Okotoks. Originally the highway engineers planned to bypass all the communities further south; however, local politics prevailed and in the case of Nanton and Claresholm the highway was routed through the towns.

High River and Okotoks are located only a few minutes to the west of Highway 2 on Highway 2A and are worth a visit.

High River, named after the Highwood River—so named because of the extensive cottonwood communities at this locale—known to the Blackfoot as Spitzee—was one of their favorite wintering camps. Peter Fidler, the first white man to explore the foothills of southern Alberta, camped here in the winter of 1792. Like the Oldman to the south, Spitzee also became a focus for the whiskey trade in the 1870s. A series of small posts were established in and above today's town. Liver Eating Johnson, later to become the famous Mountain Man, Jeremiah Johnson, of the Yellowstone Country, was one of the operators.

After the NWMP came, a stopping house was established at the crossing of the Highwood, and the town grew becoming a focus for the surrounding ranching community, as did Fort Macleod and Pincher Creek at the south end of the Porcupine Hills. The ranch lands, the finest in North America, attracted a variety of well-educated men, retired Northwest Mounted Police (many of whom were from monied families in the East and only served their required two years before retiring to take up ranching), retired British East Indian Army officers, and a group of monied young Englishmen and Easterners known as "Remittance Men" who were "black sheep" and sent out by their families to the West with a small allowance (remittance). These ne'er-do-well young men generally preferred to do anything else but work. One of the gentlemen ranchers favorite sports was polo. In the late 1800s polo clubs sprung up throughout the ranching communities in the hills. Few survived the years of the First World War. One which did was High River, the oldest continously operating Polo Club in Western Canada. Polo has once more been revived as the sport of choice along with fox hunts among the gentlemen ranchers/oil tycoons of the Calgary region. Many of these historic scenes are depicted in larger-than-life murals throughout the city.

The older sections of High River still maintain much of their historic character. You can learn about the towns' early history by visiting the Museum of the Highwood in High River, open seven days a week from the first of May to the end of August from 10:00 a.m. to 5:00 p.m. and during the rest of the year by appointment only. For more information write Museum of the Highwood, Bag 10, Highriver, AB TOL 1BO or phone 403-652-7156. Continuing north on Highway 2A, 20 km/12.5 mi brings you to the community of Okotoks, which is the Blackfoot word for Big Rock. This Big Rock, the largest glacial erratic in the world is located 7 km/ 4.4 mi west of town on Highway 7 and well worth a visit. After visiting Big Rock and Okotoks you continue north on Highway 2A rejoining Highway 2, 8 km/ 5 mi north of town. You can also quench your thirst at the Ginger Tea Room, a Victorian reproduction of an older era located in Okotoks.

Big Rock, a glacial erratic

Big Rock is one of many boulders in the Foothill Erratics Train, a string of boulders that extends from the Athabasca Valley (at the north end of the Trail of the Great Bear) down into northern Montana. An erratic is a rock that's been transported far from its place of origin. Glacial ice started the process when massive landslides spilled rock on the glacier that flowed through the Athabasca Valley (clear up near Jasper) and eastward onto the plains. After turning south, this glacier dumped boulders and may have unloaded rocks on top of lake ice.

During the ice age, an ice-free corridor existed between the mountain glaciers along the East Front and the prairie ice sheet. A chain of deep lakes existed in this corridor, the waters of which flowed south. So, as the theory goes, when the lakes froze in the winter, erratics rolled off the glacial ice and onto lake ice. (By the way, the frozen lake surfaces provided a travel route to the south for humans and other animals seeking a way to escape the cold but ice-free region of northern Alaska and western Yukon.) Come summer, the lake ice broke up and ice rafts floated the erratics south. Whatever the case, Big Rock is the largest member of the Foothills Erratic Train; other examples can be seen on the western outskirts of Calgary. To find Big Rock, at Black Diamond on Highway 22, turn right (east) onto Highway 7 and follow it 12 km/7 mi. The Blackfoot and Kootenai painted pictographs on erratics for spiritual reasons or to turn the rock into a commemorative memorial. Some panels still remain on Big Rock though they've faded due to the passage of time and cattle rubbing along the base. Blackfoot folklore offers an equally fascinating story about the origin of the erratic train.

Napi was walking along when he saw a boulder (this was a very big boulder). "You've been out here a long time with nothing to keep you warm," he said, spreading his robe over the rock. "Thank you," said the boulder. As Napi continued on, dark clouds rolled in from the mountains. "Looks like rain," said Napi and he asked a coyote to retrieve his robe. The coyote ran back to the boulder but the big rock said, "No, Napi gave it to me. What is he, some kind of Indian-giver?" The coyote passed this on to Napi, so Napi walked back and took the robe. The rock got mad and rolled after Napi. Napi was pretty scared and as he ran he called to the prairie dogs for help; this was back when prairie dogs were as big as us. They tried to stop the rock but it rolled right over the prairie dogs, which is what made them small.

Next Napi called to the birds for help. Birds swooped down from the sky and pecked at the rolling boulder. Some of those birds got their faces caved-in; today, those are the owls. Slowly the birds pecked the boulder to pieces that are scattered for a long ways up and down the prairie. The boulder finally stopped. Today we call that place Big Rock. Napi walked away with the robe on his shoulders and a smile on his face.-*Brian Reeves*

ROUTE 13B: HWY 1A CALGARY-CANMORE   135 km/ 84 mi

General description: From Calgary Route 13B, travels west along Highway 1A on the north side of the Bow Valley, passing through magnificent foothills and river valley landscapes into the Front Range of the Rocky Mountains, rejoining Route 15 at Canmore, the east entrance to Banff National Park.
Travel season: Year-round.
Services: Full services in Calgary, Cochrane, and Canmore.
Road conditions and route description: Highway 1A is an all-weather, two-lane highway.

The route: Highway 1A provides an excellent alternative to Highway 1 for traveling west from Calgary. From Calgary, you travel west through the highlands along the north side of the Bow Valley, an area of rolling ranchland and country residential development. Thirty-eight km/24 mi west lies the town of Cochrane situated within the Bow Valley at the foot of the Big Hill. Just before you descend the Big Hill there is an unimproved pull-off on your left from which you have a sweeping view of the Bow Valley foothills and Rocky Mountains.

Cochrane is named after the Cochrane Ranche, which was the largest cattle lease ranch established in the west in 1881. The Cochrane Ranche Company leased 190,000 acres/76,000 ha for $1.00 per acre, brought cattle in from Washington and Montana, purchasing an additional 4,500 head in 1882. Most of the cattle died in the blizzards of the following winter. A self-guiding interpretation of the ranch history is provided at the Cochrane Ranche Historic Site operated by Alberta Culture and Multiculturalism on the west side of town. The historic site includes the original ranchstead, with a reconstructed bunkhouse situated alongside Big Hill Springs Creek. For more information on the Cochrane Ranche write: Cochrane Ranche Provincial Historic Site, Box 1522, Cochrane, Alberta TOL OWO; 403-427-2022.

The Western Heritage Centre is also located on the Cochrane Ranch property (you access it from Highway 22). When opened the center will provide a multi-media interpretation of the ranching and rodeo industry. It will be a must for western buffs to visit. For more information on the center write: Western Heritage Centre, Box 1477, Cochrane, Alberta TOL OWO or phone 403-932-3514.

Highway 1A continues westward up the Bow Valley passing through magnificent grassland and forested foothills. Twenty-two km/14 mi west you cross the Ghost River, a tributary of the Bow, which is here dammed by the Ghost River Dam, the easternmost of three hydro dams constructed on the Bow in the early decades of this century. There is a day-use picnic area and boat launch.

Ten km/6 mi west from the crossing of the Ghost along Highway 1A is the Morleyville Mission and Settlement established in 1873 by the Methodist missionary Reverand John MacDougall. The mission site is located immediately east of the Stony Indian Reserve in a historic setting. The mission church, built in the 1870s, stands today. It is a designated Provincial Historic Site and open on a limited basis to the public. The mission was the first Christian church and Methodist mission in southern Alberta. For more information on the mission write McDougall Mission Historic Site Tours, 3707 Utah Drive NW, Calgary, Alberta T2N 4A6.

Highway 1A continues westward through the Stony Indian Reserve, passing by the community of Morley where the tribal administration and school buildings are located. West of Morley, the reserve landscapes have been the setting for many Hollywood westerns (including Buffalo Bill and the Indians) and recently the Japanese epic movie "Heaven and Earth." Ten km/ 6 mi west of the turnoff to Morley lies Stony Indian Park. Located here are day and overnight recreation facilities, a bison paddock, a convenience store, and service station.

The site of Old Bow Fort is also located in the Park. This post (also known as Peigan Post) was established in 1832 by the Hudson Bay Company to create a post south of Rocky Mountain House (located on Route 16), to compete for the Blackfoot Indian trade with James Kipp's American Fur Company post, Fort MacKenzie, located on the Missouri River below today's Fort Benton. Peigan Post was abandoned in 1834 in favor of reopening Rocky Mountain House. The post's architecture was unusual in that it was a pentagonal shape. There is a plaque to commemorate the site and an excellent view up the Bow from Fort Point.

Continuing west, 2km/1.2 mi, just before you cross Old Fort Creek is the turnoff to Nakota Lodge, a cultural and conference center with lodge, restaurant, and gift shop developed and operated by the Good Stony band. (There are three bands on the Stony Reserve—the Good Stony, Chiniki, and Bearspaw.) For more information write Nakota Lodge, Box 149, Morley, Alberta TOL INO, or call 403-881-3949.

The foothills now give way abruptly to the limestone walls of the Rocky Mountain Front. Bow Valley Provincial Park is located on the south side of the Bow (see Route 13) and is accessed by Highway 1X, the connector between Highway 1 and 1A. West of 1X, 1A continues to wind along the north side of the Bow, passing by two limestone mining communities— Kananaskis, where lime works were first started in the 1880s, and Exshaw, the location of a major cement factory. At one time the eastern boundary of Banff National Park—then known as Rocky Mountain National Park— encompassed all the Front.

Gradually it was "trimmed" back to accommodate various interests. Canadian park boundaries, unlike those in the United States, once established were not inviolate.—*Brian Reeves*

Events and Services

Calgary Visitor and Convention Bureau: 237 - 8th Avenue SE, Calgary, Alberta T2G 0K8; 403-263-8510 or 800-661-1678.

Glenbow Museum: 130 9th Avenue SE, Calgary, AB; 403-264-8300 or 403-237-8988.

Fort Calgary: 403-269-7747.

Wildlife Viewing

Chain Lakes Provincial Park: 403-646-5887 in summer and 403-627-2021 in winter.

Sheep River Wildlife Sanctuary: Fish and Wildlife Division, Calgary, Alberta; 403-297-6423.

Fish Creek Provincial Park: Provincial Parks Service, 403-297-5293.

Inglewood Bird Sanctuary: Calgary Parks and Recreation, 403-269-6688.

East Kananaskis Country Information for Elbow Valley and Sheep River Wildlife Sanctuary: Kananaskis Country, Suite 100, 1011 Glenmore Trail S.W., Calgary, Alberta T2V 4R6, 403-297-3362, or Box 280, Canmore, Alberta TOL OMO, 403-678-5508.

Provincial Parks

Bow Valley Provincial Park: 403-673-3663.

Fish Creek Provincial Park: Provincial Parks Service, 403-297-5293.

A Short Course in Comparative Religions
(From *These Are Our Sacred Mountains,* By Chief John Snow)

Does not wisdom call, does not understanding raise her voice? On the heights beside the way, in the path she takes her stand; beside the gates in front of the town, at the entrance of the portals she cries aloud. [From the Bible: Proverbs 8:1-3.]

Wisdom of Nature calls at all seasons, when will you learn from her instruction, understanding speaks aloud and gives sound reasons, when will you listen, hear and take discretion. At the entrance of the forest wisdom hails, at the entrance of the prairies she is at hand, at the heights beside the mountain trails and in the valleys she takes her stand.

[From Stony elders.]

Fisherman on the North Fork of the Oldman River. Darrin Schreder photo.

Kananaskis Country

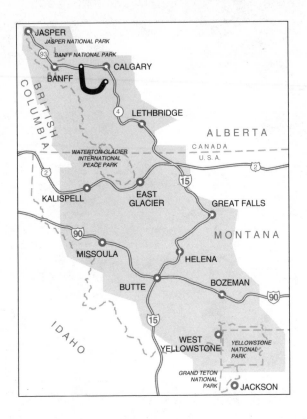

"For the fate of the sons of men and the fate of beasts is the same; as one dies, so dies the other. They all have the same breath, and man has no advantage over the beasts; for all is vanity."

The Bible, Ecclesiastes 3:19.

ROUTE 14

LONGVIEW to BOW VALLEY PROVINCIAL PARK

159 kilometers/99 miles

General description: From the subdued and rolling foothills traversed by Highway 541 to Canada's highest driveable pass crossed by Highway 40, this section presents some of the most diverse and impressive country found on the Trail of the Great Bear. While Section 14 provides few cultural or historic attractions, it offers a rich variety of natural surroundings and outdoor activities.

Unique features: Kananaskis Country, Peter Lougheed Interpretation Centre, William Watson Lodge.

Wildlife viewing opportunities: Highwood Pass and King Creek in Peter Lougheed Provincial Park.

Activities: Mountaineering, backpacking, snowmobiling, cross-country and downhill skiing, mountain biking, golf, fishing.

Travel season: Highway 40 is open year-round to the winter gate just beyond the turnoff to the Kananaskis Lakes; from there to Highway 541 is closed from December 1 to June 15.

Services: Basic grocery needs and gas at Longview, Highwood House, and Fortress Junction Service Centre; meals and lodging at Longview and Kananaskis Village.

Road conditions and route description: At Longview, turn left onto Highway 541, a good, two-lane road, and drive 50 km/31 mi to Highwood House and the beginning of Highway 40, a well-maintained, two-lane road (closed from Highwood House junction to Peter Lougheed winter gate between December 1 to June 15). Highway 40 extends 109 km/68 mi to where it intersects with Trans-Canada Highway 1.

The route: Highway 541 traverses rolling foothills west of Longview as it follows the Highwood River towards the Rocky Mountains. The scenery for all but the last 8 km/5 mi of Highway 541 is fairly subdued; but at the border of the Kananaskis Country a dramatic transformation occurs. The area takes its name from a story told to Captain John Palliser, who, along with Lieutenant Thomas Blakiston and Dr. James Hector, led an exploratory expedition from 1857-59 that was as important to Alberta as the Lewis and Clark Expedition was to Montana. Palliser wrote that he had heard of an Indian named Kananaskis, "giving account of his most wonderful recovery from the blow of an axe [to the head] which stunned but failed to kill him." Palliser named two lakes, two passes, and a river Kananaskis; apparently the word conveys a dual meaning, "man with a tomahawk in his head" and "meeting of the waters." That the Kananaskis Country possesses a name with two completely different meanings seems appropriate; here, people can drive past oil wells and slalom around grazing cattle while headed for a backpack trip through country wild enough to support grizzlies and, upon return to the trailhead, dine on haute cuise in a world-class restaurant.

Financed since 1978 by the Alberta Heritage Savings Trust Fund, the Kananaskis Country encompasses more than 4,000 sq km/1,600 sq mi of incredibly scenic country that ranges from rolling montane foothills on the eastern side to the almost surrealistic alpine peaks that flank Highway 40. While the area contains wildlands, forest reserves, a natural area, and a wildlife sanctuary, it also accommodates livestock grazing, mining, logging, oil development, and more.

Whatever your opinion might be, there's no denying that in terms of car-camping and outdoor recreation such as cross-country skiing, mountain biking, and interpretive trail walking—this is *the* most user-friendly natural area on the entire Trail of the Great Bear (especially Peter Lougheed Provincial Park). For cross-country skiers, there are more than 300 km/185 mi of groomed ski trails. More than 425 km/264 mi of trails await snowmobilers at the McLean Creek/Sibbald Flat and Cataract Creek areas. Kananaskis Country also offers 3,000 auto-accessible campsites divided between twenty campgrounds, 400 winter auto-accessible campsites, and thirty backcountry campgrounds for backpackers and horsepackers.

Up from the Highwood Junction

At the Highwood House junction, Secondary 940 leads down to the Cataract Creek area which is specially designated for snowmobiling in the winter, and Highway 541 becomes Highway 40; this is also where the (south) gate closes during the winter from December 1 to June 15 for the benefit of wildlife. Chinook winds clear away snows and help make this valley bottom critical winter habitat for elk, moose, deer, and bighorn sheep. In addition, the drainage supports mountain goats, cougar, black bear, grizzlies, wolves, and wolverine. And throughout the summer, as you'll see while continuing up Highway 40, the area also furnishes feed to cattle.

People must love lost gold mines because they're scattered all over the continent, at least in folklore. In Arizona's Superstition Mountains, the Lost Dutchman defies rediscovery. Here in the Highwood area, it's the Lost Lemon Mine. Legend tells of two prospectors, Lemon and Blackjack, who unearthed a rich vein of gold. Consumed by greed, Lemon murdered Blackjack, trekked out with a little gold, and never returned. The Stonys, realizing how gold affected whitemen and wanting to safeguard their hunting grounds, placed a curse on it. A number of fortune seekers have been the victims of strange and sudden deaths. Once, hikers found a skeleton with a pouch of gold clutched in its boney fingers. Even though their curse played havoc with prospectors, it didn't prevent the Stonys from losing their hunting grounds.

Canada's highest driveable pass

The road (surrounded by the Highwood Road Corridor Wildlife Sanctuary) passes incredible fairytale-like mountains in its ascent to Highwood Pass. This route runs right through the heart of some wonderful mountaineering opportunities; the bases of many of these mountains are extremely accessible. Be sure and observe the vegetation changes as you ascend to the top of the pass that, at 2,206 m/7,236 ft, is the highest driveable pass in Canada. Two trails take off from Highwood Pass (and it's a rare treat to begin a hike so close to timberline). The easy and short (0.9 km/.55 mi) Highwood Meadows Trail extends (one-way) through a subalpine meadow; the trail is barrier-free and designated wheelchair accessible. The Ptarmigan Cirque Trail is a 5 km/3 mi loop trip that ascends to an alpine meadow with a grand view.

If you didn't stretch your legs on either of the previous two trails, at least allow yourself a little ART (Attitude Readjustment Time) at the Rock Glacier

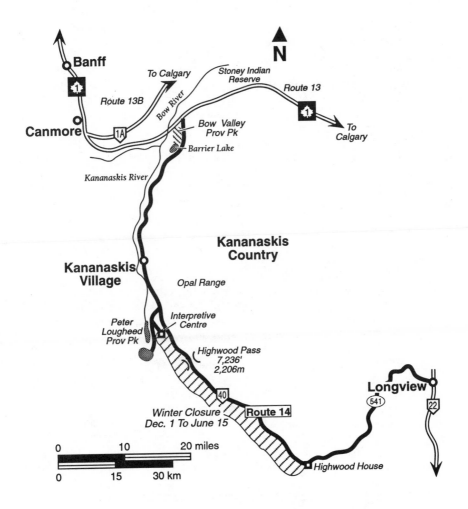

Interpretive Trail. Here you can learn about rock glaciers and, if you're quiet and patient, a pika might crawl out from beneath a rock to sun himself. These little grey lagomorphs (like rabbits and not a rodent like mice) are heard more than seen. They're also known as rock-rabbits and live, all along the Trail of the Great Bear, in alpine rockfields near vegetation. Pikas consume a portion of their waste because the first time through, the grasses, sedges, and leaves are barely digested. Recycling first-time-out pellets renders much more nourishment.

While traveling this route, you really should be prepared to stop often and explore this country from different vantage points. A short drive up a dirt road to Elpoca leads to a pleasant picnic area and a grand view of the Kananaskis Lakes, Peter Lougheed Provincial Park, the Spray Range, and the mountains that form the Continental Divide. Surprising as it might seem, these spectacular mountains—with their serrated and steep ridges, stacked one behind the other and topped with precipitous spires and pinnacles—once laid flat. Between 380 and 155 million years ago, an inland sea (that extended from the Gulf of Mexico to the Arctic) inundated this portion of Alberta. This warm sea supported lots of life that, when it died, drifted to the ocean floor along with other sediment. The sediment stacked, layer upon layer, and the weight of the upper layers squished the moisture out of the lower layers; this, in addition to chemical actions, transformed the sediment into sedimentary rock. Later, a huge chunk of the earth's surface, the Pacific Oceanic Plate, collided with the North American Continental Plate causing it to buckle. The buckling tilted layers of sedimentary rock up almost perpendicular to their original position. Add liberal quantities of rain, ice, and wind-induced erosion and the result is the striking mountains we see here today.

Peter Lougheed

The north winter-closure gate is located just south of the turnoff to the Kananaskis Lakes Trail (Park Road). After turning left (west) onto this road and crossing a bridge, watch for Pocaterra Hut; this wetlands is a good place to watch for deer, elk, and aquatic mammals. The Peter Lougheed Interpretive Centre is the best interpretive centre found on the Trail of the Great Bear; the place makes learning just plain fun. In fact, if there's any criticism that can be leveled at the centre, it's that children become so engrossed with the interactive programs that they end up staring at video screens for hours on end instead of exploring natural wonders for themselves out in the woods. Programs provide information about mountain building, glaciation, the effect on vegetation from low mountain passes, mountain waters, and living things, eco-insights, and wildlife. The mammal habitat interactive program is especially fun and creative. All of the innovative people that developed the material in this centre and the helpful staff that answer questions and keep the ball rolling deserve a major pat on the back.

The Kananaskis Lake area of Peter Lougheed Provincial Park also offers paved bike trails and five interpretive trails. A morning hike up the 2 km/1.25 mi "1982 Canadian Mount Everest Expedition Trail" begins the day with excellent views of the surrounding mountain ranges (the mountains to the east form the Opal Range). There are six auto-accessible campgrounds in this area. The extent and quality of the facilities offered to handicapped and disabled people at William Watson Lodge are unmatched on the Trail of the Great Bear. The lodge is named for an Albertan who worked much of his life to improve conditions

Kananaskis Village.

for disabled people. From birth, Watson lacked the use of his paralyzed arms but that didn't prevent him from learning to write, ski, swim, and earn a bachelor's degree and law degree. Due to his disability, he wasn't allowed to practice law so he commited his life to improving conditions for disabled people so that they could lead as normal and productive a life as possible. The lodge's philosophy rests on the concept of providing disabled persons access to a wilderness setting via accommodations (not special programs). The eight cabins (with a total of eighty single beds) and the lodge were designed to minimize natural and structural hindrances and to allow increased accessibility to people whose mobility is limited. The facility also maintains a five-unit, barrier-free vehicle campground, a six-unit, barrier-free tent campground, eight picnic sites, an observation deck, a marsh lookout, a group campfire circle, paved or compacted trails, and wintertime ski trail access to the park's 75 km/47 mi of cross-country ski trails. There is also an accessible fishing area. This, however, is a half-hour north of the lodge up Highway 40 at the Mount Lorette Ponds. Reservations can be made over the phone and confirmed by mail; call 403-591-7227 or 403-591-7229. Maximum stay at the lodge is seven nights; it's open year-round except for two-week closures in November and April, and on December 24 and 25.

Across from the Kananaskis Lakes Trail is King Creek (picnic area); a mineral lick makes this an excellent place to watch for deer, elk, moose, and especially bighorn sheep. Farther north, the route runs along the east side of the Spray Lakes/Ribbon Creek Area where you find highly developed recreational sites. Two eighteen-hole golf courses, Mount Kidd and Mount Lorette, provide a challenge. Kananaskis Village offers resort accommodations, first-class restaurants, shops, and boutiques. There are two regular car-camping campgrounds in this area. The Mt. Kidd Recreational Vehicle Park is anything but regular. In addition to 229 campsites, the park offers tennis courts, whirlpools, cycling paths, fast food, and more. Two downhill ski areas, Fortress Moutain (403-591-7108) and Ski Nakiska at Mount Allan (403-591-7777), operate in this area.

Near the north end of this route, in the Barrier Lake area, rock-climbers have established a number of routes. From Barrier Lake, the route continues a short ways to Trans-Canada Highway 1.

Lake from the top of the Mount Everest Expedition Trail in Peter Lougheed Provincial Park.

For More Information About Route 14:

Events and Services

Chinook Country Tourist Association: 2805 Scenic Drive, Lethbridge, Alberta T1K5B7; 1-800-661-1222, or 403-329-6777.

William Watson Lodge: 403-591-7227 or 403-591-7229.

Kananaskis Country: Suite 100, 1011 Glenmore Trail SW, Calgary, Alberta T2V 4R6; 403-297-3362.

Kananaskis Village: 1-800-332-1013.

Provincial Parks

Peter Lougheed Provincial Park Visitor Information Centre: 403-591-7222.

Where Mountains and Ice Reign Supreme

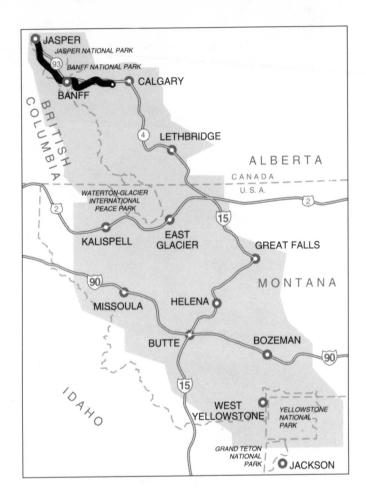

"...like some fantastic dream from a tale of the Arabian nights."

William McCardell's description of the cave at Cave and Basin, the hot spring that led to the creation of Canada's first national park.

ROUTE 15

BOW VALLEY PROVINCIAL PARK to LAKE LOUISE
103 kilometers/64 miles

General description: Some of the most spectacular mountain country on the Trail of the Great Bear is found on this final section. Trans-Canada Highway 1 enters Banff, Canada's first national park, and continues, via the Bow Valley Parkway, to Lake Louise.

Unique features: Banff National Park, the Cave and Basin Hot Springs, Banff Springs Hotel, Johnston Canyon, Lake Louise, Jasper National Park, Parker Ridge, Athabasca Glacier and Columbia Icefield, Maligne Canyon.

Wildlife viewing opportunities: All along this section, travelers commonly see elk, deer, eagles, bighorn sheep, ravens, and coyotes; it isn't unusual to also spot wolves, moose, grizzly, and black bear.

Activities: Hiking, mountain biking, fishing, golf, cross-country and downhill skiing, backpacking, mountaineering, sailboarding, river rafting.

Events: Banff Festival of the Arts, Banff Festival of Mountain Films, Jasper Winter Festival, Banff/Lake Louise Winter Festival.

Travel season: Year-round.

Services: All services are readily available along this section and especially concentrated in Canmore, Banff, and Jasper.

Road conditions and route description: Trans-Canada Highway 1 is an excellent, four-lane freeway. West of the Banff townsite, a more scenic and less speedy option exists to follow the Bow Valley Parkway (Highway 1A), a well- maintained, two-lane road. Highways 1 and 1A merge at Lake Louise Village.

The route: The route begins where, 20,000 years ago, the Kananaskis and Bow Valley glaciers (both of them more than 600-m/1,968-ft thick) merged and scoured the spacious montane Bow Valley. The main Bow Glacier started up near Lake Louise and flowed out to the prairie near Calgary. While this entire route passes a landscape of unsurpassed mountain beauty, the beginning of Route 15, where limestone quarries strip away the flanks of Grotto Mountain, provides an excellent abject lesson about what happens to an area that lacks formal protection.

Canmore is a must for anyone who cross-country skis in the winter or mountain bikes in the summer. Canmore started, in 1883, as a train stop for the Canadian Pacific Railway and became an industrial town with discovery of coal soon after. However, the town has since taken advantage of the tourist industry. Today, the Canmore Nordic Centre, site of the 1988 Olympic Winter Games Nordic Ski Events, offers 56 km/35 mi of groomed trail for track-skiers and skaters. This extensive network of trails is available, free of charge, to skiers in the winter and to mountain bikers and hikers in the summer. (For more information: Canmore Nordic Centre, Box 1979, Canmore, Alberta TOL OMO1; 403-678-2400.) A Travel Alberta Information Centre is located on Highway 1A on the west end of Canmore (403-678-5277).

ROUTE 15 *BOW VALLEY TO LAKE LOUISE*

Mistaya Canyon.

Across from Canmore, located on a unpaved road (signs point the way), the Alpine Club of Canada operates the Canmore Clubhouse. While Canadian climbers may be accustomed to such pleasant accommodations, climbers from the United States are bound to be surprised by this facility, that overlooks the Bow Valley and the Three Sisters above Canmore. It has a full kitchen, sauna, showers, laundry, licensed lounge, and an extensive library of mountain literature. The bunk and dormitory-style lodging helps keep the cost of staying at the clubhouse low. Protection of the mountain environment has been a focus of the Alpine Club of Canada ever since A.O. Wheeler formed it in 1906. The club is also dedicated to mountaineering and wilderness travel education and maintains eight mountain huts in Banff National Park and four in Jasper National Park; huts are equipped with Coleman stoves, lanterns, dishes, and foamies. The Canadian Alpine Centre and International Hostel at Lake Louise offers accommodations similar to the Canmore Clubhouse and access to classic ascents of mountains in the Lake Louise area. (For clubhouse, hut, or membership information: Canmore Clubhouse, Box 519, Canmore, Alberta T0L 0M0; 403-678-5855.)

Banff

A short drive beyond Canmore, Trans-Canada Highway 1 enters Banff, Canada's first and the world's third national park. For those stopping in the park, one-day, four-day, and annual permits can be purchased at the entry station; travel on the Icefields Parkway requires a permit. Now, you're about to begin a journey through the longest and most spectacular stretch of mountainous terrain found on the Trail of the Great Bear. When Edward Whymper (the famous mountaineer whose name is synonymous with the Matterhorn) spoke of this region, he called it "twenty Switzerlands in one."

Since you're on the verge of entering the Banff Townsite, this is a good time to discuss the difference between Canadian and United States national parks. Both countries drafted similar national park legislation that basically stated parklands would be preserved in a natural state and set aside as a public park or pleasuring-ground for the benefit and enjoyment of the people. Interpretation of this mandate resulted in some big differences between national parks in Canada and the United States.

The story of Canada's first national park opens with the skullduggery involved in the attempt of three Canadian Pacific Railway workers, McCardell and the McCabe brothers, to establish a mineral rights claim on the Cave and Basin hot springs. "Steam, Schemes and National Dreams," an exceptionally well-made documentary shown regularly at the Cave and Basin Centennial Centre, projects this story on the silver screen. The story's bottom line is that two railway magnates (one of which was William Cornelius Van Horne who will come up later) approached the federal government with the idea of turning the hot springs into a protected reserve—with the Canadian Pacific Railway

Mount Temple.

providing its expertise in developing tourism facilities, accommodations, and transport. The Prime Minister John A. Macdonald voiced the Canadian government's realization that a public reserve could be profitable when he said, "these springs will recuperate the patient and recoup the treasury."

The Cave and Basin Centennial Centre still offers a pleasant soak in addition to an interpretive centre, a fine documentary film, and, of course, a tea house.

Meanwhile, back in the past, the completion of the railroad through the Rockies created a huge deficit for the Canadian Pacific Railway; it needed to make money fast which inspired Van Horne to say, "Since we can't export the scenery, we'll have to import the tourists." He called for a grand hotel to be built overlooking the confluence of the Bow and Spring rivers. When the Banff Springs Hotel opened in 1888 it was the world's largest hotel and charged $3.50 (lowest rate) per night. Today room rates for a single begin at $160 per night (403-762-2211). It is a world class-hotel accommodating visitors from around the globe offering elegance in the wilderness.

Banff Townsite

The Banff townsite was laid out in 1886. Today Banff, with its unique international atmosphere, is a bustling little metropolis surrounded by national park. Because parking is at a premium, you're encouraged to park and walk. The Banff Park Museum, first established in 1895, is a turn-of-the-century collection of stuffed animals in a Victorian-style building. (Open daily, year-round, from 10 a.m. to 6 p.m.; no admission charged; 403-762-3324, extension 4295.) The Luxton Museum displays a wealth of Native artistic craft and the daily life of Native people of the Northern Plains and Canadian Rockies. (Open May 15 to October 15 from 9 a.m. to 6 p.m.; winter hours are noon to 5 p.m.; admission charged; 403-762-2388.)

In 1958, artists Peter and Catharine Whyte established the foundation that runs the Whyte Museum of the Canadian Rockies (403-762-2291). On the advice of a Stony friend, they named it "Wa-Che-Yo-Cha-Pa Foundation," which basically means "a place where all things good, wise, and beautiful are brought together in harmony." Anyone interested in mountains, mountaineering, or mountain life could easily spend hours here. The museum's mandate is to be "an international centre for the celebration of the relationship between culture and mountains." The museum exhibits, preserves, and interprets mountain materials from the Canadian Rockies and around the world. The Archives of the Canadian Rockies houses the largest collection of historic and artistic information (4,000 volumes) about the surrounding mountains. The museum also hosts lectures, films, and other special events throughout the year. The Whyte Museum of the Canadian Rockies charges nominal admission and is open from mid-May to mid-October, 10 a.m. to 6 p.m. daily—in the winter, Tuesday through Sunday from 1 p.m. to 5 p.m. Another event for mountain enthusiasts is the Banff Festival of Mountain Films held in early-November. Billed as "the event in the adventure community for people who love mountains and films, camaraderie, adventure, adrenalin and fun!" For more information write The Banff Centre for Management, Box 1020, Banff, Alberta T0L 0C0 or call 403-762-6422.

Banff Centre for the Arts (403-762-6100) provides students with advanced instruction in an environment that can't help but inspire artistic endeavors; the spin-off benefit to the community comes in the form of the Banff Festival

The Bow Falls and Banff Springs Hotel.

of the Arts (Theatre Box Office: 403-762-6300) that offers more than 130 performances in jazz, dance, drama, opera, visual arts, readings, lectures, and more from June to mid-August. The Banff/Lake Louise Winter Festival, during the last week of February, offers a torchlight parade, town party, snow sculptures, "mountain madness" crazy slalom and alpine ski races, snow golf, and dog sled races.

Should Banff's pace prove overwhelming, seek the Fen Trail for a little ART (Attitude Readjustment Time). Take a picnic, eat it at the trailhead, and then digest lunch with a stroll along the self-guided interpretive trail. As the trail pamphlet says, "...minutes away from Banff, and an eternity away in mood..." The Buffalo Paddock is located at the north end of Banff; a drive inside the paddock offers people a chance to see wood bison (morning and evening are recommended times). There are three auto-accessible campgrounds in the general area; one on the Tunnel Mountain Drive and two out on the Lake Minnewanka Road—which leads to Lake Minnewanka, the park's largest lake and a popular place to boat, fish, sail, take a scenic boat ride, and take a self-guided interpretive trail at Bankhead. At the height of operations (which were conducted in a national park), the coal mining town of Bankhead supported a population of a 1,000 people. Branching off (left) of the Mount Norquay Road takes you out on Vermilion Lakes Drive past the Vermilion Lakes. The often photographed view of Mount Rundle can be seen from the lakes. Bring binoculars and you may see bighorn sheep, beaver, Canada geese, bald eagles, osprey, coyote, and deer. This area also contains a rich and significant record of Native occupation that extends back more than 10,000 years.

Two parallel roads lead to Lake Louise—Trans-Canada Highway 1 and Highway 1A, which is the more scenic and less hectic drive. Johnston Canyon is a deeply eroded limestone canyon. While Mistaya and Maligne canyons are more spectacular, the trails there follow the rim. At Johnston Canyon however, a unique trail offers a hike within the canyon that is 30 m/98 ft deep at the deepest and narrows to 6 m/20 ft. Should you travel by way of Highway 1A, look at the aspen trees; there are areas where the lower trunks appear grey or black in contrast to the upper white trunk. This darkened trunk extends up for at least 2 m/6 ft and is the result of elk rubbing the velvet that encases, protects, and nourishes new antlers. On the way to Lake Louise, you pass three campgrounds.

The chateau overlooking Lake Louise began, in 1886, as a humble cabin that was replaced with the first *chateau* which was just a larger log cabin. At that time, visitors arrived on horseback or foot. After chateau-1 burned to the ground, a split-level structure was built that housed twelve people. With the addition of two wings in 1900, guest capacity increased to 200. While the Canadian Pacific Railway marketed the Lake Louise Chateau as rustic lodging for outdoor enthusiasts, track for a narrow-gauge mini-train was laid in 1912 to make the ascent to Lake Louise easier (it ran until 1930). In 1913, the Painter Wing added capacity for another 400 people. The wooden wings burned eleven years later and were replaced by a concrete wing. In 1986, the Glacier Wing with 150 rooms was built in addition to much redevelopment (403-522-3511). A convention center is still slated for construction. Mount Victoria, the most photographed and ascended peak in the range, rises above the emerald-green waters of Lake Louise to reach an elevation of 3,464 m/11,365 ft. A popular hike from the chateau ascends 365 m/1,197 ft to Lake Agnes along a 3.5 km/2 mi trail where

The view north over Peyto Lake and towards Jasper from the Bow Summit overlook.

pika, marmots, ground squirrels, and Clark's nutcrackers can be seen along the way. A teahouse is located at Lake Agnes.

ROUTE 15A: THE ICEFIELD PARKWAY   229 km/142 mi

General description: Often called the world's most beautiful road, the Icefield Parkway (Highway 93) proceeds from Lake Louise through a mountain world full of iridescent blue lakes and glistening alpine glaciers. On the other side of Sunwapta Pass, you can nearly drive to the foot of the Athabasca Glacier. Route 15A ends at the picturesque town of Jasper.
Services: Lake Louise and Jasper, year-round; Columbia Icefield and Saskatchewan River Crossing offer seasonal services.
Road conditions and route description: Just beyond Lake Louise, the Icefields Parkway continues north to Jasper on Highway 93, a well-maintained, two-lane road.

The route: Just beyond Lake Louise Village, Route 15 exits from Trans-Canada Highway 1 and follows Highway 93 up the Icefields Parkway. The valley becomes more densely vegetated with lodgepole pine, Englemann spruce, and subalpine fir which explains why Native people, trappers, and people with good sense avoided it. Called "The Wonder Trail" by explorer A.P. Coleman, the Icefields Parkway owes its existence to numerous mountaineers that established the route while on climbing expeditions; it was constructed and first traveled by cars in 1940. Between Lake Louise and Sunwapta Pass (the boundary between Jasper and Banff national parks) there are four campgrounds.

At the upper end of Bow Lake you'll notice on the left that there are no trees growing in the valley bottom and yet trees appear above it. Oddly enough, the valley bottom is an alpine zone. This is a rare case of inverted eco-zones caused by cold air flowing off the Bow Glacier and into the valley where it forms a frost-hollow and inhibits growth; such air flows are known as *catabatic winds*. The red-roofed building situated on Bow Lake is Jimmy Simpson's Num-ti-Jah Lodge.

Bow Summit

Bow Summit, with an elevation of 2,069 m/6,786 ft, divides the Bow and Mistaya valleys. A turn left, atop the pass, leads to a short interpretive trail offering another opportunity for a little ART Signs along the trail explain adaptations made by plants to survive in such a harsh environment. The view from Peyto Lake Overlook by itself warrants a walk along this interpretive trail. At the overlook, an 1885 archival photo shows the snout of Peyto Glacier extending into the valley below; this photo displays how far glaciers have receded in the past century. The overlook is also an excellent vantage point to observe the effects of glaciation. As the trail continues up the saddle, you pass from subalpine vegetation to the alpine zone. Right at tree line (one of the few definite boundaries in nature) a krummholz forest grows. Extreme conditions and harsh winds beat these trees into stunted and twisted shapes that looks like something out of a fairy tale.

Beyond the pass, the shallow Waterfowl Lakes encourage aquatic growth that entice hungry moose; sightings are more likely in the early morning and evening. Mistaya Canyon is yet another dramatic result of the ice age. The glacier, that ground its way down Mistaya Valley, didn't erode as much valley

Mount Rundle and Vermillion Lakes.

bottom as the larger North Saskatchewan Valley Glacier. This left the Mistaya Valley hanging above the North Saskatchewan Valley; today, the waters roaring through Mistaya Canyon work to make up for the difference in elevation. And this brings up a point about life's many wonders that we often take for granted—in this case, the temporary beauty of lakes and waterfalls. The duty of water is to find a resting place and only the sea offers such a location, so water is constantly carving a channel in order to attain sea level. By looking at water in these terms, you realize that lakes are like enforced rest-stops, where something temporarily stopped the water; be it erosion-resistant material or a morainal or concrete dam, something slowed the water, but only for awhile. In the end water wins. It finally cuts through and keeps carving deeper until sea level is reached. Then it evaporates, rises over the ocean, drifts inland, floats down to mantle the mountains in snow, melts, and starts the process again.

A short ways beyond Mistaya Canyon, the road crosses the Saskatchewan River. With a bridge in place, crossing the river today is easy. But, take a good look at the river and then imagine crossing it on horseback. The Weeping Wall rises above Highway 93 forming the base of Cirrus Mountain. Once the freezing cold of winter sets in, this wall transforms itself into a haven for ice climbers. The road ascends towards Sunwapta Pass, but before attaining the summit there's a pullout; this is the trailhead for an exceptional hike into the alpine country of Parker Ridge (allow a couple hours) and a grand view of Saskatchewan Glacier (which is not visible from the highway). As Graeme Pole advises in the *Canadian Rockies Super Guide,* "If you're going to get out of your vehicle only once along the Icefields Parkway to go for a walk, Parker Ridge is the place to do it.''

The Columbia Icefield

Sunwapta Pass, at 2,023m/6,676 ft, forms the boundary between Banff and Jasper national parks. On the other side, at the base of the pass, the Athabasca Glacier comes into view. The visitor centre, on the right, displays interpretive displays about glaciers and the Columbia Icefield. The side road on the left leads down to a parking area near the front of the glacier making it the "friendliest glacier in the Rockies; [it] lets you walk right up and pet it,'' according to Ben Gadd in the *Handbook of the Canadian Rockies*. You saw the effect of catabatic winds at the upper end of Bow Lake below the Bow Summit; standing before the Athabasca Glacier you'll feel the chilled air that's often 10 degrees C/18 degrees F cooler (so pack a jacket for the walk). Foreshortening belies the length of the Athabasca Glacier that extends back 5.5 km/3.5 mi to the Columbia Icefield, the largest sheet of subpolar ice in North America. Meltwaters from the Columbia Icefield flow into three oceans, the Pacific by means of the Columbia River, the Atlantic by way of the North Saskatchewan and Hudson Bay, and the Arctic via the Athabasca and Mackenzie rivers.

A glacier is basically defined as a body of ice that moves due to the influence of gravity (thereby relegating icebergs to a separate category). Here's how a glacier forms: snow falls to the ground where it ages and changes from fluffy flakes to icy grains. The pressure caused by snow piled to a depth of 30 m/100 ft, transforms snow at the bottom to ice. Since the cooler temperatures found at higher elevations aid such a process, glaciers usually form on an incline

Mountain sheep are a familiar sight in Banff National Park.

where gravity pulls the heavy bodies of glacial ice downhill. (Also, ice is just stiff water and water is constantly seeking sea level.) The Athabasca Glacier is a good place to identify some glacial features. Starting at the top, the Columbia Icefield is the zone of accumulation, the ice factory that feeds the Athabasca Glacier. Down a little ways from the ice field, transverse (lateral) crevasses and icefalls extend across the glacier; these are the result of differential flow speeds between the bottom of the glacier and its surface. While the average Canadian Rockies' glacier cruises downhill at a speed of 15 m-/49 ft-per-year, the whole glacier doesn't move in unison. On the Athabasca for instance, ice in the icefalls area moves 125 m-/410 ft-per-year while the terminus (end of the glacier) pokes along at 15 m/49 ft. The rate of speed is also different at the glacier's side, middle, surface, and base; it's just the same as the differing speeds of water in a river which is why glaciers are called "rivers of ice." Above and to the left of the glacier are tributary glaciers and the long pile of gravel and rock immediately to the glacier's left is called lateral moraine. The ice closest to you is called the toe or snout of the glacier, the numerous piles of gravel between the snout and you are terminal moraines, and the body of water to the right is a meltwater lake (Sunwapta Lake). Snowcoach tours of the Athabasca Glacier are available at the building next to the Columbia Icefield Information Centre (for more information, 403-852-3332 from Jasper and 403-762-6735 from Banff). An extensive system of caves tunnel through the earth beneath the Athabasca Glacier. Park Service permission is required before entering the caves.

As you observed from the archival photo at the Bow Summit Overlook, glaciers in the Rockies are retreating. What is even more significant than the elevational retreat of glaciers is the vertical loss; some glaciers (at the terminus) have lost 200 m/656 ft of vertical thickness over the past eighty years. The Athabasca Glacier has shrunk thirty-two percent in volume and fifty-seven percent in area. No, this isn't a come-on for contributions to Save The Glaciers Foundation—after all, the earth has warmed, glaciers retreated, and why should we care; it's not like we can do anything about it, can we (outside of building a mondo-freezer that contains the Rockies)? Here's why we should care: glacial ice (including the Polar Ice Caps) contains more than ninety percent of the earth's supply of fresh water.

Coming into Jasper

Between Sunwapta Pass and Jasper, where there are seven auto-accessible campgrounds, the Icefield Parkway is like a well-stocked visual buffet that offers an abundance of scenic wonders. Beyond the Athabasca Glacier, the road ascends along the base of Mount Wilcox and a sign warns, "Watch For Sheep On Road." The sign is there for a good reason; mountain sheep congregate in this area and often wander about on the road. Sometimes the entire band of sheep decides to walk the road. Jasper is also one of the best places along the Trail of The Great Bear to observe wolves. In 1990, on Jasper National Park roads alone, 149 mountain sheep died. An old lateral moraine diverted the Sunwapta River through a weakness in the limestone and resulted in today's Sunwapta Falls. Athabasca Falls plunges over an area of rock that resisted glacial erosion. Here, Highway 93 divides, offering a route to Jasper called the Athabasca Parkway.

Like Banff, Jasper National Park owes its existence to the trailroad and the lesson learned by the Canadian government that beautiful scenery and watchable wildlife attracted tourists and tourists made the cash registers ring.

Maligne Canyon in Jasper National Park.

This is not to sound cynical by any means, only to point out the obvious. Today, however, we're faced with a responsibility, based on knowledge that didn't even occur to people back in 1907 when the Jasper Forest Park Reserve was established. Today we realize that the pristine portions of North America, that exist as they did two centuries ago, have shrunk dramatically. The work involved in preserving such country is never-ending, and it requires appreciation of an area; after all, why take care of something you don't care about. And appreciation stems from knowledge and use (as in camping, hiking, horsepacking, etc.) of the area. The more people that know about and appreciate an area, the more likely it is for the area to receive formal protection. However, and here's the rub, knowledge and appreciation of an area can result in its being loved to death. Like the Inuit hunter once said, "There's no easy way."

Native people lived in the Athabasca Valley 12,000 or more years ago. By the early 1800s, fur traders and voyageurs traveled through the area. In 1813, the North West Company established a fur trading post on the Athabasca River (Brule Lake), out in the Front country, and called it Jasper's House (imaginatively named after a company clerk). "This is the place at which

The Athabasca Glacier grinds down from the Columbia Icefields.

the voyageurs [left their canoes and] became horse-riders...," wrote Ben Gadd, "following the Athabasca valley to a large, snowy mountain they called la montagne de la grande traverse 'the mountain of the great crossing.' " Today it is call Mt. Edith Cavell." In 1829, the company relocated the trading post farther upstream and the area became known as Jasper.

In 1911, the Grand Trunk Pacific Railway, building a second (and northern) trans-Canadian railroad, ushered in present-day Jasper as it laid track that crossed Yellowhead Pass and continued to Prince Rupert. In an obvious case of repetitive overkill, the Canadian Northern Railway constructed a second and parallel railroad. The two lines were eventually consolidated. Today (with a population of 4,500), the community's economy works out roughly like this: a third railroad, a third government, and a third services. The prominent mountain due south of town is Mount Edith Cavell, known to Native people as the "White Ghost." O.A. Wheeler bestowed the present name (upon request from the Geographic Board of Canada) as a memorial to Edith Cavell, a nurse who remained in Brussels and was executed for helping allied prisoners of war escape. The Jasper Yellowhead Museum (which is still in the midst of growth) offers two galleries, one with a permanent collection that centers on the human history of Jasper National Park (Native people, trappers, railroad, mountaineering, and the park). The other gallery displays a variety of regularly changing exhibits. The museum also conducts educational programs and special events. In the summer it is open daily from 10 a.m. to 4:40 p.m. and winters (Labor Day to May 24) from Sunday to Wednesday 1:30 p.m. to 4:30 p.m. (For more information, contact Jasper-

On the way up Parker Ridge after a recent snowstorm.

Yellowhead Historical Society, Box 42, Jasper, Alberta T0E 1E0; 403-852-3013. Jasper Chamber of Commerce, 403-852-3858.)

Up the Maligne Road, 11 km/7 mi from Jasper, a disappearing lake and the most spectacular limestone canyon in either Jasper or Banff national parks awaits. Maligne, pronounced muh-LEEN, is french for "wicked" and was given to this tributary of the Athabasca River after Father de Smet had a tough time crossing it. At the end of the road, Maligne Lake extends 22 km/14 mi back into wild country; boat tours are offered, but it's best to call ahead from Jasper and reserve a seat. The Maligne River flows from Maligne Lake to Medicine Lake, but no water issues from Medicine Lake even though the river reappears again in Maligne Canyon 17 km/11 mi away. Despite no visible drainage, Medicine Lake changes from a scenic mountain lake into mud flats with braided stream channels. The reason for both phenomena lies beneath the ground; the sub-surface rock in this area is limestone. Water has found its way underground through cracks and created subterranean channels that empty the lake and carry water to Maligne Canyon. The longest cave system in Canada may exist beneath this area, but at this time, no one has discovered an entrance. A walk along Maligne Canyon will give you some idea of what's occurred underground. This canyon, that attains a depth of 55 m/180 ft and a width of only 1 m/3 ft in places, is billed by Graeme Pole as "the longest, deepest and most interesting limestone canyon in the Rockies."

For More Information About Route 15:

Events and Services

Banff/Lake Louise Chamber of Commerce: Box 1298, Banff, Alberta T0L 0C0; 403-762-3777.

Jasper Chamber of Commerce: Box 98, Jasper, Alberta T0E 1E0; 403-852-3858.

Canmore, Bow Valley and Kananaskis Chamber of Commerce: Box 1178, Canmore, Alberta T0L 0M0; 403-678-4094.

Banff Park Museum: 403-762-3324, extension 4295.

Luxton Museum: 403-762-2388.

Whyte Museum of the Canadian Rockies: Box 160, Banff, Alberta T0L 0C0; 403-762-2291.

Banff Centre for the Arts: 403-762-6100.

Banff Festival of the Arts Theatre Box Office: 403-762-6300.

Jasper Yellowhead Museum: Jasper-Yellowhead Historical Society, Box 42, Jasper, Alberta T0E 1E0; 403-852-3013.

Canmore Nordic Centre: Box 1979, Canmore, Alberta T0L 0M0; 403-678-2400.

Alpine Club of Canada: Canmore Clubhouse, Box 519, Canmore, Alberta T0L 0M0; 403-678-5855.

National Parks

Banff National Park: Box 900, Banff, Alberta T0L 0C; 403-762-3324.

Jasper National Park: Box 10, Jasper, Alberta T0E 1E0; 403-852-6161.

Wolves in the Northern Rockies
by Patricia Tucker
Wildlife Biologist for the Northern Rockies Field Office of the
National Wildlife Federation and Director of the Montana
Ambassador Wolf Program

*The eerie howl of a wolf pack, once a common sound in the
Rockies, was silenced in the western United States more than fifty
years ago by trapping and the widespread use of poison. Fortunately,
similar attempts at extermination in Canada failed, and due to a
more accepting attitude toward predators, both Alberta and British
Columbia now have healthy wolf populations. Some of these wolves
are now immigrating into Montana and Idaho and providing the
seeds for recovery of this powerful and magnificent animal
throughout the Rockies of the United States. Because Yellowstone
National Park is so isolated from other wild areas, there is an effort
under way to relocate (or transport) wolves there. This is still in the
talking stage, as I write these words.*

*Wolves live in family groups called packs, led by a female and
male wolf who usually produce the only pups in the pack. The pups
are born in late April and begin traveling with the pack in the
autumn. Wolves prey primarily on large animals such as deer, elk,
and moose. Because these animals are large and far from
defenseless, wolves tend to select the weaker members of the population such as the sick, old, and very young. Wolf packs commonly
number between five and fifteen animals. They are highly territorial
and post their borders by urinating and defecating and by howling to
warn strange wolves away.*

*Despite the plethora of stories about wolves' lust for human flesh,
there is yet to be a documented case of a wild healthy wolf killing a
human in North America. In contrast, bison, moose, and even white-
tailed deer kill people annually. While wolves do sometimes prey on
livestock, the percentage of livestock in wolf range killed is much
less than one percent annually. Control can and should be targeted
toward offending animals rather than toward the wolf population as
a whole.*

*Wolf survival is dependent on the maintenance of large populations
of deer and elk as well as a tolerant attitude by humans. If both of
these needs can be met in the Northern Rockies, future generations
will be able to awaken beside their campfires to the howl of the
West's most mysterious and compelling predator.*

The view from the Chateau, Lake Louise.

When Fur Was King

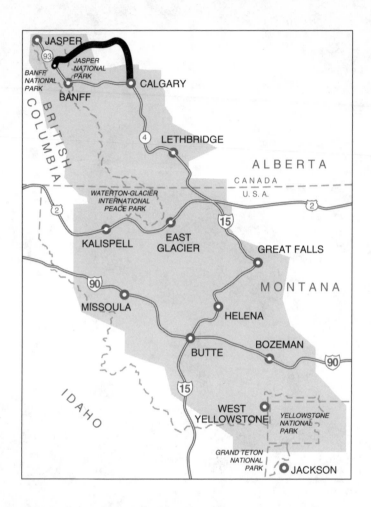

"The possibilities of Canada are truly great."

Martin Nordegg, 1910.

ROUTE 16

COCHRANE-SASKATCHEWAN RIVER CROSSING
350 kilometers/218 miles

General description: A wide variety of contrasting landscapes are encountered along this route ranging from rolling grass-covered foothills in the south through boreal forests to the spectacular mountain scenery of the north Saskatchewan Valley.

Unique features: Rocky Mountain House National Historic Park, Kootenay Plains Natural Area, Nordegg Historic Site.

Wildlife viewing opportunities: Opportunities for big game viewing throughout, particularly in the mountain section of the North Saskatchewan River Valley.

Activities: Golfing, hiking, fishing, horseback riding, whitewater rafting, mountain biking, mountain climbing, cross-country skiing.

Events: Caroline, Big Horn Rodeo (June), West Country Days (August), Nordegg, Miners Days (July), Rocky Mountain House, Rocky Rodeo (June), David Thompson Country Fair (August), Winterfest (January), Sundre, Gary Logan Memorial Rodeo (June).

Travel season: Year-round.

Services: Full services in Cochrane, Sundre, and Rocky Mountain House. Limited services in Cremona, Caroline, Nordegg, Cline River, and Saskatchewan Crossing.

Road conditions and route description: Excellent, well-paved, wide, two-lane highway throughout.

The route: Route 16 begins on Route 13 at the intersection of Highway 1 and Highway 22, where instead of turning west or east onto Highway 1 you continue north on Highway 22, 13 km/8 mi past Cochrane, the Cochrane Ranch Historic Site and Western Heritage Centre (described in route 13A), and on to Rocky Mountain House 150 km/94 mi further north. On the way you will pass through the communities of Cremona, Sundre, and Caroline. Many oil and gas wells and sour gas processing plants as well as small mixed farms, ranches, and homesteads lie along the route which provides excellent access to recreational areas and opportunities in the Clearwater Forest to the west. Campgrounds are located east of Sundre, east and west of Caroline, and in the vicinity of Rocky Mountain House.

The open, rolling, foothills grasslands which you have experienced to the south give way to aspen mixed wood and conifer forests, which you passed through before south of the Bow on Route 13. These forests are part of the Western Boreal Forest which extends in unbroken continuity for thousands of kilometers northwards almost to the Artic Ocean. Dominated by spruce and poplar and characterized by extensive muskegs "moose pasture," it was the many fur-bearing animals of this vast region that attracted the fur traders who first established fur forts at the base of the Rockies, such as Rocky Mountain House in 1799, both to trade with the Indians and to serve as a depot for the crossing of the mountains into the Columbia River and a route to the Pacific.

Rocky Mountain House National Historic Park

Rocky Mountain House National Historic Park is located on the site of the fur forts established by the Hudson Bay and Northwest companies. The first forts known as Acton House (Hudson Bay) and Rocky Mountain House established opposite each other competed for the trade from the Blackfoot, Kootenai and Stoney until 1821 when the two companies merged. Rocky Mountain House was closed and Acton House was replaced by a new fort, the second Rocky Mountian House, which burned to the ground in 1861. The third and last fort was completed in 1868, closing in 1876.

Rocky Mountain National Historic Park is Alberta's only National Historic Park and well worth a visit. It tells the story of the fur trade through indoor and outdoor interpretive exhibits, events, and living interpretation. Admission is free. Summer hours are 10 a.m. to 8 p.m. For more information write the Rocky Mountain House National Historic Park, Box 2130, Rocky Mountain House, Alberta, TOM 1TO or call 403-845-2412.

Clearwater Forest Reserve

The town of Rocky Mountain House located across the river from the historic park is the jumping off place for a vast area of wildland recreational opportunities in the Clearwater Forest Reserve to the west, many of which lie close to Route 17. At Rocky you turn westward onto Highway 12—The David Thompson Highway named after one of Canada's most famous western explorers and fur traders, following the fur traders route up the North Saskatchewan River into the Rocky Mountains—and Banff National Park, rejoining the Icefield Parkway at Saskatchewan River Crossing 174 km/109 mi west. Crimson Lake Provincial Park with camping and other recreational facilities is located north of Highway 11 just west of Rocky Mountain House. There are fourteen campgrounds/recreational areas further west along Highway 11. Be sure to check your gas, as the next services west are at the historic coal mining community of Nordegg 87. km/ 54 mi away.

Between Rocky and Nordegg, the David Thompson Highway passes through seemingly endless miles of forest with few if any signs of human or animal presence. It is much different than the endless expanses of prairie where you can see forever. No wonder the fur traders and the Natives kept to the rivers. Just east of Nordegg, two isolated mountains (geologically, really foothills as they lie well to the east of the Rocky Mountain Front) loom into view, and you pass between them through the Shunda Gap arriving at Nordegg. Off to the south you will see the remains of the old coal mining townsite and mine tipple. In 1914 the Canadian Northern Railroad (which later became part of the Canadian National Railroad) constructed a branch line west from Rocky Mountain House, developed the mines known as Brazeau Collieries and the company town of Nordegg. The mines closed in the 1950s when there was no longer a demand for steam coal. Nordegg was a very isolated community. Until the 1940s the only sure way in and out was by the train. In comparison to the usual company towns, Nordegg was a model of a planned community, built in a semi-circular plan. Focusing on the commercial district which ran along the central axis, the residential sections incorporated prefabricated houses, coordinated color schemes, and architectural controls. Nordegg is the only ghost town of its kind in Alberta.

There is an interpretive centre and gift shop. For more information on Nordegg write the Nordegg Historic Interest Group, General Delivery,

Nordegg, Alberta TOM 2HO; phone 403-721-3950.

Big Horn Indian Reserve

Continuing west from Nordegg, you will cross just east of the Rocky Mountain Front, the Big Horn River; downstream on your left is the Big Horn Indian Reserve. It is one of the outlying Stony Indian Reserves, who first came into this area around the end of the 1700s. Downstream of their reserve is the Bighorn Dam completed in 1973 for hydro generation. The reservoir behind, known as Lake Abraham, after a Stony elder who had lived upstream, flooded a 50 km/80 mi section of the North Saskatchewan River. Water-based recreational opportunities are limited. The Big Horn supplies a small percentage of Alberta's electrical generation needs. It is used mainly for peak period power generation. The spectacular double-tiered Crescent Falls is found near here.

Crown lands

The David Thompson Highway winds its way westward along the north side of this spectacular mountain valley, entering the Front Range over Windy Point (aptly named for the winds which would often hurl marble-sized gravel through the windshields of passing motorists when the highway was under construction in the early 1970s). Traveling on, you cross the Cline River. Further to the west, the Siffleur River flows into the North Saskatchewan. North and south of here are two (White Goat and Siffleur) of the four wilderness areas which Alberta's Provincial Government has set aside in the Rocky Mountains (the others are the Ghost Wilderness east of Banff and the Willmour Wilderness north of Jasper National Park). The remainder of the lands, known as crown lands, are part of the Clearwater Forest Reserve and open for energy, pulp and paper, and logging development. These lands were once part of Rocky Mountain National Park. Like the Bow Valley to the south, they were carved out by the federal government for timber and coal interests. In 1932 the government of Canada transferred these lands which were part of the federal Rocky Mountian Forest Reserve to the province under the Natural Resources Transfer Act. The only federal crown lands that remained in Alberta are those within the National Parks.

Kootenay Plains Natural Area

A few kilometers west of the Cline, you enter the Kootenay Plains Natural Area, a grassland enclave within the forested valley. The area was a traditional wintering area of the Kootenai and Stony Indians in the 1800s because it was also the winter range for herds of elk and mountain bison. The latter summered at high elevations in the headwaters of the North Saskatchewan and Howse river valleys in today's Banff National Park, moving down with the onset of the winter snows. Migrating herds were observed in this area in the early 1800s by David Thompson and by Alexander Henry the Younger.

When members of the Palliser Expedition passed through the region in 1857, no trace of any bison could be found. The Kootenai Plains owe their existence to a local rain-shadow effect created by the mountain peaks to the west. Geological and archaeological studies indicate they have existed for at least 8,000 years and been a favored place for Natives to camp for an equally long time.

From the Kootenay Plains the highway turns west past Whirl Pool point,

crossing from the steeply dipping front to the more flat lying main ranges of the Rockies. Glaciers begin to appear perched high on the mountainsides as you continue on west to Saskatchewan Crossing and the Ice Field Parkway.
—*Brian Reeves.*

For More Information About Route 16:

Events and Services

Rocky Mountain House and M.D. of Clearwater: Tourism Director W.G. Martynes, Town Office, Box 1509, 5116 50th Avenue, Rocky Mountain House, Alberta, TOM 1TO; 403-845-2866.

Rocky Mountain House and District Chamber of Commerce: Box 1374, Rocky Mountain House, Alberta TOM 1TO; 403-845-5450.

David Thompson Country Tourist Council: 4836 Ross Street, Red Deer, Alberta T4N 5E8; 403-342-2032.

ROUTE 16 *COCHRANE-SASKATCHEWAN RIVER CROSSING*

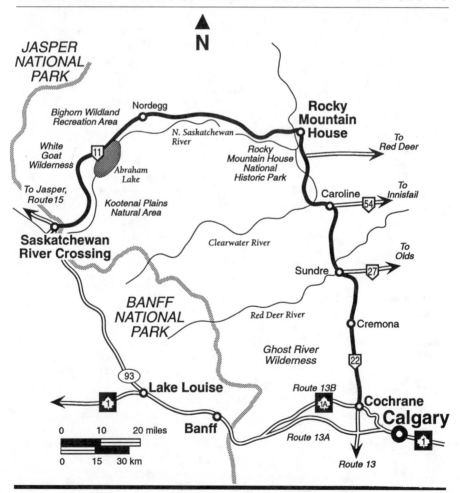

APPENDIX

Ecosystem—thinking in a fragmented world
by Kevin Van Tighem

It is late afternoon, and the sound of meltwater is everywhere. The dull thunder of avalanches fills the valley as mountains release the winter's accumulations of snow.

In the alders at the base of an avalanche slope a grizzly lies on his back, one paw poised above him and his head twisted to the side. He opens his eyes and focuses on the branches above him, then closes them again and heaves a phlegmy sigh. A fox sparrow bursts into song nearby.

Below, the rushing of Sage Creek mingles with the muted sound of wind in pines. The air is hazy with humidity and soft with spring.

The bear dozes. The long day fades.

As the evening breeze comes sliding down the gullies, bringing a fresh chill from timberline snowfields, the bear stands and shakes himself. He tests the air, then follows his nose to a newly exposed patch of brown vegetation. Uprooting a clump of hedysarum with one swipe of his claws, he munches on the stringy roots.

In the forest, varied thrushes are singing.

A bullet strikes the ground by his face, and the grizzly sits back on his haunches, shocked. The rifle's crack echoes down the valley.

Another bullet strikes, this time behind the bear.

He lumbers for the timber, head weaving as he tries to pick up a scent that will tell him what is going on.

The third bullet creases the big bear's hump just as human scent hits him. Like a ball of silver-tipped fur, the grizzly races into the trees as the last bullet ricochets into the alders.

Behind him, the hunters are left with a dilemma. They have driven by four-wheel-drive truck to the end of a logging road, through vast clearcuts, to hunt grizzlies legally during British Columbia's spring bear season in hunting zone 4-1. They know how scarce grizzlies are, especially one as big as this. They may have hit him. But it's growing dark, and neither wants to surprise a wounded grizzly at close range.

The grizzly, however, is half a kilometre away, moving steadily up the valley. The memory of the gunshots is fading as his powerful nose filters countless familiar odors from the mountain night—resin, snowmelt, mold, new buds.

By morning, the grizzly has crossed the Continental Divide, into the high country at the headwaters of the Waterton River. Wind is roaring through timberline fir as the bear descends to a small creek.

He forages half-heartedly along the stream meadow, but the ground is well frozen at this elevation. Wandering into a patch of old-growth spruce trees, he heads down. He tries to lick the sore spot on this shoulder, but his head will not twist that far. Eventually he stretches out on his side, sighs, and falls asleep.

It is unlikely that bears let worries disturb their sleep; in any case, there is no need for worry tonight. Although he is still in the same great mountain ecosystem, well within his normal home range, he has crossed an invisible line in the darkness.

Two hours ago he could be legally shot and killed as a game animal. Now, he sleeps in a national park, protected by law.

For three days the grizzly works his way downstream. The wind on this side of the Rockies seems to howl endlessly, sweeping its thawing breath down from spindrift-topped peaks into the brown foothills.

As he is digging roots one night along the edge of Blakiston Brook, still in Waterton Lakes National Park, the bear's hackles lift and he freezes, nose working, small eyes flickering. The wind has brought the scent of bear cubs.

He moves forward, pigeon-toed and stiff-legged. Something moves at the edge of the grassland. A low rumble rises in his throat.

He is answered by a loud woof.

The sow charges from a clump of silverberry, snarling and swinging her paws. She stops a few steps short of the big boar, moaning and drooling, her head swaying from side to side.

Behind her, three cubs flee, hesitate, and dash back to cower behind their mother.

The boar lowers his head as if to smell something in the grass, and walks a few paces to one side, his nostrils full of cub smell and his small brain full of blood. But the sow's desperate rage makes him cautious. The sow makes another rush and he braces for the attack, but again she turns aside. This time she herds her cubs away. The bear does not follow.

Sow grizzlies are extremely aggressive in defence of their cubs. Since grizzlies are not inclined to climb trees as black bears are, grizzly mothers often attack to protect their young.

In Glacier and Waterton Lakes national parks, grizzlies are safe from hunters but not from the growing number of people who visit the parks to savor the scenery and tramp the trails. The aggressive instincts of sow grizzlies are a constant risk, because female grizzlies react to hikers very much like they do to other bears. Attacks on humans are inevitable in the Crown of the Continent ecosystem, as more and more people crowd in on fewer and fewer bears. Human injuries usually result in dead bears.

The grizzly swims the Waterton River. The farther he travels east, the better the forage. The high passes are still locked in winter, but here at lower elevations, where chinook winds sweep away much of the winter snows, green grass and new spring flowers are everywhere. The grizzly lost almost a quarter of his body weight during his winter sleep, so the new vegetation is like ambrosia to him. This is his spring range.

Several days later he crosses another invisible boundary onto the Blook Reserve, skirting a gas well and leaving his tracks along the well road. Then, completely unaware of it, he crosses back into the national park. One end of the glacier lily patch was Indian land. By the time he ate the last lily bulb, he was in the park. They all tasted the same.

Late in June, the bear is in Poll Haven Community Pasture, well to the east of where he spent the winter. Aspen forests and meadows are misted with rain. In the fogged treetops above Lee Creek, a robin sings steadily into the sodden dusk. This piece of the Crown is owned—a human concept, alien to grizzlies and all other living things—by the Alberta government.

Green odors are everywhere. The bear steps over fallen logs and through rain-drenched buffalo berry shrubs, oblivious to the wet as he follows his nose from one wet green smell to the next. He has been gaining weight steadily these past few weeks. He is moving crosswind when a delightful smell hits him square in the nostrils; the rich, strong odor of rotting flesh.

The cow, bloated and swollen, was killed by lightning a week earlier. It is a windfall to the bear, who normally eats only vegetation.

Two days later, the cow carcass is nearly gone. Bits of hide are splattered with droppings from the ravens who argue all day long in the treetops. Three coyotes have been working on the carcass too, carrying away bits and pieces whenever the bear's back was turned.

As he emerges from the timber for one last meal, the grizzly detects a new odor, that of engine oil and exhaust. There are tire tracks in the trampled ground near the carcass.

Poll Haven used to be part of Waterton Lakes National Park. It was removed from the park in 1947 for cattle grazing. Unfortunately, it is also an important spring range for grizzly bears. When range cattle die, bears scavenge on them. Rarely, a bear will learn to kill cows.

When bears eat domestic cattle, provincial authorities remove the bears. In some cases this means trapping the bear and removing it far from the Crown. In other cases it means killing it. Either way, the ecosystem loses a bear; in 1986 and 1987 alone, ten grizzlies were removed from Poll Haven.

When the Fish and Wildlife truck returns pulling a bear trap the following afternoon, however, the grizzly is already several kilometres away, bedded just below a ridgetop in northern Montana.

He is safe now. In the U.S. the same bear that can be legally hunted in B.C., dodges hikers and cameras in Waterton Lakes National Park, and is considered an agricultural pest in Alberta grazing lands, is afforded the full protection of the U.S. Endangered Species Act. It is a criminal offense to bother this bear on this side of yet another invisible line.

None of this would make sense to the bear, if he were aware of it. This is all his home range, all the same ecosystem, and as the seasons change he will inevitably cross those invisible lines again and again. Each time he crosses another jurisdictional boundary, he will be exposed to different hazards, land-use patterns, and human philosophies. This October, when he is killed by a poacher beside a gas well road in Alberta's Bow-Crow Forest Reserve, he will have unknowingly become another victim of ecosystem fragmentation.—*This article orginally appeared in* Environmental News.

General Information
Travel Montana
The possibilities for enjoying Montana are as colorful and endless as our "Big Sky." Pick any or all of our six vacation countries, each with its own unique attractions and landscapes. Stunning scenery, abundant wildlife, fascinating history and a wealth of attractions make Montana a premier four-season vacation destination. For travel information, contact Travel Montana, Department of Commerce at 1-800-541-1447 (outside MT) or 406-444-2654 (in MT).

Alberta Tourism
Alberta Tourism, a part of the Alberta Department of Tourism, publishes a number of brochures and guides, available at no cost. They include an Alberta road map, and accommodation, campground, adventure, and winter vacation guides. They can be obtained by writing Alberta Tourism, P.O. Box 2500, Edmonton, Alberta T5J 2Z4. Toll-free, year-round travel information is available by calling (from around Canada and the continental United States) 1-800-661-8888 (within Alberta call 1-800-222-6501).

Trail of the Great Bear — Box 142, Waterton Lakes National Park, Alberta, Canada TOK 2MO.

Highway Information
In Montana: Montana Department of Transportation, Public Affairs Bureau, 2701 Prospect Avenue, Helena, Montana 59620; 406-444-6200 or 406-444-6339 for recorded information.

Area Road Reports: 1-800-332-6171
Bozeman - 586-1313	**Helena** - 444-6354
Butte - 494-3666	**Kalispell** - 755-4949
Great Falls - 453-1605	**Missoula** - 728-8553

In Alberta: Alberta Motor Association's 24-hour Road Report Line 403-246-5853. More detailed information can be obtained during business hours Monday thru Friday from the Government of Alberta Transportation Department 403-297-6311.

Weather Information
In Montana: National Weather Service - 406-449-5204
In Alberta-Calgary: 403-263-3333
Banff/Lake Louise: 403-762-2088

National Parks
Glacier National Park: Attn: Superintendent, West Glacier, Montana 59936; 406-888-5441.
Yellowstone National Park: Attn: Superintendent, P.O. Box 168, Yellowstone, Wyoming 82801; 307-344-7381.
Banff National Park: Superintendent, P.O. Box 900, Banff, Alberta T0E 1E0; 403-762-3324.
Jasper National Park: Superintendent, P.O. Box 10, Jasper, Alberta T0E 1E0; 403-852-6161
Waterton National Park: Superintendent, Waterton Park, Alberta T0K 2M0; 403-859-2224.
Grand Teton National Park: Superintendent, Moose, Wyoming 83012-0170; 307-733-2880 or 307-733-2220 recording.

Recommended Reading

Natural History

Montana Wildlife Viewing Guide Carol and Hank Fischer.

Roadside Geology of Montana David Alt and Donald Hyndman.

Rocky Mountain Landmarks: A Visitor's Guide to Banff and Jasper Parks John Root, Judith Johnson, Johanna Jacks, and Beth MacCallum.

Handbook of the Canadian Rockies Ben Gadd.

Alberta Wildlife Viewing Guide.

Canadian Rockies Super-Guide Graeme Pole.

Greater Yellowstone: The National Park and Adjacent Wildlands Rick Reese.

Bear Attacks: Their Causes and Avoidances. Steve Herrero. 1985. Nick Lyons Books.

The Birds of Alberta. W. Salt and J. Salt. 1976. Hurtig.

The Mammals of Alberta. J. Soper. 1965. Hamly Press.

The Flora of Alberta. E.H. Moss and J.G. Packer. University of Toronto Press.

Wildflowers of the Canadian Rockies. G.W. Scotter and H. Flygare. 1986. Hurtig.

The Compact Guide to the Birds of the Rockies. Geoggrey L. Holroyd and Howard Coneybeare. 1989. Lone Pine.

Birds of the Northern Rockies. Tom J. Ulrich. 1984. Mountain Press.

Birds of the Northern Rockies. 1990. George W. Scotter, Tom J. Ulrich and Edgar T. Jones. 1990. Western Producer Books.

Trees and Shrubs of Alberta. 1990. Kathleen Wilkinson. Lone Pine.

Nature Alberta. 1991. James Kavanagy. Lone Pine.

Photographing Wildlife in the Canadian Rockies. Dennis & Esther Scmidt. Lone Pine.

Bear Essentials. 1984. Peter Clarkson and Linda Sutterlin. School of Forestry, University of Montana.

Activities

Angler's Guide to Montana Michael S. Sample. Falcon Press.

Floater's Guide to Montana Hank Fischer. Falcon Press.

Hiker's Guide to Montana Bill Schneider. Falcon Press.

Hiker's Guide to Wyoming William Hunger. Falcon Press.

Hiker's Guide to Alberta Will Harmon. Falcon Press.

Backcountry Biking in the Canadian Rockies. Gerhart Lepp. 1987. Rocky Mountain Books.

Fishing Canada's Mountain Parks. James R. Butler and Rolland R. Maw. 1985. Lone Pine Publishing.

Canoeing Alberta. Janice MacDonald. 1985. Lone Pine Publishing.

Bicycle Alberta. Gail Helgason and John Dodd. 1984. Lone Pine Publishing.

The Canadian Rockies Trail Guide. Brian Patton and Bart Robinson. 1986. Summerthought.

Ski Alberta. Brian Savage and Margaret Barry. 1985. Lone Pine.

History

Montana: Land of Contrast Harry Fritz.

Montana: An Uncommon Land K. Ross Toole.

A History of Alberta James MacGregor.

More Reading

The Journals of Lewis and Clark Bernard DeVoto, editor.
Yellowstone Trails Mark C. Marshall.
Montana Golf Guide Ted Cogswell.
Hiker's Guide to Montana's Continental Divide Trail Tad Brooks and Sherry Jones.
Scenic Byways and *Scenic Byways II* Beverly Magley.
Glacier County: Montana's Glacier National Park Montana Geographic Series.
The Yellowstone Story (Volumes I and II) Aubrey L. Haines.
Lake Louise: A Diamond in the Wilderness Jon Whyte and Carole Harmon.
Bow Valley Rock (Climbing guide) Chris Perry, John Marin, Sean Dougherty.
The Rocky Mountains of Canada South American Alpine Club and Alpine Club of Canada.
Waterfall Ice (of Banff and Jasper) Albi Sole.
Backcountry Biking in the Canadian Rockies Gerhardt Lepp.
Tales of the Canadian Rockies (a series of excerpts from biographies and journals) Brian Patton, editor.
Kananaskis Country Trail Guide Gillean Daffern.
The Selling of Canada: The Canadian Pacific Railway and the Beginning of Canadian Tourism E.J. Hart.
A Grand and Fabulous Notion: The First Century of Canada Parks Sid Marty.
A Hunter of Peace (Old Indian Trails of the Canadian Rockies) T.S. Schaffer.
The Canadian Rockies: Early Travels and Exploration. Esther Fraser. 1969. Hurtig.
Parks in Alberta. Jay and Cam Findley. 1987.

Insights Into Native Peoples

Bury My Heart At Wounded Knee. Dee Brown.
These Mountains Are Our Sacred Places. Chief John Snow.
Beyond Geography: The Western Spirit Against the Wilderness. Frederick Turner.

". . . and so there ain't nothing more to write about, and I am rotten glad of it, because if I'd knowed what a trouble it was to make a book I wouldn't a tackled it and I ain't going to no more. But I reckon I got to light out for the Territory ahead of the rest, because Aunt Sally she's going to adopt me and sivilize me and I can't stand it. I been there before."

Huckleberry Finn
Mark Twain.

About the Author

Bruce Weide is a writer and film-maker. During his checkered past, he logged in the forests of Oregon, picked cotton in Arizona, made ascents of Yosemite's El Capitan, roughnecked on a drilling barge in the Red Sea, spent a month of absolute solitude in the canyon country of southeast Utah, and built an earth sheltered home in Montana. Bruce is a graduate of the University of Montana's MFA writing program and has written for *Montana Magazine, Northern Lights, Washington Magazine,* and *Boys' Life.* Currently, he is at work on, *Animals of the Mind,* a documentary film series that explores how myth, folklore, film, and stories influence our perceptions of animals such as wolves, snakes, sharks, ravens, and bears. Bruce lives in Missoula with an ambassador wolf, an ancient cat, and his wife, Patricia Tucker (after they married, he decided to keep his last name).

About the Artist

Carol Snow's pen and ink drawing of the Spirit Bear graces the cover of *The Trail of the Great Bear* and serves as the logo of the Trail of the Great Bear Society.

The Spirit Bear is a part of her predator/prey series which reflects her love for animals we share the earth with. Snow, who lives in New Mexico, is involved with a number of wildlife organizations and raised two coyote pups as part of her Master's Degree program. Snow says of her work, "The animal spirits have many lessons to teach us. I know that I am guided when I do these paintings by the spirits of the animals that I paint; it is their message that you read."

Her work is popularized through the efforts of Wintercount, American Indian Fine Art — P.O. Box 576, Glenwood Springs, Colorado; 303-984-3685.

The Trail of the great Bear Society

Travel the road less traveled, stop and smell the roses, get off of the beaten path.

These activities are becoming more important and filling more of our leisure time. The Trail of the Great Bear provides these kinds of high-quality recreation and vacation experiences, and promotes an appreciation of cultural, wildland, and National Park values. The Trail also educates visitors by interpreting the wildlife, wildlands, and historical and cultural attractions along the way—from the world's first national park, Yellowstone, to Canada's first national park, Banff.

You can become involved in the planning, development, and evolution of the Trail of the Great Bear by becoming an **Associate Member** of the Society of the Trail of the Great Bear. As a member, you will have the opportunity to participate in workshops, conferences, and promotional programs. Your $15 contribution will support a special journey through the national parks of the northwestern United States and southern Canada—because the spirit of the Great Bear acknowledges no borders.

Join now and you will receive:
* an official Trail of the Great Bear lapel pin
* a membership card
* a Trail of the Great Bear newsletter
* member discounts on unique Trail of the Great Bear publications and giftware.

☐ Yes! I support the vision and goals of the Trail of the Great Bear!!

Name _____   Address_____

City/Town_____Pro/State _____ PC/Zip _____

1992 Membership Contribution
        is just $15.00
    (+ $1.05 GST in Canada)

Mail your contribution to:

**TRAIL OF THE GREAT
BEAR SOCIETY**

P.O. Box 142 • Waterton
Lakes National Park
Alberta • Canada • TOK2MO